23

inscription 1st Ed
by author Mar 97 $3.00
Hist

to Carolyn & Ronf —
Thanks to you
twi I always enjoy
my trips to The OBS.

Keep The donuts
sealed and gary
out of town!

Best wishes,

Jim

D0354124

FOR
SHAME

Also by James B. Twitchell

The Living Dead: The Vampire in Romantic Literature

Romantic Horizons: Aspects of the Sublime in English Poetry and Painting, 1770–1850

Dreadful Pleasures: An Anatomy of Modern Horror

Forbidden Partners: The Incest Taboo in Modern Culture

Preposterous Violence: Fables of Aggression in Modern Culture

Carnival Culture: The Trashing of Taste in America

Adcult USA: The Triumph of Advertising in America

FOR
SHAME

The Loss of Common Decency in American Culture

James B. Twitchell

A THOMAS DUNNE BOOK

ST. MARTIN'S PRESS
NEW YORK

A THOMAS DUNNE BOOK.
An imprint of St. Martin's Press.

FOR SHAME: THE LOSS OF COMMON DECENCY IN AMERICAN CULTURE. Copyright © 1997 by James B. Twitchell. All rights reserved. Printed in the United States of America. No part of this book may be used or reproduced in any manner whatsoever without written permission except in the case of brief quotations embodied in critical articles or reviews. For information, address St. Martin's Press, 175 Fifth Avenue, New York, N.Y. 10010.

Design by Maureen Troy

Library of Congress Cataloging-in-Publication Data

Twitchell, James B.
    For shame :   the loss of common deceny in American culture   /
    James B. Twitchell. —1st ed.
          p.   cm.
    Includes bibliographical references.
    ISBN 0-312-15543-3
    1. United States—Moral conditions.   2. Popular culture—United
States.   3. Shame—United States.   I. Title.
    HN90.M6T95   1997
    306'.0973—dc21   97-15787
                                                                CIP

First Edition: November 1997

10   9   8   7   6   5   4   3   2   1

For RB, Diana, Rod, & Elise

Contents

PREFACE

This book grew out of a course I have been teaching on advertising and American culture. I was struck by how often shame was invoked as a way to sell things in the 1950s, and conversely, how seldom that pitch is made today. Feeling good about buying the product has replaced feeling bad about not having it. At first I thought that this was because I only see ads directed to "haves," who are set in their ways and difficult to shame. But I soon realized that my students were also being sold by being pleased, not shamed. In fact, when I looked at ads directed to them, shame was there, all right—shame of pimples, dandruff, fat, datelessness—but shaming was the exception, not the rule. And even when it was invoked it was often made fun of in an ironic way so common to Generation Xers. When I asked my students about shame I was amazed to learn that, although they certainly sense it, it is triggered by a different series of acts and events. They have a different repertoire of the shameful. It seems smaller than the one I had grown up with and not quite so virulent.

For Shame is the result of my trying to understand how and why this came to be. Was this shift a function of my growing older or did something really happen to a generation that has been plugged into electronic entertainment since birth? Doubtless you have already guessed which I will argue. But in fairness I should mention that I watched *Love Story* on television the other night, and Oliver Barrett IV (played by Ryan O'Neal) seemed such a witless twit. Meanwhile, his stern and shaming father (Ray Milland) had become remarkably intelligent and sympathetic.

On a thumbnail, I believe that we have spent too much energy trying to "get out from under shame" and not enough trying to understand and recover its social protections. Shame is the generator of much moral sense and the ignition for much moral action. Feeling bad is often good, not just for the individual but for the group.

But before I make that argument, there are certain caveats that need to be made. First, the shame I am interested in tracing is not individual shame but communal shame, social shame, tribal shame. I am aware that personal, especially family, shame exists and can be devastating to the carrier and the unloader. But that's a different book best written by psychiatrists. Next, because I will be examining how inchoate sectors of culture like entertainment, education, religion, pop psychology, and the like have effaced the restraining powers of shame, I will often use collective words such as "we" and "people" in references wherein the reader may well feel excluded. There is no way around this generalizing problem other than to pepper the text with such limiting phrases as "it seems to me," "with some exceptions," "as a general rule," and the like. As you will see from the title, I prefer polemic to precision, especially when I think precision makes distinctions of little difference. And, finally, I admit up front I am on the wrong side of this subject—at least since the 1960s. Although we can all recall instances when shame has been horribly invoked, we may need to be reminded that shame is very often a protector of individual and group liberties. When it comes to shame, I confess that I have become a graybeard, a bluestocking, a Jeremiah, and a bit of Oliver Barrett's *père*. As a baby boomer, I know I should be ashamed of this, and oddly enough, to a degree, I am.

—CHARLOTTE, VERMONT

FOR
SHAME

CHAPTER 1

WHATEVER HAPPENED TO SHAME?

> Oh, exactly. Very much so.
> —MARGARET THATCHER's response to being asked
> by a sarcastic reporter if she actually approved of
> "Victorian values."

E ARE LIVING in shameless times. The accusation of cultural shamelessness is usually uttered by sagging fiftysomethings who also say such things as, "When I was your age I didn't spend all day watching television." People who cluck this kind of statement are usually unaware that they are joining a long line of Chicken Littles stretching from the mythic killjoy Cassandra to the melancholic T. S. Eliot. That said, let me revise: we are living in relatively shameless times.

When I was growing up in the 1950s, public drunkenness, filing for bankruptcy, having an abortion or a child out of wedlock, drug addiction, hitting a woman, looting stores, using vulgar language in public, being on the public dole (what there was of it), or getting a divorce was enough to make you hang your head. Most of these reflected concerns about limiting individual behavior within a group.

Want to feel shame today? Wear a fur coat, smoke in public, grow fat, have breasts too small or a nose too big, don't recycle, eat meat. Most of these acts violate codes of consumption. Somehow things have changed.

Where did shame go? Or, better yet, how did it get redirected to such often trivial concerns? Have we lost our receptiveness to shame? Why don't we reprimand the able-bodied drunk, addict, or panhandler? Why do we countenance such psychobabble as "codependency," such sociobabble as "entitlements," and such edubabble as "invitational education"? Why do we not excoriate the unwed teenage mother? Why do we not locate, hector, and shun her reprobate companion? The American Medical Association issued a study (4 April 1996) with this simple statistic. Among unwed girls fifteen to nineteen, pregnancy was 88.7 per thousand in 1980. In 1990 it was 95.9. These are the highest rates in any developed country. Fewer than 5 percent of these pregnancies are intended. Most of the participants feel little shame. You don't have to be a soapbox-derby scientist to see what is rumbling down the road.

Instead we mock Dan Quayle when he is attempting to shame Murphy Brown for celebrating single parenthood. I can dimly remember when Ingrid Bergman was practically forced out of the motion picture business when she became pregnant by her lover. Yet a few years ago, Annette Bening's announcement that she was to become the mother of Warren Beatty's child produced a series of stories praising his impending fatherhood. All hell would have broken loose had Ms. Brown or Ms. Bening been caught wearing mink, or worse yet, baby seal.

How did Donald Trump ever get to be a central icon of American business? Will he ever give shamelessness a rest? How can we read the daily reports of bankruptcy—even of Rockefeller Center, no less— and consider it merely a cost of doing business? Watch the Lifetime channel's game show "Debt," on which three contestants compete to have their real-life debts paid off, and you will see that debt itself has become a joking matter. Once you went to debtor's prison, now you go on TV. The surge in personal bankruptcies, up nearly fourfold since 1984, has not resulted from hard times, but from changing cultural values.

And what of American businesses like AT&T, Sears, Chrysler, or IBM, which have laid off thousands of workers in part to pander to the quarterly reports of Wall Street analysts? CEOs, puffing on now-no-

longer-shameful cigars, seem to be learning their lines from Marie An-
toinette. "Chain Saw" Albert J. Dunlap, author of *Mean Business,* may
have to fire thousands of workers to keep Sunbeam shining, but does
he have to brag about it?

Although the rich are different from you and me, one of the things
we used to share was a mild shame about the distribution and disposal
of wealth. That shame underlay economic policies such as the progressive income tax and, Veblen notwithstanding, social anxieties about
ridiculous consumption. If we can take Steve Forbes's recent expendi-
ture of some $40 million in order to spread the gospel of the flat tax,
and the feeding frenzy at the Jacqueline Kennedy Onassis estate auc-
tion, as something other than aberrations, then a shift has occurred.
Who today in a world of generation-skipping trusts can understand the
meaning of Andrew Carnegie's comment that whoever dies rich dies
disgraced?

Meanwhile in the school yard, at the other end of the economic
spectrum, the sliding of one index finger down the side of the other
while making a *tsk-tsk* clicking of the tongue has almost completely disappeared, replaced by the omnipresent raised middle finger and the
grunted "Up yours."

Some years ago Daniel Patrick Moynihan coined a memorable
phrase, "defining deviancy down," to describe how we legitimize behavior previously regarded as antisocial or criminal. We now have a
curious condition: Criminal and antisocial statistics continue to rise
even though fewer and fewer behaviors fall within such classifications.
Ironically, as deviancy is normalized, so the normal becomes deviant.
When dysfunctional becomes the norm, the functional turns abnormal.

My thesis is that, like deviancy, very much the same phenomenon
has occurred with shame. We have, since the 1960s, raised the threshold, and hence the meaning, of shame. Although we think of shame as
being deep-seated in both individuals and cultures, it can evaporate
overnight. Change a few letters, let the state advertise it, and gam-

bling gets called "gaming." If you want to see shame/modesty standards shift in a generation, simply observe bathing suits. What was once a source of shame is now a source of pride.

The shifts are not always so innocuous. Consider the family, for instance. Is there a more accurate mirror of change than the state of England's royal family? The children of Elizabeth and Philip have political and economic reasons to pretend not to be shacked up with non-spouses, but the rest of us don't care. According to census data, the number of people choosing to live with each other out of wedlock rose 80 percent from 1980 to 1991. The most dramatic increase was with people over thirty-five years of age. This once widely disapproved behavior is now practiced by half the population under age forty, and in ten years it will involve half the population under fifty.[1] Has a stigma ever so quickly become a trend?

In 1991, 22 percent of white births were illegitimate; 69 percent of those single white mothers had family incomes under $20,000; and 82 percent of them had a high school education or less. Of white children born in 1980, only 30 percent will live with both parents through the age of eighteen; those born in 1950 had an 81 percent chance. Families under the poverty line are twice as likely as other families to undergo parental separations, and various studies show that single-parent children are two to three times as likely to have emotional and behavioral problems as children from two-parent families.[2]

Whatever the rates of white illegitimacy, this behavior gets magnified in poorer communities. When you remove shame from snorting coke in Scarsdale, you get crack houses in Harlem. When there is no stigma attached to raising children through serial marriages in northeast Los Angeles, all hell breaks loose in South Central. So, according to government agencies, one African-American child in six was illegitimate in 1950; by 1982 it was more than half (57 percent); and by 1989 it was about two thirds. In Harlem, four out of five babies are now born to unwed teenage mothers who are barely able to care for themselves. Although this kind of reproduction can be endured in the short term for the "haves," it ravages the "have-nots." Bad habits, hidden by privilege, can be harrowing to those living in an unprotected world of immediate economic consequences. If we have learned one thing from biology and anthropology, it is that the family unit has developed for a reason. Cultures with unstable families tend to break down, some quicker than others. Many social scientists have joined the ranks of killjoys in believing that sex education without shame does not seem to teach the necessary lessons, especially to those most at risk.

What about politics? Thirty years ago the Profumo Scandal rocked the West. What would it do today? After Richard Nixon showed no shame for being exactly what he claimed he was not, namely, a crook, stealing from us a sense of propriety in public office, we have had a steady stream of shameless miscreants. Let's just focus on the last few years. At the time, Wilbur Mills and Fanny, Gary Hart and Donna, seemed shockingly shameless; now they seem tame by comparison. Marion Barry, former videotaped cracksmoker, is reelected as mayor of Washington. Our president has been accused of spending part of twelve years with Gennifer Flowers, an Arkansas state worker and sometime nightclub singer. When she was upstaged by another Friend of Bill, Paula Jones, Gennifer marketed her phone-call "love tapes" for $19.95.

In 1995 Senator Dole tried to shame Time Warner for promoting violence in movies and music, pointing to *Natural Born Killers* and gangsta rap, while admitting he has not seen many such movies or heard the music. He conveniently neglected to mention violent films by Bruce Willis, Arnold Schwarzenegger, and Sylvester Stallone, all actor/producers who have supported Republican causes. Meanwhile Newt Gingrich tried his best to "lay a trip" (as shaming is called) on welfare mothers, threatening orphanages and cold turkey. It did not bother Senator Dole that he was supporting the National Rifle Association, which delivers more violence per capita than Time Warner, nor did it distress Congressman Gingrich that his support settlement with his ex-wife had been niggardly to the point of embarrassment.

Politicians are forever talking about how they are going to abolish crime or drugs or welfare. Ironically, what they have most success-fully abolished is public shame. It is news when one-time Secretary of Housing and Urban Development Henry Cisneros admits that he had not helped a former lover as promised. He actually said, "I feel some shame." Of course, he was married at the time. When Dick Morris found out that the wages of sin are a $2.5 million book contract, it was hard for him to drop his head in shame.

Had he run for public office, Colin Powell intended to make the re-covery of shame a central part of his campaign. In his words:

> We've got to teach our youngsters what a family means, what giving to your community means, what raising good children means. We've got to restore a sense of shame to our society. Noth-ing seems to shame us or outrage us anymore. We look at our television sets and see all kinds of trash, and we allow it to come into our homes. We're not ashamed of it anymore.[3]

Alas, he decided not to seek public office.

So what's new? Politics is old news. Here's some new news, tabloid news. Mike Tyson, convicted rapist, is celebrated as a conquering hero, at least until he started ear biting. Woody Allen proclaims he saw "no moral dilemma whatsoever" in having an affair with the twenty-year-old adopted daughter of Mia Farrow, with whom he'd raised a family. His box-office appeal takes only a minor dip. O.J. Simpson, on trial for a double murder, gets $1 million for his book on how he didn't kill his ex-wife. The title tells much about the celebritized nature of cultural authority in a shameless culture. *I Want to Tell You* is not "What You Want to Know." When Joey Buttafuoco was released from prison after serving a few months for having sex with a minor, who also shot his wife in the head, he was welcomed by a crew from the TV tabloid "A Current Affair." The show's producer reportedly paid him $500,000 for TV rights to his story.

Meanwhile Tonya Harding, who knew of a little mafioso knee work on a competitor, has been paid a handsome six-figure sum for her appearance on a TV tabloid show. Before her descent into oblivion, other lucrative offers (magazine spreads, a book, a movie) arrived, including a $2 million proposal from the All Japan Women's Professional Wrestling Association. And what of Mr. John Wayne Bobbitt, accused of raping his wife before she cut off his penis, who reportedly has made hundreds of thousands of dollars on a "Love Hurts" media tour featuring appearances in which he autographs steak knives and plays "Stump the Bobbitt," a contest testing his knowledge of Bobbitt-castration jokes. Charles Manson wanted royalties from his own line of apparel and residuals from his songs. Donald Trump conducts his courtship, divorce, fatherhood, remarriage, and another divorce, all in the pages of *People*. As I write this, The Donald is trying to protect New Yorkers from gambling anywhere but in New Jersey. He is even contending that since his casino is called Taj Mahal, an Indian restaurant should be forced to change its name. Could this paragraph go on? You bet. But you get the point: in the last few decades the cultural spotlight has swung from illuminating the gatekeeper to focusing on the gate-crasher.

This list of the shameful will evaporate by nightfall. By the time you read this you may well wonder who these characters were. That's just the point. Since we have lost the boundaries between here and Shameland, we need to map them out anew each day. One foot over the line yesterday is colonized turf today. Where the lines were once drawn in concertina wire, they are now sketched in chalk. Worse yet, the only ones who claim they can really see them as bright lines and are willing to invoke shame are either on the reactive Christian right or among the trivializing Politically Correct left.

SHAME!

…on you trash talk show **PRODUCERS** who fill our children's minds with moral rot.
…on you **TV STATIONS** which bring these perverse programs into our communities.
…on you greedy **ADVERTISERS** who sponsor trash talk shows simply to fill your coffers with money.
We are **FED UP** with your calloused and arrogant disregard for the impact your filth is having on our children. We are not going to take it any more.

WE ARE FIGHTING BACK!

THIS IS THE KIND OF TRASH THEMES **THESE COMPANIES** *(below left)* HAVE BEEN SPONSORING:

- **Women chasing married men**
- Men who want their wives to look sexy again
- People obsessed with ex-lovers
- Housewives vs. strippers
- **Fathers who think they're studs**
- Teen criminals and parents who encourage them
- I have the hots for a former Jenny Jones case
- Is there life after a career in porn?
- Women who marry their rapist
- **Mom, I'm a teen prostitute**

- Get bigger breasts or else
- **A woman in love with a serial killer**
- Baby-sitter accused of killing two children
- I'm marrying a 14-year-old
- **Teens who have sex for status**
- My daughter's in love with a 76-year-old
- **My mom dresses like a tramp**
- My daughter is living as a boy
- **Virgins who are choosing their first sex partners (including a homosexual couple)**

Imagine the vulgar dialogue that these topics generated!

YOU CAN HELP by contacting the trash TV talk show sponsors listed on this page. Your action is needed TODAY if we are to SAVE OUR CHILDREN, our families and our society from the glut of TV trash talk show hosts – society's "cultural assassins."

Here's what three writers have said:

"When [the SPONSORS OF THESE SHOWS] – and/or their spouses – start to get hassled and harangued about the talk shows by their buddies on the golf course, at the health club, the boat yard, the hairstylist's and the charity ball – then you might get some action." – *Eric Mink, New York Daily News TV critic.*

"Good idea. LET THE HASSLING AND HARANGUING BEGIN." – *John Leo, contributing editor of U.S. News and World Report, citing Mink's comments in his November 9, 1995, column.*

"Fire away at daytime DEGENERATE EXPLOITATION SHOWS, but don't aim at the performers. Aim at the people who pay them to perform. AIM AT THE ADVERTISERS WHO SPONSOR THESE SHOWS." – *Charley Reese, writing in the Orlando Sentinel.*

SEND IN THE PETITION TODAY.

Help us run this ad in other papers ALL ACROSS AMERICA. Return the petition along with a tax-deductible contribution to support this fight. Let us JOIN TOGETHER to stop this ATTACK on our children. ACT TODAY! The time is now. Join other Americans who are FED UP with what the trash TV talk shows are doing to our CHILDREN. We will keep the sponsors informed about the number of petitions received. Now it is UP TO YOU.

TOP SPONSORS of trash TV talk shows

DONAHUE: Hasbro, Clorox
GERALDO: Unilever, Warner-Lambert
JENNY JONES: Procter & Gamble, Remington Products
MAURY POVICH: American Home Products, Philip Morris
RICKI LAKE: Hasbro, Grand Met
SALLY JESSY RAPHAEL: Hasbro, American Home Products

Remington Products Company
Chrm. Victor Kiam II
92 Main Street • Bridgeport, CT 06604
Phone: 203-367-4400 FAX: 203-366-6039
Products: Remington appliances and shavers

The Clorox Company
Chrm. G. Craig Sullivan
P. O. Box 24305 • Oakland, CA 94623
Phone: 510-271-7000 FAX: 510-832-1463
Toll free: 1-800-877-2624
Products: Brita water filtration system, Clorox, Formula 409 cleaners, Hidden Valley dressings

American Home Products Corp.,
Chrm. John R. Stafford
5 Giralda Farms • Madison, NJ 07940
Phone: 201-660-5000 FAX: 201-660-5771
Products: Advil, Dimetapp, Robitussin cold remedies, Centrum vitamins

Grand Metropolitan, Inc.,
Chrm. George Bull
200 S. 6th St. #M5380 • Minneapolis, MN 55402
Phone: 612-330-4966
Products: Burger King restaurants, Green Giant vegetables, Pearle Vision Centers, Pillsbury food products

Hasbro, Inc.,
Chrm. Alan Hassenfeld
P. O. Box 1059 • Pawtucket, RI 02862
Phone: 401-431-8697 FAX: 401-727-5779
Products: Hasbro, Kenner, Playskool toys, Milton Bradley games

Philip Morris Companies, Inc.,
Chrm. Geoffrey C. Bible
120 Park Avenue • New York, NY 10017
Phone: 212-880-5000 FAX: 212-878-2165
Toll free: 1-800-343-0975
Products: General Foods International coffees, Kraft food products, Maxwell House coffee, Post cereals

The Procter & Gamble Company
Chrm. Edwin L. Artzt
P. O. Box 599 • Cincinnati, OH 45201
Phone: 513-983-1100 FAX: 513-945-9155
Toll free: 1-800-426-9254
Products: Cover Girl cosmetics, Crest toothpaste, Oil of Olay skincare, Pantene haircare products, Tide detergent.

Unilever United States Inc.
Pres. Richard A. Goldstein
390 Park Avenue • New York, NY 10022
Phone: 212-688-1260 FAX: 212-906-4411
Toll free: 1-800-598-1223
Products: Calvin Klein fragrances, Lipton tea & foods, Mentadent toothpaste, Vaseline skincare

Warner-Lambert Company
Chrm. Melvin R. Goodes
201 Tabor Road • Morris Plains, NJ 07950
Phone: 201-540-2000 FAX: 201-540-3761
Toll free: 1-800-223-0182
Products: Benadryl, Sudafed remedies, Listerine mouthwash, Schick razors

WHO IS AMERICAN FAMILY ASSOCIATION?

AFA is a 19-year-old organization working for better TV. Help us run this ad in papers across the nation. Help us recruit millions more who are willing to get involved. AFA is composed of nearly 1.9 million supporters. We are not a political organization.
AFA is a member of the Evangelical Council for Financial Accountability (P.O. Box 17456, Washington, DC 20041), the Better Business Bureau and registered in every state which requires registration. The Roanoke (VA) Times & World-News checked on AFA and wrote: "The American Family Association...has operated WITH A GOOD RECORD OF HONESTY. We checked four sources...No one doubted the money will be used as the donors specify. Words like 'sincere,' 'up front,' and 'pretty clean ship' were offered in describing the American Family Association."

A PETITION TO THE SPONSORS OF TRASH TV TALK SHOWS

Mail to: American Family Association
P.O. Drawer 2440/107 Parkgate
Dept. AA
Tupelo, MS 38803

Mr. Sponsor, we are FED UP with the trash you are paying for. We are DISGUSTED that you would use the money we spend with your company to help promote such FILTH. We are HOLDING YOU ACCOUNTABLE. It is time to clean up your act! To show my commitment to this effort, not only am I sending this petition, but I'm also enclosing a gift of $_____ to help AFA run this ad in other papers. It is time to stop this moral rot.

Name _____

Address _____

City/State/Zip _____

P.S. All gifts are tax-deductible. If you cannot contribute at this time, but still want to participate in helping fight the trash TV talk shows, please return the form without a contribution. Whether you contribute or not, this project is so important that we ask that you reproduce the information in this ad and distribute it. It is going to take all of us working together to defeat the big money of the producers, sponsors and TV stations.

A project of American Family Association, Dr. Donald E. Wildmon, President
Approved by the I.R.S. as a 501-c-3 not for profit organization

---

MODERN INVOCATIONS OF SHAME FOR FURTHERING SOCIAL AGENDAS, 1995 (AMERICAN FAMILY ASSOCIATION AND THE HUMAN FARMING ASSOCIATION).

How safe is drug-laced veal? Don't expect an honest answer from the veal industry.

According to the USDA, drugs such as sulfamethazine (a known carcinogen), penicillin, streptomycin, and neomycin have all been found in veal.

The industry tells us not to worry about tainted veal. The meat board even claims that the drugs used in veal have been "approved" by the Food and Drug Administration (FDA).

Industry promotional materials also claim that the FDA regulates "the doses permitted and withdrawal time" of drugs used in veal.

Here are the facts: **The drugs commonly used in veal have _not_ been approved by the FDA** or _any_ government agency.

Furthermore, the FDA has repeatedly warned the industry that, due to the veal calf's deficient diet, no safe drug use and withdrawal regulations exist.

According to federal law, products may not be sold based upon false assurances of safety.

That's why we have brought this matter to the attention of federal authorities — and have filed a formal petition with the Federal Trade Commission (FTC) in order to halt deceptive veal industry claims.

A "milk-fed" veal calf is _not_ fed mother's milk — nor is he allowed solid food. Instead, he's fed a liquid mixture laced with antibiotics. _His entire life is spent chained in a crate._ He can't even turn around.

You can take action to stop the abuse — and to stop the deception.

• Mail the attached coupon to the FTC. This will hasten government action to stop the meat board from distributing false assurances about drugs in veal.

• **Say no to anemic veal.** Don't reward an industry that flagrantly disregards consumer safety, animal welfare, and the truth.

• And please, if you can, support our work. The Humane Farming Association (HFA) is leading a national campaign to stop factory farms from misusing chemicals, abusing farm animals, and misleading the American public. Please join us!

Veal factories say the drugs used in veal are "approved."

But don't buy it!

Bureau of Consumer Protection
Federal Trade Commission, Room 470
Washington, DC 20580

Please take action. The FDA has not approved the drugs used in veal. Sulfamethazine, for instance, is a known carcinogen. Order the meat board and veal companies to immediately retract, recall, and cease distributing misleading information.

NAME _____

ADDRESS _____ CITY _____ STATE ___ ZIP.

The Humane Farming Association
Toxic Veal Task Force
1550 California St., Suite A, San Francisco, CA 94109

Keep up the pressure. Hold the veal industry accountable. Factory farms must be stopped from misusing chemicals, abusing farm animals, and misleading the American public. Here is my tax-deductible contribution:
__$15 __$35 __$50 __$100 __$500 ____other

NAME _____

ADDRESS _____ CITY _____ STATE ___ ZIP

You may obtain a copy of HFA's latest financial report by writing us at our office address, or by writing New York State, Department of State, Office of Charities Registration, Albany, NY 12231.

Still there is a pattern in this contemporary, albeit ephemeral, litany. Here is an instructive retelling of *The Scarlet Letter*. Jessica Hahn was once a devout Pentecostal. Employed as a church secretary, she was sexually victimized by televangelist Jim Bakker in a Florida hotel room. She felt such shame that she was later paid $265,000 by this modern Reverend Arthur Dimmesdale. All she had to do was keep quiet. She almost did. Still, she felt some lingering residual shame. In the modern mode, rather than have the Rev confess his sin and expire of grief on the town scaffold, she sold her story to the tabloids. She was finally washed clean, however, by reconstructing her prow and posing topless for *Playboy* in 1987. This act, she said, "made me feel clean again." Feeling cleaner still, she made her own Playboy video. Then, as if to show that beatitude was close at hand, she became a regular on "The Howard Stern Show," and a featured star in such Stern videos as *Butt Bongo Fiesta*. Having seen the video, I can assure you that she does not go off at the end into the woods with a scarlet letter pinned to her breast.

Nor, for that matter, does the modern Hester Prynne. In the 1995 movie version of Hawthorne's screed on shame, Demi Moore plays the Puritan as babe, and screenwriter Douglas Day Stewart (best known for his script for *An Officer and a Gentleman*) makes the story relevant. Thanks to an upbeat ending, Dimmesdale and Hester ride off to start a new life. The adulterous sexual act is not so bad; in fact, it allows the repressed Rev to learn a little about life. If only Tammy Bakker had seen the movie, she might have understood what Jim really wanted was not sex but a deeper understanding of his repressed feelings. Anyway, Chillingworth has committed suicide in this version and Pearl doesn't exist, so what the hey? A victimless crime is really no crime at all. At movie's end, Hester and Dimmesdale have had enough of suffocating Puritan hypocrisy and head off to the West. As they reach the edge of the forest, Hester unfastens the scarlet letter, letting it fall into the muck. The rear wheel of their wagon rolls over it. Ah, Hollywood, ah, mores.

What we see on television, is not just shaming but shamelessness. We see the Madonna from upstate Michigan, not the one from Bethlehem—the one who published a book of sexual fantasies that featured the pop diva with several partners, including a seventy-year-old man, lesbian skinheads, and a dog. Just watch the Fox network for a few days. We have gone from being a nation of shameless consumers to being a nation of consumers of shamelessness. Spend a few hours watching "Cops," one of Fox's premier shows, and you'll see the most ungodly group of stupid people trashing their spouses, their neighbors, their trailers, and themselves, all in full view of the video camera and bright lights. Why do they do it? Better question: why do we so love to watch it?

Although it has now cooled off, the hottest genre on television was ambush talk shows. It still won't die. The hosts are not Oprah and Donahue, but a new breed. They have cute, diminutive names like Jenny, Ricki, Sally, and Jerry. We'll meet them later. But here's what happens in a typical show: A mother and daughter bare their souls between commercials to tell the world how they have both fallen in love. What they don't know is that the man they have fallen for is one and the same. They also don't know they are both entertaining his sexual advances. But they do know that there is "another woman" in *his* love life. We watch the man in question waiting backstage, smirking. Another commercial. Out he comes. The women look at each other in embarrassment and shock. The studio crowd roars. The host feigns distress. How could you be sleeping with both mother and child? Isn't that close to . . . incest? Not difficult, he says. The crowd roars again. Well, who are you going to choose? an audience member asks. Both, he says.

No area of American culture has gone untouched by the desire to remove shame from the self and settle it on others. Shamelessly, we try to shame others. In psychology we have the Recovery industry run by such guru-entrepreneurs as reformed alcoholic John Bradshaw. Warning: Shame is toxic to the psyche. You need to recoup your self-esteem by unleashing your inner child and settling the shame where it belongs—on your dysfunctional family. Mr. Bradshaw believes 97 percent of American families are dysfunctional. Hum, does that mean that 3 percent are functional? Am I missing the logic of what is normal/abnormal here? When everyone is a victim, no one can be. When everyone is shame-free, no one can be shamed.

What of religion? When the Devil goes, so goes sin. And when sin goes, shame is not far behind. The ultimate shaming figure is, of course, the jealous God who, if He sees every falling sparrow, certainly sees us. He carries the biggest shame stick and is not afraid to use it. This force has loomed over the American landscape since preacher Jonathan Edwards's early warning that we were all "sinners in the hands of an angry God." If you have gone to any fundamentalist Protestant church recently, you will realize that you are safe. Stay in this congregation and you will escape His grasp. Others will not. *They* are sinners, we are safe. I'm okay, you're not.

In less fundamentalist climes, shame has just about disappeared. Episcopalians can't find it. In New Rochelle, ministers developed a ceremony to celebrate divorce. They have market-tested it about five hundred times. For around $400 the celebrants get an invocation, a chance to return rings, and a ritual in which they can burn some testament to their vows, like the marriage certificate. "When vows are broken, rights are returned," we are told. Not for nothing has the Catholic church, ever mindful of where the competition is coming from, renamed confession "reconciliation."

Need we turn to education? In shelving the canon and the standard it implied, the gatekeepers of the "best that has been thought and said" may deserve their own current irrelevancy. In giving up the "myth of high culture," academics have drained our culture dry of the grandest explorations of shame. For, as we will see, shame is taught, and some of its teachers are the creators of the world's great art. That is why shame is all through, say, Renaissance art, Victorian poetry, and the English novel. You can major in English at Georgetown University and never be assigned a work by Chaucer, Milton, or Shakespeare.

Slave narratives and Victorian cookbooks are important, but they are not great literature. Saul Bellow suffered public opprobrium for raising the question, but it is still worth a go: "Who is the Tolstoy of the Zulus? The Proust of the Papuans? I'd be happy to read him." Much of what is taught in courses on Women's Studies is stuffing to fill up the semester. You don't need Christina Hoff Sommers's *Who Stole Feminism?* to show you this, just look at a typical syllabus. Attend a class. Until recently, literature was not thought to be social therapy. In this context, lily-white (and overwhelmingly male) Deconstruction, which essentially says art is whatever critics want to call it, and that there is no real distinction between criticism and art, is as well a sign of our times. Any text will do.

If you want to be howled at by colleagues in the academy, mention that you think that there is literary quality in canonical works that transcends the concerns of race, gender, class, nationality, politics, and the like. At best you will be considered naive; at worst, deceptive or stupid. Students, however, know exactly what you are talking about. They hunger for it.

Shamelessness pervades educational bureaucracies. Consider grade inflation. There is almost the same percentage of cum laude students in the Ivy League as supposedly "dysfunctional" families. To define excellence downward, the SATs had to be racheted upward. Consider athletics. The graduation rates of those on athletic scholarships tell much about how much their caring institutions really care.

What's really going on in an institution that uses such concepts as "mastery learning," "integrated learning," "invented spelling," "continuous progress," "portfolio assessment," and "child-centered learning"? What can be made of the fact that a frighteningly large number of professional educators, as they often call themselves, argue that the emphasis on right and wrong answers is culturally oppressive, unfair to minority children? Could such mumbo jumbo be brought to us by the same folks who have drained the shame from language? They have countenanced the transformation of "relief" into "welfare" and "welfare" into "entitlement," "wrong" into "inappropriate," "bad habits" into "lifestyle choices," "illegitimacy" into "nonmarital child-bearing," "promiscuous" into "sexually active," and—most frightening—"heinous killer" into "victim of an abusive family." The Political Correctness Movement is a school-based movement in part because this is where much of the we-feel-good-but-you-should-feel-bad voodoo of America is currently being brewed.

American education has been so busy manufacturing self-esteem, pasting gold stars on everyone's report card, posting "My Child Is an Honor Student [Sorry about Yours]" bumper stickers on vans, being nonjudgmental and supportive, and listening—forever listening!—that it has forgotten what Carlyle, Emerson, and even John Dewey and Horace Mann have said: at home you can be loved just for being you, but in school you are what you do, and what you do is learn. I'm not at all surprised that so many high-school graduates think Oliver Stone movies are based on fact. Nor am I surprised that Madonna is one of the most sought-after college commencement speakers. It's not that I can't imagine what she could possibly have to say to kids entering adulthood, it is that I know exactly what she would say. At least before her "this has changed my whole life" motherhood.

Recently the Joseph & Edna Josephson Institute of Ethics surveyed nine thousand students aged fifteen to thirty. A large number, according to an Associated Press report on the study (26 April 1995), admitted to lying, cheating, and stealing. One third of high school students and 16 percent of college students admitted stealing something within the past year. Sixty-one percent of high school students and 32 percent of college students admitted to cheating on a test. More than a third said they would lie on a resume to get a job, and 18 percent of college students said they had already done so. A survey by Tulane University found that 20 percent of suburban high school students said it was okay to shoot someone who had stolen something from them, and 8 percent said it was okay to shoot someone who offended or insulted them. The most depressing parts of these studies may not be all the lying and cheating and stealing and even shooting but the shamelessness of those surveyed to admit it. Deal with it. Make shameful acts repeatedly public and they soon become shameless.

Western culture, led by American popular culture, is rapidly removing central shaming events that developed over generations and replacing them with often trivial and short-lived concerns. Instead of viewing shame as a powerful socializing device, we see it as a hindrance to individual fulfillment. Of course shame inhibits behavior—that's the point. It retards action, it increases reticence, it invokes self-censorship. Of course it makes the individual feel bad. But it does so in the name of a higher social good. Shame is the basis of individual responsibility and the beginnings of social conscience. It is where decency comes from.

Appropriate shame separates and degrades the offender, true, not to exile but to instruct, not to scorn but to educate. The final object of such shame is not banishment, but reintegration. You say "I'm sorry" not on the way out, but on the way back in. The next words you should hear are "Welcome back."

I have no conspiracy theory to explain the current shamelessness of American culture. I don't believe it occurred because the church fathers dropped their guard and let the heathen in, or because college professors caved in to moral relativism and oppression studies while throwing out the shaming canon of Spenser, Milton, Pope, Carlyle, and Tennyson, or because craven politicians realized that shaming others while maintaining their own contrived integrity won votes, or because defeat in Vietnam destroyed our self-confidence, or because professional therapists—called counselors—promulgated a phony "you deserve a break today" empowerment nonsense to patients—called clients. But they all had a hand in it.

To be sure, the desire to coat oneself with Teflon while coating others with Velcro is the ineluctable result of losing a shared sense of community values. Certainly this effacement of shame norms started with the industrial revolution, but it really picked up momentum in the 1960s with the advent of television.

None of this observation is new. However, what is original is that this resettling of shame thresholds has much to do with the rise of *commercial* entertainment. The demands of advertisers in the new media of radio and especially of television have resulted in a tectonic shift in the centering of culture. Thanks to this culture, norms of acceptable behavior have moved from adults to adolescents; from those who have fixed patterns of consumption to those who have not yet made their brand preferences known; from those in the control room to those whose fingers are on the remote-control wand. As long as adolescents have plenty of time and disposable income, and as long as there are plenty of channels of entertainment, there is no reason to think that this situation will change.

It seems doubtful that we will confront, let alone solve, the social problems that result from this resettling of shame. "Letting the government do it" ironically only exacerbates the problem. We are still knee-deep, whether we like it or not, in a world organized not around solutions, or enlightenment, or even political or economic conquest, but around advertiser-supported good feelings. The "feelies" are here. Every medium of culture, be it religion, politics, advertising, the law, or psychology, is having to live by the rule: Make me feel good or be gone. Entertain or die. So say good-bye to shame, at least as we have known it, at least for a while.

CHAPTER 2

THE SENSE OF SHAME

Shame is by nature recognition. I recognize that I *am* as the Other sees me.
—JEAN-PAUL SARTRE

THE FORCE OF SHAME

EARLY IN 1995 Scott Amedure saw a notice flashed during an episode of one of his favorite early afternoon television talk shows. This notice requested calls from lovers who have a secret "crush" they would be willing to divulge on national television. The object of your crush would also be there and, for a moment, at least, you would be famous. Your fame would not last as long as Warhol had predicted, but if you lived in a trailer park, as Scott did, and if you were down on your luck as Scott was (he had recently been beaten up, his truck had been trashed, and he was unemployed), the risk/reward ratios were in your favor.

The show was "The Jenny Jones Show," and if you were lucky enough to be chosen, you would be given free air travel to, and accommodation in, Chicago for a few days. A limo would even come to your hotel and take you to the studio. So Scott called. He told one of the show's assistant producers, called talent brokers, that he had such a crush on a man eight years his junior.

Jonathan Schmitz also lived alone in a mobile home a few miles from Scott. He had a job as a waiter. When he was called by the talent broker and told he had a "secret admirer," and that he would be given a trip to Chicago, and be seen on national television, he jumped at the chance.

17

Like many other young people, he had seen the curious genre of ambush TV. How could you watch afternoon television and not run across the good-humored Ms. Jones and her colleagues Ricki Lake, Montel Williams, Rolonda, and Jerry Springer? They were all over the syndicated airwaves, often broadcast twice a day. Three years ago you would have tuned in to their predecessors Sally Jessy Raphael, Geraldo Rivera, and Maury Povich, and ten years ago you would have seen the Ur-talk shows of Oprah Winfrey and Phil Donahue. These titans, who have transcended show business to become household names, have now spurned the format they hatched. Phil has retired and Oprah even did a two-part show called "Are Talk Shows Bad?" At the end of it she swore off shame TV as if it were a bowl of Ben & Jerry's ice cream, and watched her ratings slide. Happy to say, her new interest in books and a flagging popular interest in ambush TV has restored her to daytime dominance.

To find the prototype of the entire genre, recall "Queen for a Day" of the 1950s, in which the "woman next door" was honored, if not for a whole day, then for part of a half hour. The otherwise unknown woman became Queen for some act of generosity or heroism. Her act was celebrated with adulation and lots of brand-name presents. In the modern version, however, the talent broker goes bottom-fishing for desperate people without moral judgment—unfaithful spouses, incestuous stepfathers, sex addicts, bisexual white supremacists—willing to talk about their most hurtful private acts. True, their acts are celebrated with derision, but celebrated nonetheless. In short, what separates the current generation of "yes, even *you* can be noticed" television from its roots is that, while guests are still treated with cloying dignity, a generation ago the reward was to be publicly honored; now it is to be publicly exposed, and often shamed.

Make no mistake—this is very exciting television, made more so by the appalled and/or solicitous face of the host and the intercut shots of the audience members' faces, showing horror, or maybe just glee. The main attraction of all these shows seems to be the sense of moral superiority viewers derive from watching an endless succession of hapless misfits boast or whine about their failed lives. Sometimes a kindly therapist with a PhD is trotted out at the end to deliver a little psychological mumbo jumbo as if this tale needed a McMoral.

Like the proverbial fawn, Jonathan Schmitz was caught in the headlights of fame. Here is what happened on March 6, 1995, according to Sheriff's Lieutenant Bruce Naile:

> Mr. Schmitz came out on stage before a studio audience, and there was a woman [Debbie Riley] sitting there that he knew. He figured she was his secret admirer and walked up and kissed her. But then they [Jenny] told him, "Oh, no, she's not your secret admirer, this is"—and out walked Scott Amedure. The show was about men who have secret crushes on men.[1]

When it turned out that it was Scott, not Debbie, who had nursed the crush on him, Jonathan sat still. The audience tittered. His shoulders slouched and his head slightly tipped forward. Although he was not conscious of it, he was making himself smaller. He was becoming less of a target. He politely said he was a heterosexual and that he was not interested. Like a good sport, he seemed to go along with the joke.

Was it the anxiety of waiting for the show to air, was it an unsigned sexually suggestive note on his trailer door that he thought was from Scott, was it post-traumatic stress syndrome, or was it homophobia that so disturbed him? Whatever it was, Schmitz went home to Orion Township, Michigan, and bought a twelve-gauge shotgun and five shells of double-ought buckshot. On March 9 he fired two blasts of that buckshot into the body of his secret admirer. "I just walked into his house and killed him," he told the 911 operator. "He was after me day and night." After turning himself in, Schmitz pleaded not guilty to charges of first-degree murder. He was convicted of second-degree murder—his lawyers said he had been fighting depression, alcoholism, and a thyroid condition—and is now serving twenty-five to fifty years in prison.

To Burn with Shame: The Self in Flames

Although we will never know exactly why Jonathan Schmitz responded as he did, we do know this: Here was a human who had been humiliated in a very special way. He felt he had been vivisected in public. He had been, in a word, shamed. In his own words, he told the press that he had been "eaten away" by the show. It was not a haphazard description. He might have used the older expression. He had "lost face."

Specifically, his sexuality had been questioned, but it could have been his honesty, duty, social status, or any number of other perceptions of self that we depend on each day for our sense of position. When we lose this sense, as we momentarily do when we are shamed, we go into free-fall, and our actions can sometimes become violent. Such massive shame causes disorientation; hence the biblical curse "shame and confusion" as a formula for weakening one's enemy. Shame experienced at these levels is profound degradation and can trigger the fight-or-flight mechanism.

Individuals are not alone in their vulnerability. Shame can melt down the nuclear family. Shame can permeate civic organizations, those private groups that spring up between family and state like charities, church-study groups, book clubs, and the Loyal Order of the Moose. One can hear shame being passed around these "intermediate institutions" by just listening to the colloquy between pro-life and pro-choice sides of the abortion issue. Shame on you for slaughtering the unborn. No, no, shame on you for violating a woman's right to choose.

And, as we saw in the outbreak of World War II, shame can cause entire nations to erupt in violence. Many historians blame the rise of the Nazi movement on the brutal shaming of Germany after the first war.

In fact, once shame gets settled on a nation, it can linger for generations. Why else do the Japanese still have such trouble accounting to their neighbors for their behavior a half century ago? Clearly it is so difficult to say, "Sorry, we were wrong" that they will go through endless public hand-wringing lest they experience the onset of dreaded shame. In the lingo of the Recovery movement, putting Vietnam behind us was the American shame-work of the 1980s, and according to Stuart Schneiderman's *Saving Face*, the work is still going on.

Holding families, associations, and other cultures aside for a moment, we can learn more about our own handling of shame by staying with Jenny Jones. Whatever Mr. Schmitz experienced, it was something that could gather not just a studio audience but a massive television crowd. Sleaze is entertaining. Often it is riveting. The trigger finger stays off the remote-control clicker. A month after the shooting during the February "sweeps," the Nielsen figures revealed that Jenny Jones's show boasted a 61 percent improvement over the previous year, Jerry Springer enjoyed a 52 percent improvement, and Ricki Lake managed a 46 percent increase.[2] More people were watching, most of them young.

Crowds always cluster around the guillotine, the car wreck, and the freak show. If you ask them why they have gathered, many will say they know they are not supposed to like this, but they do. "There but for the grace of God go I" is clearly part of the attraction. "I may not be much, but I'm better than they are" may be the rest. Still, it is a nifty conundrum that we are ashamed of being so interested in the shaming of others.

"The Jenny Jones Show" is packaged by Warner Bros. Domestic Television Distribution, a subsidiary of Time Warner, a multinational conglomerate well known in these circles as the one-time major distributor of gangsta rap and signatory to a long-term contract with one of the most successful franchisers of shamelessness, Madonna. Time Warner's job is not to merchandise shame, but to make money for its shareholders by trading entertainment for cash. The connections are instructive. All the large suppliers of television product (Viacom, The Tribune Co., Sony, King World, Multimedia, Columbia TriStar, News Corp., and even Disney, to name a few of the biggest) have a stake in this type of transaction. Naturally they do not call it shame TV; they call it emotional-confrontation or surprise-revelation TV. They are just giving the sponsors what they want: access to the difficult-to-reach eighteen- to thirty-year-olds.

The sponsors were quick to say it wasn't their fault either. You won't find their fingerprints on the shotgun. They were just giving the audience what it wanted. Accidents happen. The distributor made the telling point that with 260 episodes a year, they certainly couldn't be second-guessing Jenny and her talent brokers. But they were certainly not pleased and would reevaluate their sponsorship. Meanwhile, like guppies gleefully eating their own, the day after the slaying, a public-relations executive in Chicago says she got a call from the Montel Williams staff. They wanted a psychologist to discuss the "Jenny" murder on an upcoming show.

What we may see in the matter of Jonathan Schmitz is that there is plenty of shame to go around. But there is always plenty of shame in culture, because shame is part of what stabilizes culture. "I never wonder to see men wicked," wrote Jonathan Swift in *Thoughts on Various Subjects*, "but I often wonder to see them not ashamed." Societies can be evil, but never shameless. What changes are the objects of shame and the thresholds necessary to trigger it. When triggered, however, shame can be as powerful as any gun, as confining as any jail cell.

THE PARADOX OF SHAME

Ironically, we can never be free of shame. A key to unlocking the conundrum of shame is that *shameless* and *shameful* are synonyms. Only the crazy are shame-free. To be shame-free is to be devoid of a self.

Shame is but one direction point on the compass of self. Shame points one way, honor points the other. Have too much shame and an individual/culture will throttle itself—too introjected. Have too little and an individual/society will dissipate—too aggressive. Vice versa with honor. They are both social leashes, or better yet, electric fences forever being dug up and replanted. Until recently, the process occurred over generations. Now it happens monthly.

Social contracts depend on how much individuals care about the good of the group, and how much the group cares about the good of individuals. Shame/honor gauges that concern. What gives shame its particular power, however, is that it is usually unacknowledged by both shamer and shamed. Usually, only long after the act will one or both parties realize what has occurred. In fact, to acknowledge shaming as it is happening is to remove, or at least lessen, its intensity, loosen its rein, lower the voltage. No one said to the lazy schoolboy that he was wearing the dunce cap so that he would associate embarrassment with bad behavior. No one ever says to the chain gang that public display is the object of their work, not the making of pebbles. Nor does Jenny Jones ever say to her guests that they are being ridiculed as entertainment for her young audience.

One of the reasons so little has been written on shame is that no one feels very good about discussing something so unfortunately awkward. Until recently, most of us were often embarrassed not just of being ashamed, but of seeing others publicly shamed. Feeling *schadenfreude* (that wonderful German word for pleasure in another's pain) is one thing; expressing it is quite another; merchandising it is yet another.

Having said that, let me try to acknowledge shame by defining it. There are many approaches. There is individual, familial, political, and religious shame, to name the most obvious. There is existential shame, racial shame, sexual shame. Shame also overlaps a number of related degradations like humiliation, guilt, chagrin, and embarrassment. We will never pin it down. But this much is clear: whatever

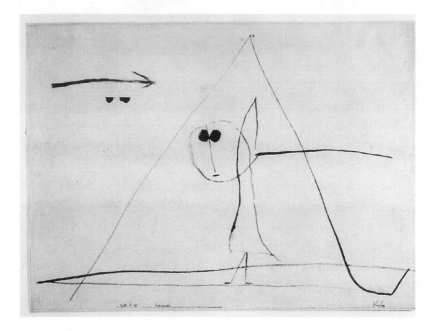

PAUL KLEE, *SHAME,* 1933 (KUNSTMUSEUM BERN, PAUL-KLEE-STIFTUNG).

shame is, it profoundly affects our selves, families, politics, economics, entertainment, conduct of international affairs, and even our approach to nature and the Beyond. Shame is a social taproot, perhaps even the master emotion.

The easiest way to tackle shame may be to describe what it feels like. As opposed to other deflating emotions, when you experience shame you usually blush intensely, your head drops slightly, your shoulders stoop, your knees may buckle, and your feet feel leaden. There is often a mild experience of nausea. To be "put to shame" is profoundly disorienting in most every culture. Everything literally shuts *down:* eyes down, face down, slouch down. You lose muscle tone. You melt down. In extreme cases you even fall over. Although a staple of medieval and Renaissance art (witness the countless exiles of Adam and Eve on church walls), shame is rarely pictured today. Above is Paul Klee's ink-and-brush rendition of the sensation.

What is instantly noticeable to others is your face. You lose it. It goes away. "Losing face" is no haphazard metaphor, nor is the attempt to ward off shame by "saving face." Being shamefaced is having no face to face others. I can't face it, you say, not just about the object of the shame, but about the others around you. You hide your face in shame. You have been defaced. Sociopaths are exempt. They smile and look up. Strangely, however, although the face is so central, this is one emotion with no special facial signature other than the blush, which is why Mr. Schmitz looked so normal.

When the sensation of shame moves from the individual to the group, a different reaction occurs. Coded stigmata appear. The anxiety of being seen and shamed by the Other becomes ritualized. For instance, a veil sometimes appears to cover the face. So Middle Eastern women wear the chador in daily life, and some Western women don a veil in church settings. Both are dim vestiges of a shared sense of routinized humiliation expressed across the face. Not by happenstance does the modern Christian define his cultural origins as the shaming and exile of Adam and Eve. "The eyes of both were opened, and they knew that they were naked" (Genesis 3:7). Moses turns his face down lest he should see the face of God. We bow our heads in prayer. Yet the bride lifts the veil and shows her face after the wedding vows. Her shame, albeit a highly contrived and pantomimed affair connected to mating rituals, is over, at least for the moment.

The Blush of Shame

The reason the face disappears in shame is that it is in pain. Although it may seem strange to speak of the face as if it were an elbow or a foot, shame is a pain in the face. The face is wounded. "O shame! Where is thy blush?" asks Hamlet in Act Three, doubtful that his mother really is distraught. He is right to wonder if shame can travel without the blood rush. The Talmud calls shaming "shedding blood," and Jean-Paul Sartre moves the bleeding inside, calling it an "internal hemorrhage." Little wonder that, once it is experienced, we all become erythrophobic—the fear of blushing is almost as intense as the act itself.

Silvan Tomkins, a research psychologist, studied the blood-rush symptom. The pain of shame is literally caused by a kind of hemorrhage to the blood vessels in the face. Glands, which we need not be familiar with, muscles, which we need not name, and skin receptors, which we have not even discovered, go into spasm. Shame to Tomkins is all very biological. It is a series of involuntary responses within the limbic system. Let's just be old-fashioned and say that blood vessels dilate. Or let's be really Victorian and say you become rubescent. You burn with shame.

I mention the medical component because some people do seem more receptive to this facial blood rush than others. For example, the Romantic poet John Keats considered it an admirable family trait; more women blush than men; more Mediterraneans than Teutons blush. Blushing *is* triggered by chemicals. What pulls the trigger, however, is cultural.

Dr. Donald L. Nathanson, a psychiatrist interested in Tomkins's work and author of a number of books on shame, postulates the existence of a "shame chemical" secreted in a subcortical portion of the brain that starts the chain reaction resulting in the "internal hemorrhage." If he is correct, a shame antidote is possible. In the future we may be able to drink a shame-freeing cocktail before heading off to don the lampshade and insult the boss. After all, the medications called "monoamine-oxidase inhibitor antidepressants," MAOI drugs, and the family of antidepressants represented by fluoxetine (Prozac), do seem to lessen the facial effect. In addition, if they are used with alprasolam (Xanax), "shame panics" can be pushed aside by tricking the brain to turn down the pump and lower the blood pressure.

Drs. Tomkins and Nathanson stand in an illustrious group, for Victorian scientists were also curious about what was going on in the face. Thomas Burgess of the Royal College of Surgeons composed *The Physiology or Mechanism of Blushing* in 1839, stressing its providential design (the "divinity which stirs within us"). At almost the same time Charles Darwin was concluding his more scholarly *The Expression of the Emotions in Man and Animals* with an exploration of "Self-attention, Shame, Shyness, Modesty and Blushing." By the end of the century even Havelock Ellis had a go at it in "The Evolution of Modesty" (1899), considering the blushing discomfort of shame a central step on the road to Cultureville.

As we all know, the Victorians were very concerned about shame. One of the less obvious reasons for this concern has to do with their scientific interest in establishing equitable social policy. Dark-skinned people have always provided a puzzling enigma. Baron von Humboldt, the German explorer and collector, raised the question when he asked, "How can those be trusted who know not how to blush?"[3] and these Victorian scientists attempted an answer. Since blushing is the central signifier of shame, and since you cannot see blush on dark skin, many assumed that the Indian and Negroid races were shame-free. Shame-free = shameless = subhuman. While this made conquest and the slave trade easier to conduct, it was based on mistaking the absence of expression for the absence of affect.

While the blush may indeed be the mark of humanity, humans can't resolve its peculiarities. Here are just a few. You can tickle almost any people in any culture and make them laugh, you can pinch them and make them cry, but you can't make them blush. The crimson glow is biological, but the mechanism that operates it is social. Why is a little blush, a little controlled shame, a key to perceived sensitivity; else how to account for the millions of dollars to be made from producing rouge? Gender seems secondary. In the seventeenth century—the century of the most intense patriarchy (the divine right of kings, the Great

Chain of Being, and all that)—men wore rouge. And in the nineteenth century the sentimental novel was a man's way of practicing the blush. Henry Mackenzie's *The Man of Feeling* and Oliver Goldsmith's *The Vicar of Wakefield* were primers for budding Romantics to work on their feelings.

And what about this: Can a man, blind since birth, blush? And if he can't blush, can he feel shame as intensely as the seeing man can? Can you blush in your sleep? Will we blush less in the dark? Alone?

And what of animals—are they capable of shame? Jeffrey Masson and Susan McCarthy, authors of *When Elephants Weep*, think so, but they are in the minority. Friedrich Nietzsche, who was fascinated by the centrality of shame, used shame to separate man from the animals by asserting that "man is the creature who blushes." And Mark Twain, who was fascinated by what that separation means, continued the description, ". . . or needs to." Until science explains the chemistry of shame, we will have to be content with our rather prosaic understanding of the blush.

What is known about the blush of shame is this: The sudden pain in the face and shrinkage of the self will happen to you regardless of race, sex, culture, or intelligence all over the world. Almost anything can trigger it. Shame is therefore not like honor or guilt, which cannot be seen by others. Rather it is like fear or laughter, which either lifts the hairs on the nape of the neck or causes the mouth to turn up. No one teaches you the physiology of the fight-or-flight response; no one teaches you how to turn your mouth. These responses are hardwired. No one teaches you how to blush. So shame, too, comes with the territory; it has evolved with us, most probably for a reason.

Feelings of shame begin to emerge in the second year of life, at the very formation of the infant's sense of self. As the infant realizes that he is a separate person, he is first able to understand that others are directing emotional messages to him. Pride and shame appear: pride at pleasing others and shame at displeasing them. Moments of intense shame will continue through childhood into adolescence. Then they abate. A few of these experiences will be memorable, some positively cauterizing, but most will be assimilated and forgotten. If the socializing process is successful, the adult will have learned where the electric fence is and memorized the map. The mature and socialized human is not often shamed. Shame has set the moral compass and acts become seemingly free, but only within certain limits.

What We Share for Shame

One finds all this tucked into the history of the word itself. Most European languages have at least two meanings for the word *shame:* one to denote the feeling, one to denote the fear of feeling it. This double view acknowledges that one does not have to be in the painful blush of shame in order for the codes to be read. So, for instance, the French have *honte,* which is pain that you feel after misbehaving, and *pudeur,* which is warning before the bashful-making event. The Germans have *scham* and *schande.* This distinction between disgrace-shame and discretion-shame is also present in Greek, Latin, Spanish, and Russian.

We all know the difference between *I am shamed* (humility) and *I feel shame* (pain). But our language doesn't. The duality is simply not in English. We have only the single word *shame,* which is derived from a Germanic root: *skam/skem* from Old High German *scama* via Anglo-Saxon *scamu,* meaning a sense of shame and being shamed *(schande).* When you trace that root to the East you find the Indo-European *kam/kem,* which means "to cover, to veil, to hide," which picked up the prefix *s/skam* to mean "to cover oneself." While the linguistic trail may be complex, the notion of hiding/covering is clear. Protection is intrinsic to, and inseparable from, the concept of shame.

Clearly the notion of shame is located in the very hub of selfhood, for it establishes the concept of inside and outside. From this develops the distinction of *me* from *you,* and *us* from *them.* And from that comes the most central aspect of culture: privacy and a sense of self.

Although the subjects and intensity of what is considered private will differ by culture, a few similarities are present. No matter where you are, you will feel shame for haphazard public excretions, difficult-to-manage eating/suckling habits, nonreproductive sexual behavior, and, strange to us, dying. A shame rule of thumb: if you do it in private, if covering/uncovering is important, or if the act is surrounded by a lexicon of expletives and euphemisms, you can guess that shame is near. When shame fails, disgust ensues.

No one defecates carelessly in public; no one, not in any culture. We have repressed our primate heritage. Even in China, where defecation is often very public, there is a rigorous decorum. This taboo is fierce and clearly has hygiene as its surface rationale. But we go crazy over toilet training and bed-wetting for more reasons than disease and laundry costs. Elimination of waste is also a socializing concern, a proximity/separation gauge that takes constant recalibration. How deep into the woods do you go? Here is the initiation of self and the concept of personal space. From this comes the central building block of any society—modesty. Once it is learned, any weakness of bowel and urethral control is shameful. If you don't believe this, simply look at how Depends and other elimination-control devices are advertised to older people. When people talk in whispers, you know something serious is being said.

While we come into this world between shitting and pissing, or in the more polite words of Saint Augustine, *inter urinas et faeces nascimur,* we never admit it. In India, for instance, where there is little indoor plumbing and few outhouses, many castes defecate outdoors. With space at a premium, however, privacy is maintained by the conditioned reflex of others not looking. Or pretending not to. Oddly enough, as V. S. Naipaul wrote of life in Kashmir, "If you surprise a group of three women, companionably defecating, they will giggle: the shame is yours, for exposing yourself to such a scene."[4] When anthropologists have asked both participants and nonseeing observers to explain what has transpired, all parties deny any elimination event took place. So, too, in Turkey the latrine is referred to as "the house of shame," in Brazil workers demand "shame pay" for unloading toilets, and members of many tribes will let a fellow drown in a communal cesspool rather than attempt a rescue.

Shame associated with eating is a bit more complex than elimination shame. We think of eating as a communal behavior, but since we have well-defined eating spaces and very rigid rules, we should think twice. The electric fence is all over the dining room table. Eating is highly ritualized, done at certain times, with special instruments, and demands a prescribed behavior. The fact that etiquette first becomes codified as table manners and can result in such bizarre occurrences as the codes concerning the placement of the napkin, the proper techniques of carving, or the use of some specialized fork, shows us how uneasy we are about eating close together. In most preindustrial cultures the concept of rigid meals, divided into courses and consumed around a table, is unknown. As anorexics know, we relate eating to social activity, not to hunger.

In the industrialized West, regular meals are the tribute we pay to the machine. The words *coffee break* and *lunch break, Miller Time* and *cocktail hour, daytime* and *nighttime shift* show where the control of diurnal rhythms has gone. But every culture has table manners, although it may not have tables, and bad eating behavior is sometimes so shameful that violence can result. Pass food improperly in some cultures, or try reaching over to another's plate for "just a little taste," and you will find out.

Ironically, some of us are ashamed to eat alone, although private grazing and gorging is indeed how most humans eat, and have eaten.

We are so anxious about being seen eating alone in public that we usually read newspapers and sit in the corners. Our more modern cultural shame at seeming friendless can trump our ancient anxiety of eating too close to others. Still, we like space around us when eating, which may account for the popularity of drive-through fast-food restaurants, as well as eating in front of the TV set. The success of the TV dinner eaten on a tray may be attributable more to the pleasures of solitary eating than to the quality of the food.

Sex, as we all know, is a veritable rumpus of shame. Not for nothing does the Latin *pudenda* mean both the organs and covering. To say that someone is impudent means that he or she is shameless, like uncovered organs. So the Bible asserts "the shame of nakedness" and our culture reiterates this concern, naming the genitals "shameful parts," "privy members," or "parts of shame." English is not alone. This barely veiled censure is present in most languages.

Nakedness, however, is a cultural construction. There is a famous example, put forward a century ago by Max Scheler in his treatise on shame, of a nude female model posing for a male artist. As long as the model perceives she is being painted as a form, she feels no shame. But the moment she feels that the artist is looking at her not as a model but as an object of desire, she blushes.[5] To make this modern and give it the proper shame spin, the same model, now a go-go dancer at the Café Risque, may feel shame if the audience is *not* perceiving her as a sexual object, but as a form in space.

There is, as well, a revealing story told by anthropologists about how early explorers to New Guinea kept themselves covered in the European manner. Finally they were just too embarrassed by seeing the nakedness of others and insisted the natives cover up their genitals with cloth. The natives did, but then attempted to cover their now-clothed selves with their hands just as we would do if naked. Their heads dropped and shoulders slumped. They then rushed into the bush to remove the offending rags. Although it was not obvious to Caucasians, they blushed.[6]

The primordial connection of shame is not with nakedness but with the reproductive organs erotically observed or nonreproductively used. Although the degree of shame differs, all lasting cultures stigmatize sterility, small organ size, incest, masturbation, and usually homosexuality. As with eating and elimination, sex is highly regulated, not by overt acknowledgment, but by the buried electric fence. Shame is the ultimate prophylactic, and when it is not working efficiently, as is currently the case in modern America, unwanted and uncared-for babies multiply.

And let us not forget death, which is another universal shaming event. We have done our best to remove death from visible culture, not just because it is a nuisance but because at some level we, too, are ashamed. Is this really how it all ends—not with a bang but a whimper? Thomas Browne, that most cranky genius of elegant Augustan prose, knew this well:

> I am not so much afraid of death, as ashamed thereof. It is the very disgrace and ignominy of our natures, that in a moment can so disfigure us that our nearest friends, wife and children stand afraid and start at us. (*Religio Medici*)

Browne was not alone. Read Leo Tolstoy's *The Death of Ivan Ilych* for a disquisition on the shame of dying. Ivan lies in the dark not because he does not want to see, but because he does not want to be seen. With the exception of heroic death, expiration is totally undignified. We make a point of asserting death with dignity, of having living wills, of hospices, of composing elegies, of elaborate religious ceremonies in which the sting is removed. But we know better. Such death *is* shameful. We lose face forever. We say we almost die of shame, that shame is a little death, but in truth, death is the big shame.

As we codify social behavior into etiquette and modesty in order to deal with the shame of certain aspects of living, we generate religion to deal with the shame of dying. As Nietzsche said, wherever mystery is, shame is close behind. In most cultures, even sleep, the poetic cousin to death, is mildly shameful. Is this because it has all the flags of a death event? We lose consciousness. Else why are we ashamed to be "caught" sleeping at the wrong time—caught napping? It is not simply a Puritan work ethic taboo—too many cultures have the prohibition.

But this is about all we share for universal shame triggers: aspects of eliminating, eating, copulating, and death. These are the hardwired shame events. They are in machine memory. However, there is one more type. If you believe that there is entirely too much shame in modern culture—a view that has characterized the baby-boom generation since the 1960s, which sees shame as an obstacle to self-esteem—you should be reminded that long-lasting cultures share another generalized shame event. The opposite of shame is shameless. And shamelessness, the absence of certain default levels of blush-producing behavior, is a cultural toxin. It is feared everywhere. If in the beginning of cultures there is shame, at the end there is shamelessness.

The electric fence keeps certain behaviors from getting out, but it also keeps certain threats from getting in. In this sense, to really mix the metaphor, shame is the canary in the mine shaft of culture. The point is not to throw out shame and enthrone autonomy, but to recover an appropriate sense of shame and the boundary protections it affords.

Although we tend to think of shame as a Puritan and Victorian affliction, it most definitely is not. The sentiment behind the ancient German proverb "So long as there is shame there is hope for virtue" is repeated again and again in Western cultures. When Edmund Burke wrote in *Reflections on the Revolution in France*, "While shame keeps its watch, virtue is not wholly extinguished in the heart," he was speaking a commonplace.

Admittedly, from often high-minded principles, we have in the last generation tried to push shame aside. The human-potential and recovered-memory movements in psychology; the moral relativism of audience-driven Christianity; the penalty-free, all-ideas-are-equally-good transformation in higher education; the rise of no-fault behavior before the law; the often outrageous distortions in the telling of history so that certain groups can feel better about themselves; and the "I'm shame-free, but you should be ashamed of yourself" tone of political discourse are just some of the instances wherein this can be seen. Most important, the merchandising of shaming and shamelessness as entertainment has recently come to dominate American popular culture. Shame that was once thought natural is now considered something to be sloughed off, to be free of, even to be made fun of. In our short-lived Pyrrhic victory over shame, we have given up much of value. As the carnival culture of adolescents has become the dominant culture, we have neglected many of the crucial ceremonies of adult decency.

CHAPTER 3

THE CONDITION OF MODERN SHAME

Where the heart's past hope, the face is past shame
—Scottish proverb

WHAT SEPARATES HUMAN cultures is that while the jolt of shame remains the same (the meltdown blush), for unknown reasons, the fence is buried in different places. As we have seen, there are certain fence lines we all share, certain acts that are beyond the pale, regardless of time, place, and culture. But other than those, it's a free-for-all. As Eric Heller, the cultural anthropologist, has written, "In the first place (if not also the last), man is capable of being ashamed of almost anything that is about him."[1] So a fellow blowing his nose in Japan, a woman going out in Baghdad without a veil, disparaging songs sung about you by fellow Eskimos, a waiter being tripped while serving food in Iceland, a bridal couple not receiving proper wedding gifts in China, a prisoner having his head shaved in Muslim cultures, a golfer not replacing his divot in Scotland—all these will evoke a most powerful, and *learned,* response.

Never underestimate the power of shame. Jonathan Schmitz was hardly the only one to feel its mortal power. In the spring of 1996 the chief of U.S. Naval Operations shot a .38-caliber bullet through his own chest. He did this because one of the minor ribbons he wore on that chest had a small *V* pinned to it. The *V* signified that the award was for combat action, and the admiral was never formally authorized to wear that *V.* Civilians found it ludicrous that such an accomplished man would be driven to suicide by such a minor impropriety. Many military men did too. But clearly, what seems to be just surface decoration, or, irreverently, "fruit salad," is sacramentally serious to a few. Napoleon Bonaparte said that a soldier will "fight long and hard for a bit of colored ribbon," and just as clearly some soldiers will be mortified if that ribbon (and all that it signifies) is not won (and worn) properly.

Suicide is the ultimate response to shame. Thankfully, the sensation is usually expressed in a less extreme measures. In fact, it is usually expressed and conveyed in culture-specific subtle gestures. When I was an adolescent, drawing one index finger down the side of the other while *tsk-tsk*ing with the tongue was a slightly ironic sign that you should "hang your head." To communicate shame in Jordan and Syria, you hold your extended right thumb near your chin with the heel of your hand out. Just next door in Saudi Arabia you stroke your chin with the fingers of the right hand with downward a motion. The Indians of the American plains made the motion of pulling a blanket up over the face. Meanwhile, the French close the fingers, raising the thumb and index fingers, making the "horns" of the cuckold. In Italy you make an imaginary slap on the wrist. In many cultures the pantomime act of cutting hair communicates the shame message. No matter what the sign, the significance is quickly decoded, especially by the young. Or else.

Shame vs Guilt: How Necessary Is the Distinction?

A generation ago, in an attempt to explain why shame codes were so different, cultural anthropologists suggested that the distinction between shame and guilt might serve as a guideline. Perhaps one could differentiate among cultures on the basis of whether shame (external conformity) or guilt (internal sense of self) was the prime motivator of behavior. This hypothesis, popularized by Ruth Benedict, led to such assertions that there was a fault line in Europe between the wine-drinking countries of the South and the beer- and whiskey-drinking North, between those who follow ties of kin and fealty and those who follow the social rules. Guilt up North, shame down South. Moving to a global scale, what separated the Germans, with a Judeo-Christian guilt culture, from the Japanese, with a Shinto shame culture, was, they argued, that Occidentals could admit responsibility for what they and their countrymen did while Orientals could not.

Alas, as one can see even from the preceding examples, the taxonomy has proven neater for writers of scholarly articles than for observers of culture. It just didn't work. Eskimos are not more susceptible to guilt than equatorial Africans. Easter Islanders are drenched with shame, but then so are the Amish. And just what is Germany, anyway: a shame or a guilt culture? If it is a guilt culture, why has communal honor been so central a concept? Why the focus on Aryan ancestry?

Clearly, all cultures use internal, unarticulated controls, and just as clearly, one culture will seem more shame-riven than another. The observer will have a great deal to do with the assessment; Heisenberg's uncertainty principle works in anthropology too. The guilt and shame bugaboo, which has also plagued psychology (guilt supposedly is the ego dissatisfied with itself, while shame is the superego dissatisfied with the ego), needs a rest. The differences between shame and guilt are matters of degree, not kind. Maybe it sounds precise to say such things as that shame is the basis of *public* virtue, while guilt is the basis of *private* value; that shame concerns failure of *being,* while guilt points to a failure of *doing;* that shamed people are bothered by *shortcomings,* while the guilty notice *transgressions;* or that a shamed person fears *abandonment,* while the guilty fears *punishment.* But such distinctions don't really add much. Try applying this either/or distinction to real life and you will see it has more heuristic than practical value.

If it is necessary to distinguish between them, let's leave it at this: Both shame and guilt are an "internalized other." With shame, the internalized other is a watcher (thus, primitively, it is shameful to be seen naked, but not to be naked), while with guilt, the internalized other can be imagined as a voice, speaking as victim or judge. In our ordinary lives we know both shame and guilt together, as do all socialized humans.

All cultures depend on shame, all cultures abhor shamelessness, and all cultures think other cultures have more inappropriate shame than they do. So, too, all cultures think they are "free" relative to others; they just define the state differently. In this sense, shame is rather like language; it communicates what it has to, and one should be wary of saying Eskimo is better than Tuareg. One does a better job with snow, the other with sand.

The Example of Japan

Having said this, it is instructive to look briefly at Japan, because whatever they have for shame, it is certainly different from what we have. Dishonor in the group is a stronger force on behavior than a personal sense of universal right and wrong—the central trait of Western individualism. Hence, the Christian notion of singular sin, repentance, and salvation gets little traction in Japanese culture. The possibility of expulsion from the group is what they have for the fires of hell. Little wonder that Billy Graham was met with polite wariness. This same sense of inside/outside maintains the Japanese group system of obligation, honor, and deference—a social ecology that produces efficient corporate teams, crimeless streets, and a safe wonderland of indulged, yet obedient, children.

Even on the surface, Japanese shame doesn't look like our shame.

They are forever apologizing to each other. Listen to them on the telephone. "I am unworthy to take your time," the conversation begins. It ends, "I apologize for interrupting you from your important tasks." And this is a call to a best friend! Go to a Japanese house for dinner and you will think from the host's comments that the delicious meal you are enjoying has been scraped from a Dumpster.

We may well wonder, since shame rituals are so prevalent, why the Japanese should have such a hard time taking a little blame for killing ten million of their neighbors a generation ago. Apologies have the same deep meaning for Chinese and Koreans. That's why they have focused so intently on Japan's unwillingness to even acknowledge the atrocities committed during World War II. Japan has stalled and dithered about the wording of an apology for generations because the ramifications of shame are so far-reaching. Public apology for them calls a whole world view into question, and is every bit as painful as individual nausea.

Japanese shame is a two-way street. Criminals draw reduced sentences if they apologize and show shame. Business leaders save their companies from the wrath of stockholders by bowing deeply and affecting the blush of shame. Politicians save their careers and survive to run again by abjectly apologizing for anything from accepting bribes to keeping mistresses. Even miscreant husbands can reenter the good graces of their wives by invoking routinized mea culpas.

The point is simply this: Shame codes look different, often bizarre, but they always do the same thing. They maintain boundaries, they separate public and private, they resolve ambiguity, they limit excess and danger, they control individuality, they provide for dignity and honor and pride. They exile *and they let back in*. Admittedly and importantly, they appear—especially to the young—heartless.

A Thumbnail History of Western Shame

Moving from the cross-cultural to the specific culture, we can see the continual battle for control of the codes within our recent history. Take the Victorian codes, for instance. Although Victorian shaming is much ridiculed today, it was a crucial aspect of the industrial revolution, and lasted well into the twentieth century. Until recently, much of what we took as immutable human behavior resulted from endless tinkering with human social interactions to make efficient the production and consumption of mass-produced goods. Divorce-free families, intense nurturing of children, longtime job affiliations, regularized consumption, communal worship, and routinized celebrations like Christmas were all maintained by shaming. As has often been pointed out, the success of capitalism was in large measure because Christianity had already set the system in place.

The demands of the machine were easily layered onto already-established demands of the Church. If the Church had shown how shaming could produce a cohesive culture using such institutionalized formats as excommunication and the Inquisition, the modern industrial state could do the same with wages and economic shunning. But all was not negative goads; you need the stick *and* the carrot. The carrot of salvation remained, achieved through consumption in this world, not faith in the next.

As one might imagine, the Church itself was both the magistrate and the medium of Renaissance shame. The great biblical stories—Job, Abraham and God, Adam's fall, Abel and Cain—were all shame stories. Many of the great works of Renaissance art were of shame. Think only of Michelangelo's *Tree of Knowledge* or Masaccio's *The Expulsion from Eden*, in which Adam and Eve are bent double with shame.

The Church even sanctioned the *pitture infamanti,* or shaming cartoons, which were placed on the outside of church walls in much the

Masaccio, *The Expulsion from Eden*, 1425–27 (Brancacci Chapel, Santa Maria del Carmine, Florence).

same way that the local paper now runs an insert with the names of overdue taxpayers. These pictures, painted in fresco on masonry, were caricatures (the most feared were human images upside down) and could be changed with a little plaster as the culprit redeemed himself.

The Church participated in other shaming events. It acted as judge, jury, and police. The priest would lead his parishioners to publicly shame a deadbeat, say a man who had abandoned his family, by sur-

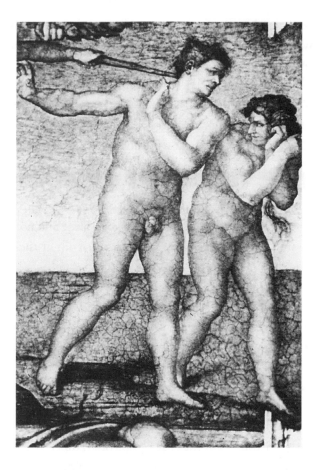

MICHELANGELO, *EXILE FROM EARTHLY PARADISE,* 1508–11 (DETAIL OF THE CEILING OF THE SISTINE CHAPEL, THE VATICAN, ROME).

rounding him while pounding on pans and banging sticks together. Boom-box pain in reverse. In Mediterranean cultures, this ceremony, called "rough music," continued through the nineteenth century, and was even picked up and made part of high-culture music in the French *charivari.*

The early codifiers of modern shame were self-conscious spokesmen of the military-ecclesiastical complex. They were churchmen who attempted to regularize behavior by establishing manners, that is to say, the behavior expected of a gentleman. To fill in the blank spaces of the church code, they added bits of the chivalric code governing the court practices of the knighthood. In Rotterdam, Erasmus published *De Civilitate Morum Puerilium* (translated as *On the Manners of Children*) in 1530. What to wear, not to stare, how to eat, how to blow your nose, what to do with spittle, and such were all covered. A few decades later in Italy, Annibale Pocaterra published his *Duo Dialogi della Vergogna (Two Dialogues on Shame)*, which again attempted to place behavior developed in monasteries into the ordinary home. Its focus on eating together, on "waiting" table, on staying in your place and not grabbing food from the serving plates, shows how modern our at-the-table eating really is.

English culture's primary shame manual was also one of the central documents of the Renaissance, Thomas More's *Utopia* (1516). Shame is the primary organizing system in this never-never land, a world that promises social peace at a price. In More's ideal social system, shaming is the central method of enforcing conformity. Individuals merge with the utopian state because the threat of publicized separation is so intense. No prison, no death penalty, no parole; you make a mistake and you pack your bags. And, if you are really misbehaving, you take your loved ones with you. So in the case of out-of-wedlock babies, you do not receive Aid to Families with Dependent Children; just the opposite. You receive a bus ticket to the Yukon. You take your partner with you. And your parents are shunned: "Both father and mother of a family in whose house the offense was committed incur great disgrace as having been neglectful in doing their duties."

The key, of course, is to make membership in the group so rewarding that exile is an anathema. To do this, the Utopians spurn much of what we consider valuable. Jewels, gold, gems, and all objects whose value is based on rarity are drained of worth. In fact, such objects are draped around the necks of those who have been shunned, those called "slaves." When potentates come from afar to observe the Utopians, the children run and hide. They have been taught to associate jewelry with antisocial behavior.

The ecclesiastical paradigm did not survive. Capitalism did. The jewels went to the captains of industry, and so *not* having them became shameful. Although academic Marxists may see the resetting of shame thresholds as the infantalization of workers and reification of consumers, the industrial revolution produced the lasting stability of Victorianism, a stability that endured until it encountered electronic entertainment. More, Erasmus, and Pocaterra were primarily concerned about interpersonal microrelations; they were trying to move the concerns of the Church and the Court *downward* into everyday homes. Modern shame (what we might call Victorian shame) has been concerned about economic macrorelationships and moved *outward* from the middle class to the working class. What made it powerful was that while the earlier system was static, the modern one allowed improvement. Learn the codes, do the job, and pretty soon you had access to all the things your superiors had. Well, almost everything.

TELL ME A STORY: HOW SHAME IS COMMUNICATED

While earlier shame thresholds had been carried in various catechisms and etiquette books (often in a typeface still called civilité), modern/Victorian shame was conveyed in popular culture, in what we now call literature. Take the novel, for instance. You cannot read most nineteenth-century novels and not be aware how suffused they are with social conventions. Shame sweeps through the English novels of Jane Austen, the Brontës, George Eliot, William Makepeace Thackeray, and Thomas Hardy. It permeates the American vision of Hawthorne, Poe, Melville, James, Dreiser, and Crane, as well as the Russian works of Tolstoy and Dostoyevsky and the French creations of Hugo, Flaubert, and Balzac. A visitor from a distant galaxy would

have surely concluded from the novel that shame was not just culturally central, but omnipresent. It was.

If you were looking for a *vade mecum* of shame in the novel, you
need look no further than the central works of arguably the most important novelist ever, Charles Dickens. Commentators never tire of
pointing out that Dickens's novels represent his working out of the
intense childhood embarrassment of an incarcerated father and the
dreary days working at the stove-blacking factory. What they don't
mention is that here was a reading public that lined up ten deep to buy
the latest installments of his fictional vision for *exactly* that experience.
Which of his works is not suffused with shame: *Our Mutual Friend,
Oliver Twist,* or *Great Expectations?* Here, for instance, is Pip, unaware
of his Victorian condition, in a typical Dickensian passage:

> I was so humiliated, hurt, spurned, offended, angry, sorry—I
> cannot hit upon the right name for the smart . . . that the tears
> started to my eyes. The moment they sprang there, the girl
> looked at me with a quick delight in having been the cause of
> them. This gave me power to keep them back and to look at her;
> so, she gave me a contemptuous toss . . . and left me . . . When she
> was gone I looked about me for a place to hide my face in, and
> got behind one of the gates.

One need not trust the text alone. The copious illustrations to the
Victorian novel provide a visual gloss to the important scenes. Take
David Copperfield, for instance. When Hablot Browne conferred with
Dickens on which scenes to illustrate, they decided on those of emotional distress. The scene of David's introduction to his aunt shows
the shame of social ostracism, while the interlaced scenes of "Martha"
and "Mr. Peggotty's dream comes true" depend on our sensitivity to the
tradition of the fallen woman. She has been shamed by out-of-wedlock
sex. The imagery is not haphazard. In "Martha," for instance, Browne

Hablot Browne, "I make my-self known to my Aunt," 1849–50 (*David Copperfield,* no. 5).

Hablot Browne, "Martha," 1849–50 (*David Copperfield,* no. 8).

Hablot Browne, "Mr. Peggotty's dream comes true," 1849–50 (*David Copperfield,* no. 16).

arranges the characters to approximate the figures in the mantle scene
of Christ blessing Mary Magdalen. The picture forms the top of a tri-
angle linking Martha, who is identified with the Magdalen by her similar posture and isolation from the group. As well, Browne makes the
heads of his characters follow an ascending diagonal like that of

Christ's in the picture. Sin, downfall, shame, redemption, is the message.

An entire genre of the novel is dedicated to shame. The gothic novel, from Horace Walpole's *Castle of Otranto* onward, always centers around acts of profound embarrassment and shame. In the three most important examples—Mary Shelley's *Frankenstein*, Bram Stoker's *Dracula*, and Robert Louis Stevenson's *Dr. Jekyll and Mr. Hyde*—the story hinges on the shame of inappropriate and unguarded adolescent sex. Victor Frankenstein has no business creating life alone, by himself, and then not tending it. Lucy Westenra has no business wandering alone in the cemetery to be courted by the Prince of Darkness, Dracula. Dr. Jekyll has no business subjugating his sexual urges, so that his buried self gets loose and comes out of Hyding to do violence. There is no more terse definition of shame in all literature than Jekyll's comment about what his "other" self has done: "He, I say, I cannot say I." In each of these central novels a callow and brittle youth has to confront the monster of shame, and in each case the frisson of horror we feel observing them conducts the socializing lesson to be learned. Behave! lest their fates become ours.

The novel is hardly the only place one could learn the social role of shame. In a world before Big Bird and Barney, children were glutted with socializing information. In America, for instance, youngsters were brought up on print, often written by schoolteachers or pastors, melodramatic in nature and stern in punishing the wayward child through shame. Have a look at such Puritan primers as John Cotton's *Milk for Babes*, James Janeway's *A Token for Children,* or *The New England Primer* and you will see a world steeped in Calvinist theology. In this world the child is depraved by birth and made social by shame. Later authors, like Martha Finley with her series about Elsie Dinsmore, Louisa May Alcott, and Thomas Bailey Aldrich, tempered this zeal, but still cast the child as at risk in a world of danger. Protect yourself, behave properly, learn the manners, then success may be yours.

Could there be a more pervasive text than the *McGuffey Readers*? First published in 1836 and read by almost every child in America, it remained a keystone of Victorian culture for generations. Although expanding their reading, writing, and speaking skills, the books taught primarily the importance of patriotism, parental respect, cleanliness, industry, and . . . shame. The books instilled moral principles, emphasizing—in accordance with the educational aims of the day—adherence to Christianity, allegiance to country, and consideration for others. In place of the loving acceptance of Barney and the Cookie Monster were warnings of dire consequences if the nation ever stopped observing the Sabbath with proper reverence; stories stressing the mutual obligations between young and old, rich and poor; excerpts from an essay by Oliver Goldsmith on how happiness comes from within, not from external objects; numerous tales of children who strive to support their families by doing such menial tasks as selling matches or shoveling snow lest the shame of poverty descend; and, above all, the importance of getting an education—Little Lucy, in the First Reader, would "rather read than play" because children who "do not know how to read cannot learn anything but what is told them."

One can literally see the lessons taught all over again in popular Victorian art prints and mezzotints. These were the most popular images produced by the massive steam-driven presses and distributed through magazine solicitation. They were suitable for framing, to be hung in the parlor. They were what was seen instead of *Nick at Nite* reruns. So here are a few: John Absolon's *Opie, when a Boy, Reproved by his Mother* (1862), Thomas Armstrong's *The Test* (1865), and Thomas Brooks's *The Captured Truant* (1850). These are genre paintings and the genre is clear: the disciplining of youth by shame. The word *shame* is never mentioned, but if you look at the postures of the young people, the message is unambiguous. Lest the message be forgot, such images were produced by the literal ton. These were not works intended for the downtown aesthete. They were not to be displayed under spot-

THOMAS BROOKS, *THE CAPTURED TRUANT,* 1850 (SOURCE: CHRISTOPHER WOOD, *THE DICTIONARY OF VICTORIAN PAINTERS,* 1978).

lights on the gallery wall—no little polished bronze plaque with painter's name and title. They were produced for the burgeoning middle class, to be hung in family space. That they looked like art—after all, they *could* be framed—made them all the more compelling. No wonder Horace's definition of art as *utile et dulce* ("useful and pleasing") was embraced by the Victorians.

SHAME AND VICTORIAN VALUES

No doubt such institutionalized opprobrium as we see in nineteenth-century Anglo-America reflected the social (read, economic) needs of the Puritan-Republican, producer-capitalist culture. Shame was often more a cudgel than a lever. No doubt it was heartlessly and unsympatheticly applied to those who strayed. Flogging and the pillory were literal and figurative. Such shame suited a culture in which men and women were judged on the basis of character, on the basis of their moral qualities, their principles, their rectitude and especially their

JOHN ABSOLON, *OPIE, WHEN A BOY, REPROVED BY HIS MOTHER,* 1862 (SOURCE: CHRISTO-PHER WOOD, *THE DICTIONARY OF VICTORIAN PAINTERS,* 1978).

work habits. There was plenty wrong with Victorian society—bigotry, exploitation of labor, racism, genocide in empire building—but there was also plenty right. They were right in their attention to first individual and then group decencies. Victorian shame was most often directed toward the excesses of romantic narcissism. Its focus was on creating the independent self: *self*-help, *self*-discipline, *self*-respect, *self*-control, *self*-reliance, *self*-interest. Responsibility was situated first in

THOMAS ARMSTRONG, *THE TEST,* 1865 (SOURCE: CHRISTOPHER WOOD, *THE DICTIONARY OF VICTORIAN PAINTERS,* 1978).

the individual, then in the group. Public and private were well defined, and private came first. Private life. Private charity. Individual responsibility. You pull yourself up by your bootstraps. You were entitled to what you earned, the sweat of your labor. As individuals matured, however, private values became immutable public virtues. Noblesse oblige was all the more powerful because it was voluntary.

In our newer culture of plenty, the standard of judgment has become sociability, the ability to interact effectively with others, to win their affection and admiration—to fit in, to join. The focus is now on the interdependent self: on its relationship with the state, the law, a fully vested retirement community. You are entitled to some of what others have earned, especially if they are perceived to have too much.

In the older culture, aspirations to material comfort were sharply restricted by the limited capacity of the economy to produce. In the modern world, much greater material satisfactions lie within the range even of those of modest means. Hence a producer culture becomes a consumer culture, a hoarding culture becomes a surplus culture, a segmented culture becomes a mass culture, a work culture becomes a therapeutic culture. "Deal with your pain" becomes "I feel your pain." Responsibility is situated primarily in the state. You can't pull yourself up by your bootstraps. How silly to think so. Just try it and you'll see. You'll fall over. Public life is central. That the safety net for some becomes a hammock for others is a cost worth paying. Virtues become relative values.

This is all quite glib, to be sure, because it is already part of what we take for granted. Mickey Mouse has not taken over from Mrs. Grundy, but the torch has been passed.

Gross generalization that it is, we have gone from an "ought" culture where superego was central—where there were rules for everything from how to commence courtship to how to tip the porter—to a "want" culture—in which "Question Authority" and "Shit Happens" are more than bumper stickers. They are theologies.

The shift has become obvious recently because (1) the piper has appeared and insists on being paid for the social costs of these changes, and (2) a highly sentimental culture—oft misnamed a counterculture—emerged since the 1960s in which modern/Victorian shame has essentially disappeared. Paradoxically, the group most threatened by the absence of shame has been the most willing to countenance its effacement. The educated middle class, thanks primarily to the narcotic allure of "free" worldwide electronic entertainment and the transitory pleasures it carries, has in effect said, "Push the remote and change the channel" when reality programming interfered with fun. Although we will see how the struggle to become shame-free has dominated religion, psychology, politics, and education, let's see first what the piper is presenting as a bill.

Here is what the reality check looks like using illegitimacy as an example:

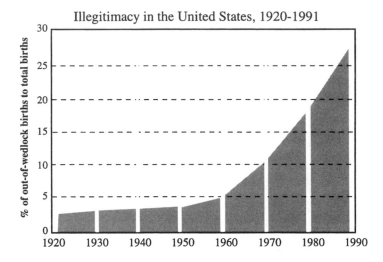

Illegitimacy in the United States, 1920–1991 (adapted from Gertrude Himmelfarb, *The De-Moralization of Society*) source: U.S. Bureau of the Census, Vital Statistics of the United States, 1940; for 1940–1991 U.S. Department of Health and Human Services, National Center for Health Statistics.

As recently as the fifteenth editions of *Encyclopedia Britannica* (1974–86), "Victorian" was described as a time associated with the at-

titudes of "insularity, materialism, complacency, hypocrisy, and especially censoriousness," in which "gentility, respectability, and propriety
were often regarded as the greatest public virtues." What, one wonders, will it say of us? For the sake of comparison, here is what the lines
of that horribly repressive Victorian culture looked like. Note the
steady descent of bastardy from the 1850s to past the turn of the century as Victorian "insularity, materialism, complacency, hypocrisy,"
and the rest made certain individuals unhappy but benefited the group.
The next two spikes to the right are during the world wars, but then
look what happens in the 1960s:

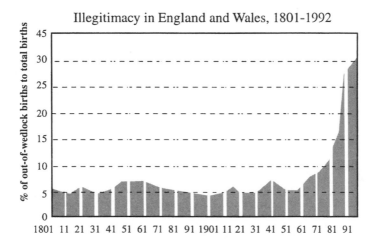

ILLEGITIMACY IN ENGLAND AND WALES, 1801–1992 (ADAPTED FROM GERTRUDE HIM-
MELFARB, *THE DE-MORALIZATION OF SOCIETY*) SOURCE: UNITED KINGDOM OFFICE OF
POPULATION CENSUSES AND SURVEYS.

Okay, okay, let us admit again that Victorian England was able to
"moralize" itself on the backs of urchins, destitute farmers, prostitutes,
coal miners, and innocents the world over. That Victorian respectability was more often than not based on draconian shaming was
not news to them. When Jack Tanner in George Bernard Shaw's *Man*

and Superman says, "We live in an atmosphere of shame. We are ashamed of everything that is real about us; ashamed of ourselves, of our relatives, of our incomes, of our accents, of our opinions, of our experience, just as we are ashamed of our naked skins," he is not telling anyone anything new. The middle class knew the British Empire was no Arcadia.

"Victorian values" have been much misunderstood and, indeed, quite unfairly calumnized as little more than hypocrisy, cruelty, misery, drudgery, squalor, and ignorance. But, as Gertrude Himmelfarb demonstrates in *The De-Moralization of Society: From Victorian Virtues to Modern Values,* Victorian values above all meant a continuous improvement in British society between the 1840s and the 1900s. Crime was high before Victoria came to the throne in 1837, and continued to be a source of concern until the 1850s. But from then it fell year upon year, even though the population increased. "In 1857," writes Himmelfarb, "the rate of indictable offenses per 100,000 population was 480; in 1901 it was 250—a decline in less than half a century of almost 50 per cent. The absolute numbers were even more graphic: with a population of 19 million in 1857, there were 92,000 crimes; with a population of 33 million in 1901, there were 81,000 crimes—14 million more people and 11,000 fewer crimes."[2] The reason for this progressive reduction in crime throughout the latter half of the nineteenth century was not more police, or more "entitlement" programs, a larger safety net, or more security measures, but more morality. The Victorian ethic of improvement and especially *self*-improvement, based largely on shaming, brought remarkable social rewards to the vast majority.

The Victorians were willing to put up with shame because they felt that, while shaming could certainly be abused, it also served a higher social good. Recall that the middle class, which so intimidated the poor, the meek, and the female with the shame stick were themselves often cowering before it. Who was more a pillar of Victoriana than William Gladstone, the most eminent statesman of his time? Open one of his innumerable volumes of diaries and you see this kind of sentiment: "He spake no word, he thought no thought / Save by the steadfast rule of Ought."[3] It was not elite culture but middle-class culture that maintained the so-called cult of respectability. They were the ones forever reiterating bromides by the likes of Edmund Burke—"Manners are more important than laws"—and needlepointing *"Laborare est Orare."* They were the market for Bulwer-Lytton novels, didactic illustrations for the parlor, and *Palgrave's Treasury.*

The middle class believed in such pith and treacle, to some degree, because of the generation that had come before them. The Victorians had had enough of Wordsworth's solipsistic nonsense:

> One Impulse in the vernal wood
> May teach you more of man,
> Of moral evil and of good,
> Than all the sages can.
> ("The Tables Turned")

Enough of Shelley claiming that incest is the highest form of love. Enough of Byron dragging his bleeding heart across Europe. Enough of Coleridge and De Quincey and their opium eating. To them, Romanticism was shameless bunk. "Close thy *Byron,*" Carlyle advised, "open thy *Goethe.*" Quit moping, he continually implores, there is work to be done. The working class, eager to improve its lot, did.

Victorian values were not peculiarly or uniquely Victorian. They were the values developed for generations, disturbed only by the revolutionary irruption of Romanticism. The Victorians knew that a child untutored in morality will not grow up innocent and pure, as Jean-Jacques Rousseau and William Blake thought he would. The *philosophes* of the earlier Age of Reason knew that too. The Victorian did not need any *Lord of the Flies* to show them the savagery lurking below the surface; they had a better text. They had the work of Darwin.

While we think of shame as a communicable disease, the Victorians saw it as an immune system. The two do look alike. However, shame is really spread not just by a stern eye, a rap on the wrist, a spank on the backside, but by a culture telling stories, creating a shared reality that makes certain behavior forbidden and other behavior rewarded, certain acts honorable and others abhorred. As we have seen, Victorian culture spread shame not just in church but in all manner of media: in the novel, in parlor illustrations, in songs, in etiquette books, in primers, in public spaces like parks, and especially in the peculiar construction of the royal family. If you want a nifty barometer of how much things have changed, think only of the royal family today.

Victorian media were tended by gatekeepers who decided exactly what got through. Ministers and parents were the least of the gatekeepers—they were cultural bowdlerizers putting the apocryphal skirts on piano legs and rewriting fairy tales. No adolescent ever takes them seriously. True, every time Queen Mary visited the Victoria and Albert Museum, a vast plaster fig leaf was hooked onto the cast of Michelangelo's *David*. But the real powers were editors, publishers, teachers, manufacturers, shopkeepers, and all the bourgeois who knew that while the shame disease is bad, there is something worse. The still palpable fear of the middle class was what they could dimly remember from the French Revolution, and from what they knew was occurring in the midcentury uprisings in Europe. Their fear was of the *mobile vulgus,* the lower class on the move, or what it had been Anglicized into—the shameless and mindless *mob*.

So Who's to Blame?

Social evolution works both ways, toward and away from stability, toward and away from barbarism. The middle class had the most to lose if the gates were thrown open, and so they, not the elites, maintained the shame myths of family, of culture, of class, and of empire. And they did it with great success through the mid-twentieth century. What was said by a contemporary historian of the nineteenth century would have applied as well to America of the 1950s: "One is continually struck, when reading nineteenth-century reports of housing conditions, by the extent to which the poor strove in the almost impossible circumstances of their lives to conform to middle-class standards of morality."[4] Then around 1960, something happened. Shame antibodies went the way of the top hat and spats. Cultural programming started being generated from below, not above. The center would not hold. The dreaded *mobile vulgus* was slouching toward Cultureville to be born.

The asleep-at-the-remote-control-switch intelligentsia is usually blamed for this rebarbarizing of culture. Here they are as most recently excoriated by Christopher Lasch in *The Revolt of the Elites and the Betrayal of Democracy*. The betrayers of Upper Aesthetica who have let the Vulgarians take over are

> brokers, bankers, real estate promoters and developers, engineers, consultants of all kinds, systems analysts, scientists, doctors, publicists, publishers, editors, advertising executives, art directors, moviemakers, entertainers, journalists, television producers and directors, artists, writers, and university professors . . . who control the international flow of money and information, preside over philanthropic foundations and institutions of higher learning, manage the instruments of cultural production and, thus, set the terms of public debate.[5]

This "elite" doesn't give a hoot for the world around them. They only care about their careers. Giving Wordsworth a turn, "Getting and spending, they lay waste *our* lives." These gatekeepers now live in gated towns with color-coded garbage cans. They live in comfy isolation, Lasch says, by ensconcing themselves in the suburbs, sending their children to private schools, and employing security guards. In short, they have removed themselves from the general culture and let others tell their stories.

But that is not the whole story. True, a culture is held together by shared myths, but these myths are not told by the elites. It has been argued that it is not the elites but the refugees from middle class who are responsible for the cultural revolution that produced the foregoing graphs. Shame became trivialized on their watch. This was the legacy of the short-lived, self-styled "counterculture," which tried to free itself from the stultifying atmosphere of Victorianism by trying drugs, sex, and rock 'n' roll. This was Romanticism revisited, personified by the hippies, who, in many ways, both typified and caricatured the entire movement from the Beats to the deadbeats.

The hippie culture that believed in guilt-free thrill seeking, no-fault divorce, "doing your own thing," recreational drugs, Marxism, funding social programs for the poor with money, not morality, and "let it all hang out" was not without consequence. "If it feels good, do it" and "Turn on, tune in, drop out" were the mantras. Although hippie culture seems innocuous, even quaint in retrospect, it wasn't. It had real intellectual content and real social consequences. It was a rebirth of Romanticism. Close your *Carlyle,* reopen your *Wordsworth,* or, if that was too tough, read Erich Segal's *Love Story* or see the movie. More demanding required undergraduate reading: Thomas Szasz, *The Myth of Mental Illness*; Erving Goffman, *Asylums*; Ken Kesey, *One Flew Over the Cuckoo's Nest*; and R. D. Laing, *The Politics of Experience.* Required graduate reading: Michael Harrington, *The Other America*; William Ryan, *Blaming the Victim*; and John Rawls, *A Theory of Justice.* Well, at least they were still reading in the 1960s.

According to Myron Magnet's *The Dream and the Nightmare: The Sixties Legacy to the Underclass*, the hippies were not the problem. They were harmless enough. For them the sixties were a lark. They went on to get jobs, pay taxes, move to suburbia, vote Republican, buy computers, and write books on *The Loss of Common Decency in American Culture*. Recall that Jerry Rubin became a stockbroker. Your current correspondent, now listing to starboard, was once an SDS wanna-be. The problem was that the lower classes were also swept along. They were not savvy enough to sell out before this market crashed. The have-nots, in Magnet's terms, got caught holding the bag. This underclass—especially inner-city blacks—got caught. They were the ones to become addicted to drugs, welfare, casual sex, and poverty. They ended up with the chump change of economic expansion, with the demoralizing war on poverty, filthy public housing, cosmetic affirmative action, dead-end job training, desultory "special education," minority set-asides, a wicked concept of entitlements, a sense of consequence-free behavior, and worse yet, no sense of redemptive and reintegrative shame.

This underclass became dependent not on Victorian incentives to succeed but on what Charles Murray has called in *Losing Ground* "incentives to fail." Behavior that could be permitted, even sanctioned, in small doses will ravage if experienced in excess. Remove the shame markers and what else do you expect? While superannuated hippies ended up with lots of tie-dyed T-shirts and Polaroids of memorable marches, the poor ended up with chronic unemployment, fatherless children, school-free adolescence, drug dependency, rampant crime, and you know the rest. As Irving Kristol has written, "It's hard to rise above poverty if society keeps deriding the human qualities that allow you to escape from it."[6] And as sociologist Christopher Jencks says in an interview with Magnet: "One way to read the sixties is to say it was a failed experiment whose price was paid by the Have-Nots. The rest of us landed on our feet."[7]

I would like to suggest a variation on the themes developed by Messrs. Lasch and Magnet. All agree, the character of a culture is determined by the stories it tells itself. While it is tempting to blame the elites for forgetting to tell the stories, or blame the hippies for telling the wrong kind of stories, it should also be noticed that storytelling itself profoundly changed in the 1960s. It became electronic. And it became completely commercial, that is, completely advertiser-supported. Say what you want about television, the one thing that is self-evident is this: the stories that free-market (i.e., advertiser-supported) television transmits are those that most of the non-brand-aligned consuming public (i.e., adolescents) want to hear, at least most of the time. The hippies had nothing to do with this, nor did the intellectual elites. This was a technological phenomenon.

As we have seen, the stories of Victorian culture were told by a middle class that controlled the flow of culture, and they were heavily weighted toward shame. In an electronic culture the stories are controlled by those hearing them. Advertisers pay the freight, but they care little, if at all, what gets transmitted. What they want is audience attention, and their prime audience is young, affluent, and eager to experiment. In the old style, the crusty gatekeeper decides. In the new style, the pubescent audience does the job. No wonder the stories of the modern advertising-supported culture are heavily weighted toward entertainment and away from shame.

CHAPTER 4

IT'S THE CULTURE, STUPID

We're in the business of selling audiences to advertisers. They [the sponsors] come to us asking for women 18 to 49 and adults 25 to 54 and we try to deliver.
—ROBERT NILES, vice president of marketing for NBC, 1986

The salient fact is that commercial television is primarily a marketing medium and secondarily an entertainment medium.
—SONNY FOX, now an independent producer, at a lecture series sponsored by the Annenberg School at USC, 1980

The people are the boss. We listen to the audience, see what they want, and try to accommodate them. I know it sounds simplistic, but that's exactly what it is.
—ROGER KING, in charge of syndication for King Brothers ("Wheel of Fortune," "Jeopardy"), 1989

I'm not interested in culture. I'm not interested in pro-social values. I have only one interest. That's whether people watch the program. That's my definition of good, that's my definition of bad.
—ARNOLD BECKER, CBS's vice president for research, 1980

Our business imperative is to make sure we're covering our base, 18-to-49s, but as broadcasters we try to bring everyone else into our universe.
—WARREN LITTLEFIELD, president, entertainment division, NBC, 1995

TO UNDERSTAND WHAT has happened to shame since the 1960s, we need first to understand what has happened to storytelling. Although we may be hardwired to experience the blush of shame, our culture provides the software, and the software is loaded by the stories we tell each other, and especially by the ones we are told when we are young.

In the early modern world, the lessons were downloaded from above. They were told vertically, as it were, from the Church and the

Court down to the people, and from there down to the children. These stories were told first in song and later in paint. With the advent of the printing press, they were told horizontally, sideways-out, from the writers to editors and publishers and then fanlike outward to the readers in books, magazines, and newspapers.

In the contemporary world, the electronic world, stories are told bottom-up, from the audience *backward* to the storytellers. Those now in control of the storytelling machinery can be wonderfully amoral— they don't care which stories are told, as long as they can gather a particular audience together for a period of time, and then essentially rent that audience's attention to an advertiser. The only gate they keep is the bottom line.

This point cannot be stressed enough. Most of our shared stories are told on commercial television, and commercial television is a most peculiar medium. The storyteller has no idea what to tell and so he continually asks the audience what it wants to hear. His job is to accurately gauge what the audience wants, gather that audience together, and then sell their attention to a third party for money. *That* is his livelihood, not storytelling.

What provides the power in the modern system is advertising. And what separates commercial television from all previous media is that it is totally supported by companies trying to sell something. This fact is a key to understanding whatever has happened to shame.

True, print media also carried advertising, but it was almost always subservient to the text, used as a way to lessen purchase price. Historically, book, newspaper, and magazine publishers saw their connection with the reader as one of friend and guide. They saw their connection with advertisers as one of unfortunate commercial necessity. In the nineteenth century pitched battles were fought between those who owned and assembled the print media and the advertising agencies who desperately wanted to "get a word in" about their clients' products. Often ads were bundled up in ghettos in the back of the book, placed in agate type, or moved off to the corners rather than allowed to intrude on the text.

In the last generation electronic media have profoundly influenced print. Rather like the children's game of paper/rock/scissors, the commercial electron has forced printers' ink to knuckle under. It has forced print to see itself as delivering consumers to advertisers rather than delivering information to readers.

Until the rise of "free" television, the power of print was vested in editorial hands. Often these hands belonged to members of the same family—the Scribners, the Holts, the Curtises, and the like—who had a tradition of caring for their readers in an admittedly paternalistic way. Publishing was run like a secular church. It was a sacred trust. The "gentle reader" idiom was part of a culture that also included a weekly "Letter from the Editor" or an occasional "Notes from the Publisher's Desk." If this also sounds like a note from the teacher, it should, because that was also the implied (and sometimes even stated) relationship.

Thumb through an old copy of the *Saturday Review of Literature,* the *New York Times Book Review,* or *Publishers' Weekly* and you will see that this relationship really lasted well into the 1960s. Publishers ran ads in which they subtly but insistently touted their wares as beneficial to common culture. So Simon & Schuster ran "From the Inner Sanctum," Doubleday had its "Page," Oxford University Press held forth from its "Amen Corner," and Alfred Knopf ran a series called "Borzoiana" in which they discussed publishing. They often mentioned books by competitors. True, publishers more usually announced publication dates, sales figures, and tidbits of gossip, but it is clear they were concerned about the world around them. Perhaps this was a clever merchandising ploy to shame readers into increasing consumption, but I think not. Many of the great publishers saw themselves as "merchants of light." Today their counterparts in large conglomerates call books *units* and authors *talent* just as their cousins in Hollywood do.

Here is a modern story about publishing. In 1996 Joan Collins, the Dragon Lady of TV's "Dynasty," was taken to court by her publisher, Random House, a subsidiary of Advance Publications. When she was a still-rising star, she had been signed to a multimillion-dollar contract for two books. Her star had flamed out and now the publisher wanted to be relieved of a costly mistake. Presumably they had read her previous books, but they now said her submitted manuscript was simply unreadable. "Don't *you* have any shame?" asked an unironic Richard Callagy, publisher's lawyer, to Ms. Collins.[1] After winning her lawsuit, she might have asked him the same question, seeing that Random House has made a niche publishing books often not even written by media stars.

Here is an older story about how print once behaved. After the Civil War, George Rowell, the Boston advertising agent, offered $18,000 for the back page of *Harper's Weekly*. Fletcher Harper not only spurned Rowell's offer, but literally kicked him out of the office. Harper would have been ashamed of selling what he took to be space shared by himself and his readers. Rowell was attempting to buy space not for some outrageous patent medicine, but rather for the Howe Sewing Machine. Another time Rowell asked Harper for circulation figures, only to be told they were none of his business. To punish the effrontery, Harper refused to accept any of Rowell's placements for months.[2] Admittedly, Harper was eccentric, but many of his colleagues shared his disdain for selling their personal space and exploiting a relationship with readers based on trust and companionship.

SHAME AND THE HARD SELL

When advertising entered print, it did what advertising has always had to—it tried to make itself part of the plasma, inconspicuously conspicuous. Yet it had to bite the unwary reader. Have a look at a handful of pre-television print ads. You don't need the surrounding text to see that this is a culture that responds to the blush of shame.

Whether you wanted to sell a car, toothpaste, gasoline, breakfast cereal, air-and-water bread, hand cream, a laundry service, shaving cream, life insurance, books, furniture, music lessons—you name it, in the pre-TV world you made the "pitch" by asserting the shame of not having your product.

Consider Listerine, which started as a wall disinfectant. At the turn of the century, had you swirled it around in your mouth you would have been ashamed of yourself. This stuff was to be used in privies and in operating rooms. But swirl in 1930 and you would have been thought polite. Why? Looking for a way to extend product application, Gerard Lambert, the mildly dissolute heir of the family business, came across the term *halitosis*. He also understood the power of shame. Linking them together, he made bad breath into the cause of spinsterhood, divorce, lost love, and even alienation from your own children. Having a smelly mouth was shameful. It lowered you in the estimation of others. Young Lambert steadily increased his shame-filled advertising until he had saturated magazine and newspaper culture. By 1928 he was the third largest advertiser in magazines. By the 1930s, the mouth was his.

In advertising jargon this approach is called the *hard sell*. It is based on being able to mildly mortify your audience. If you have a homogeneous audience who cannot easily tune you out, it works. But if you have a mixed audience who can easily change the channel, turn the page, or switch entertainment media, forget it. Shaming still works in print better than on radio or television, in part because the audience has already had to pay something in order to hold the product in their hands. It is an effort to turn the page. But the hard sell will also work in electronic media if the choices are few and it is difficult to switch

"Jones Must Be Broke"

SURFACE appearances ... snap judgments . . . hasty conclusions. No matter how beautiful your home may be within, an outside surface of dilapidated paint is sure to give an unfavorable impression of your circumstances.

Confidence, consideration and respect surround the family whose home, inside and out, bears the beaming look of prosperity that only the proper use of Paint and Varnish can impart.

But remember... you can't get more out of the painting job than the manufacturer has put into the paint. For five generations Devoe has meant supreme quality in Paint and Varnish products.

When you paint with Devoe you get all the beauty and durability you can get out of any other product . . . plus a guarantee, backed by the Oldest Paint House in America, that Devoe will cost less money per job and give better results than any other paint you can buy.

This Coupon is WORTH 40 CENTS
Use It To-day

Fill out this coupon and present it to any Devoe Agent within 30 days. He is authorized to give you FREE a 40 cent can of any Devoe Paint and Varnish Product you want, or a reduction of 40 cents on a larger can. If you do not know the name of the Devoe Agent notify us.

Your Name................................Address.............................

Town..State................................

Devoe Agent's Name..

Your Dealer's Name...(A4)
One coupon to a person. To be used by adults only.

New York   DEVOE & RAYNOLDS CO., Inc.   Chicago
Founded 1754

DEVOE
Paint and Varnish Products
THE OLDEST, MOST COMPLETE AND
HIGHEST QUALITY LINE IN AMERICA

[1923]

MID-CENTURY INVOCATIONS OF SHAME FROM MADISON AVENUE — THE "HARD SELL" AT WORK.

Ashamed of Corns

As People Should Be—They Are So Unnecessary

The instinct is to hide a corn. And to cover the pain with a smile.

For people nowadays know that a corn is passé. And that naught but neglect can account for it.

It is like a torn gown which you fail to repair. Or a spot which you fail to remove. The fault lies in neglecting a few-minute duty—just as with a corn.

Any corn pain can be stopped in a moment, and stopped for good. Any corn can be ended quickly and completely.

All that is necessary is to apply a little Blue-jay plaster. It is done in a jiffy. It means no inconvenience.

Then a bit of scientific wax begins its gentle action. In two days, usually, the whole corn disappears. Some old, tough corns require a second application, but not often.

Can you think of a reason for paring corns and letting them continue? Or for using harsh or mussy applications? Or of clinging to any old-time method which is now taboo?

Or for suffering corns—for spoiling hours—when millions of others escape?

Can you think of a reason for not trying Blue-jay? It is a modern scientific treatment, invented by a famous chemist. It is made by a house of world-wide fame in the making of surgical dressings.

It has ended corns by the tens of millions—corns which are just like yours. It is easy and gentle and sure, as you can prove for yourself tonight.

Try Blue-jay on one corn. If it does as we say, keep it by you. On future corns apply it the moment they appear. That will mean perpetual freedom. A corn ache, after that, will be unknown to you.

Blue=jay
For Corns

Stops Pain Instantly—Ends Corns Completely

Large Package 25c at Druggists
Small Package Discontinued   (888)

How Blue-jay Acts

A is a thin, soft pad which sti-mulates the corn. Usually it takes only 48 hours to end the corn completely.

B is the rubber which gently relieves the pain by relieving the pressure.

C is rubber adhesive which sticks without wetting. It wraps around the toe and makes the plaster snug and comfortable.

Blue-jay is applied in a jiffy. After that, one doesn't feel the corn. The action is gentle, and applied to the corn alone. So the corn disappears without soreness.

BAUER & BLACK, *Makers of Surgical Dressings, etc.*, CHICAGO and NEW YORK

[1918]

A Cough is a Social Blunder

People who know have no hesitation in avoiding the cougher. They know that he is a public menace. They know that his cough is a proof of his lack of consideration of others.

And they know that he knows it too, so they are not afraid of hurting his feelings.

For there is no excuse for coughing. It is just as unnecessary as any other bad habit. For it can be prevented or relieved by the simplest of precautions—the use of S. B. Cough Drops.

S. B. Cough Drops are not a cure for colds. They are a preventive of coughing. True, they often keep a cough from developing into a sore throat or cold. And they are a protection to the public because they keep people who already have influenza, colds and other throat troubles from spreading them through unnecessary coughing. Have a box with you always.

Pure. No Drugs. Just enough charcoal to sweeten the stomach.

One placed in the mouth at bedtime will keep the breathing passages clear.

Drop that Cough
SMITH BROTHERS *of Poughkeepsie*
FAMOUS SINCE 1847

[1919]

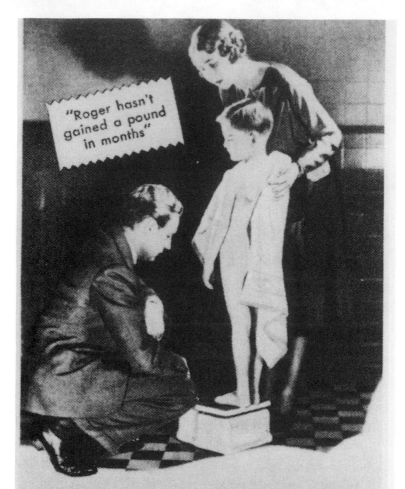

"Roger hasn't gained a pound in months"

Whose fault when children are frail?

So easy now to put on weight

"WE THOUGHT we were giving Roger the best possible care. You can imagine how awful we felt when we discovered he was underweight, and

and minerals supplied by Cocomalt that make children gain so wonderfully.

Vitamin D—important!

!

ashamed

It brought him untold misery; yet only he himself was to blame.

HE had neglected his teeth so long that he was actually ashamed to visit his dentist. And like so many people, he kept putting it off.

Finally he became so sensitive about their appearance that in conversation he habitually distorted his mouth in an effort to hide them from view.

A reasonable effort on his own part—consulting his dentist, conscientious use of his tooth brush and the right dentifrice—might have saved him this humiliation. But he even neglected these things. He was uncomfortable wherever he went.

Listerine Tooth Paste cleans teeth a new way. At last our chemists have discovered a polishing ingredient that really cleans without scratching the enamel—a difficult problem finally solved.

You will notice the improvement even in the first few days. And you *know it is cleaning safely.*

So the makers of Listerine, the safe antiseptic, have found for you also the really safe dentifrice.

What are your teeth saying about you today?— *LAMBERT PHARMA-CAL CO.,* Saint Louis, U. S. A.

LISTERINE
TOOTH PASTE

Large tube—25c

[1924]

DON'T FOOL YOURSELF

Since halitosis never announces itself to the victim, you simply cannot know when you have it.

Halitosis makes *you unpopular*

It is unexcusable . . . can be instantly remedied

No matter how charming you may be or how fond of you your friends are, you cannot expect them to put up with halitosis (unpleasant breath) forever. They may be nice to you—but it is an effort.

Don't fool yourself that you never have halitosis as do so many self-assured people who constantly offend this way.

Read the facts in the lower right hand corner and you will see that your chance of escape is slight. Nor should you count on being able to detect this ailment in yourself. Halitosis doesn't announce itself. You are seldom aware you have it.

Recognizing these truths, nice people end any chance of offending by systematically rinsing the mouth with Listerine. Every morning.

Every night. And between times when necessary, especially before meeting others.

Keep a bottle handy in home and office for this purpose.

Listerine ends halitosis instantly. Being antiseptic, it strikes at its commonest cause—fermentation in the oral cavity. Then, being a powerful deodorant, it destroys the odors themselves.

If you have any doubt of Listerine's powerful deodorant properties, make this test: Rub a slice of onion on your hand. Then apply Listerine clear. Immediately, every trace of onion odor is gone. Even the strong odor of fish yields to it. Lambert Pharmacal Company, St. Louis, Mo., U.S.A.

The new baby—

LISTERINE SHAVING CREAM

--you've got a treat ahead of you.

TRY IT

READ THE FACTS
⅓ had halitosis

68 hairdressers state that about every third woman, many of them from the wealthy classes, is halitoxic. Who should know better than they?

LISTERINE
The safe antiseptic

[1928]

LISTERINE COLONIZES THE MOUTH USING THE SHAME OF HALITOSIS.

CRITICAL EYES
ARE SIZING YOU UP
RIGHT NOW

keep your face
FRESH, FIRM, FIT

Let your face reflect confidence—not worry! It's the "look" of you by which you are judged most often. Try for a many slant on life. Let Williams Shaving Service help you. It can! Cover your beard with the thick, quick lather that Williams is famous for (hard water or soft, hot or cold—it doesn't matter with Williams). What an easy shave! Your taut skin relaxes . . . feels cool, supple. Williams conditions, revives, gives you the world's smoothest shave. It's a mental tonic too. How alert you look now! A Williams Shave gives you the satisfaction that brings confidence.

Then give your face a bracer of Aqua Velva . . . to *keep* what you've just gained. Dash it on your still-moist skin. Feel your face tingle. There's a tonic in it. It firms the skin. Helps care for unseen nicks, abrasions.

Protects from dust. Conserves the natural moisture that keeps your face flexible and fit all day long.
Williams Shaving Cream and Aqua Velva . . . wherever toilet goods are sold.

● MAIL THIS! *It will show you the way to Face Fitness*
THE J. B. WILLIAMS COMPANY, Dept. P-300
Glastonbury, Conn., U. S. A.
Canadian Address: 3552 St. Patrick St., Montreal
I am anxious to try Williams Shaving Service. Please send me free trial sizes of Williams Shaving Cream and Aqua Velva.

You can't lose this cap

Williams
Luxury
Shaving
Cream

LARGE

Williams

JUST NOTICE THE FINE SKINS OF MEN WHO USE

Williams

SHAVING CREAM ——— AQUA VELVA

channels. Early television ads were far more shaming than current ones.

So what happened? As choices proliferated, in order to deliver the audience to the sponsor, advertising itself had to change. That change is known as the Creative Revolution and it happened in the late 1950s just as television was entering the bloodstream. The central figure was

Bill Bernbach of Dane Doyle Bernbach and the central campaign was first the print, and then the television, ads for Volkswagen. This was not the get-tough advertising of Claude Hopkins or Rosser Reeves (Anacin works fast, Fast, FAST), but rather feel-good entertainment. These ads were fun. They still are. Cute ads still are watched, as shown by the successes of the Nike campaign from Wieden & Kennedy, the Absolut vodka images from TBWA, the Apple Computer and Energizer battery ads from Chiat/Day, and the Pepsi series from BBDO.

They better be fun or we'll blink them off into oblivion. Ironically, television, which started as advertiser-friendly, has often turned out to be advertiser poison. The coaxial cable and the remote-control clicker have moved the power to the viewer. Lots of choice and easy channel changing are the cross to the vampire of hard sell.

Still, the explanation of what has recently happened is more complex than just the advertising and goes to the very nature of electronic communication and *broad*casting. Electronic broadcasting profoundly transformed the nature of stories because it changed the very process of storytelling.

Electronic Media: Who Pays the Piper Chooses the Tune

To understand commercial television, you need to realize that it was destined by radio. Radio started with high hopes that it could be used to educate the nation. The first licenses were issued to universities, which controlled about one fourth of all the airwaves. Radio would be used only for the highest purposes, passing along the "best that had been thought and said" to everyone. "Schoolroom of the air" was how radio was described in early documents. If this schoolroom was going to be anything like the one reflected in the *McGuffey Readers,* shame would be central.

During the Depression, the universities sold their schoolrooms to the highest bidders, thereby allowing companies like NBC and CBS to wire the nation. The networks assured Congress that they would be responsible, and by the time it was clear that they had no such thing in mind, it was too late. In the late 1930s the Wagner-Hatfield bill, which was to have returned the licenses back to the schools, was defeated and the die was cast. Entertainment, not education, was the goal of radio, and the entertainment was delivered "free," provided a "few words from the sponsor" could travel alongside. Those words came from the great advertising agencies like N. W. Ayer & Son, J. Walter Thompson, Lord & Thomas, and Young & Rubicam, who provided *both* the programs and the ads.

When television appeared in the 1950s, the same networks controlled its distribution from the same Manhattan offices (now DuMont and ABC were in the loop), and the same agencies (now clustered up and down Madison Avenue, often with names made up of initials like BBDO, DMB&B) supplied the programming. Radio shows were simply picked up and dumped into television. So soap operas like "As The World Turns," or comedies like "Amos 'n' Andy," and westerns like "The Lone Ranger," were just moved across the street and made into pixels. "The $64 Question" on radio became "The $64,000 Question" on TV.

Television didn't have a prayer. From the first narrow broadcast, it was going commercial. No schoolroom-of-the-air arguments were ever made. The prophetic Philo T. Farnsworth presented a dollar sign for sixty seconds in the first public demonstration of his television system in 1927. Once Hazel Bishop became a million-dollar company in the early 1950s, based solely on its television advertising, the direction of the medium was set.

Certain systemic changes in both broadcast media did occur; most important, the networks recaptured programming from the agencies. Although this shift away from agency control took scandals to accomplish (most notably the quiz scandals rigged by advertising agencies, not networks), it would have happened anyway. Simple economics made it more lucrative to sell time by the ounce than by the pound. The "nets" could make more by selling minutes than by selling half or full hours. Only the behemoths could afford time chunks for their "Philco Television Playhouse," "Kraft Television Theater," "Firestone Hour," or "U.S. Steel Hour." What about all the little companies? Magazines maximized ad revenues by selling space by the partial page; why not television? The rise of "segmented sponsorship" meant that sponsors would have even less control over content. Often the sponsor had no idea what the show was about, he only knew what the time period was and the supposed ages of the audience.

Having the networks tell the stories meant that they also had to produce and guarantee the viewers. In the polite language of the time, these guarantees were called "assurances." Now the "nets" could sell one-minute insertions, six per hour, and they could sell them as part of a time period, not part of a show. The agencies could resell them to anyone, just as newspaper space brokers did in the nineteenth century. The motto of this new medium became "Programs are the scheduled interruptions of marketing bulletins." How could it be otherwise?

Call television whatever you want—"idiot box," "American dada," "child molester," "plug-in drug," "thief of time," "painkiller," "chewing gum for the eyes," "a toaster with pictures"—this electronic space is the greatest cultural medium ever concocted, bar none. Only the Holy Roman Church comes close. And this medium, supported almost entirely by commercial interests, is at the center of where shame has gone in our culture.

Television is *the* primary force in our lives. Whereas generations ago, growing up was defined by a progression of books read, then for my parents by movies seen, for those of us born since World War II, it has been marked by a progression of television jingles memorized. Print took about two centuries to gain currency as communal memory;

photography was in general use after 1900; the telephone took half a century to become part of everyday life; radio was absorbed in thirty-five years; and the cinema, in twenty. Television happened overnight. At some mysterious point in the 1950s, television ceased to be just an odd-looking gizmo—a radio running a picture track—and entered the bloodstream. It became part of our nervous system. It is who we are. It is what we do. And more important, it is how we feel.

In our culture most people watch it for most of their "free" time. After sleeping and working, watching images on a video tube is what we do with ourselves. It is our favorite way to pass time. More than 97 percent of American households have at least one television set and it is on more than six hours a day. We spend the equivalent of a day a week watching it. Well over eighty million households have this thing as part of their lives, and when asked if they would give up the thing or a family member for a week or so, most children respond that the thing stays.

The experience of watching television has become the social and intellectual glue that holds us together, our "core curriculum." Television has co-opted many of the ceremonies of American life. Religion, politics, psychology, and education have gone into the box. "Did you see . . . ?" has replaced "Do you know . . . ?" "Did you read . . . ?" and "Have you heard . . . ?" Television displays most of what we know and much of what we believe. There is only one forbidden act: *never make the viewer feel bad*.

One indubitable result of television is the erosion of any life outside the home. Take voluntary associations, for instance. Civic groups like the PTA, the Elks, the League of Women Voters, the Odd Fellows, Red Cross, and even the neighborhood bar and bowling leagues have fallen on hard times because, as Harvard Professor Robert D. Puttnam has contended, the allure of watching the little screen has proved so powerful. Surveys of average Americans over the last thirty years show that participation in such voluntary associations is down between 25 and 50 percent.[3] It is from engagement with these groups—just as it is with religious ones—that one learns the codes of conformity (or morality, if you prefer) that underpin a shared sense of shame.

How Advertising Culture Knows What Stories to Tell

Just as tax collection is the unacknowledged heart of government, audience measurement is the heart of modern advertiser-sponsored culture. This is how the storyteller knows what to tell, and the advertiser knows how much to pay for the telling. This measuring started with Rowell's *Directory* for newspapers, continued to the Starch Ratings of magazines, the Crossley and Arbitron surveys of radio, and came full flower with the Nielsen Ratings on television. Since the networks cannot depend on copies sold, coupons returned, or gross receipts at the box office, programmers have to guess at the audience.

In radio days, AT&T noted that calls dropped 50 percent during "Amos 'n' Andy," and water departments found that pressure decreased in the evening on the half hour, but these were hardly sophisticated counters. In the mid-1930s, two professors at MIT developed an ingenious device called the "Audimeter," which measured where and when the dial on a radio was moved. Each time the dial was turned, a mark appeared on a moving spool of paper so a history of specific listening habits could be constructed. Not only could the Audimeter provide a quantitative measure of audience, it could also tell who was listening to what. Hooking the meter up to Junior's set, or to Grandmother's set, would produce a different chart and let a station know what percentage of its audience was working-class, male or female, adolescent, retired, or whatever profile they wanted.

In 1936 A. C. Nielsen purchased the Audimeter, and the history of broadcasting—and culture—was forever changed. Nielsen gathered and sold audience profiles. Since broadcasters are in the business of selling the attention of an audience to advertisers, here was a way to tell where the audience was and how long it would pay attention.

The networks, in consultation with the agencies, have five age categories in their demographic analysis: (1) up to eleven years of age, (2) between twelve and seventeen years of age, (3) eighteen to thirty-four, (4) thirty-five to fifty-five, and (5) over fifty-five. The heaviest watchers are in categories 1 and 5, but unfortunately for TV critics, they are the smallest consumers. Those with the most disposable income are in 4, but those who are most willing to part with it are in 3. In the 1950s, only 4 and 5 had access to sets and so programming was for them.

Essentially, the history of TV has been the shifting downward of demographic clusters, until the 1970s when the medium was omnipresent. Now we are experiencing the very gradual rise of the median age, as the baby boomers start wearing bifocals and full-bottomed jeans. However, as long as groups 2 and 3 are the target audiences, the entertainment and the advertising will reflect their concerns regardless of their percentage of the population. One of the concerns of this audience is definitely not to experience shame. Watching other people experience it, however, is another story—an increasingly popular one.

No one currently is very happy with television on Madison Avenue. True, cable has allowed networks to narrowcast to demographic target audiences or "niches," and true CPM, or cost per thousand, has dropped as competition has increased, but the fact is that, although the machine is everywhere and always on, it is never really paid proper attention anymore. Although advertising dollars were constant between 1980 and 1990—about 20 percent of total expenditures—and although ads still reached about 98 percent of the audience, that audience has so fractured into network, cable, and independent that fewer people are likely to watch a single ad. To reach a hundred gross rating points (a common measure of media weight), it now takes nine spots to do the "work" of six. There are simply too many ads, and too many of them are short (fifteen-second) ads. The networks are broadcasting about six thousand commercials a week, and more than a third of them are these shorties.

You don't have to be a rocket scientist to know that if you double the ad pages in your magazine, and then make many of them quarter-page ads, your reader will be less likely to be reached by any particular message. Now make it easy for him to jump over your ads and follow the text without being interrupted and you have the present situation of advertising on television. What this has meant is that if your ad has any potential to make the viewer feel uneasy, you are wasting your money to show it. Try to shame your consumer, if only for a second, and you will be passed by. With the exception of a few products like pimple creams, dandruff shampoos, and diet aids, the hard sell—the shame sell—is dead.

To make matters still more complicated, we magnify haphazard programming by the way we consume it. We do not "watch" television programs; we sample, taste, choose, reject, and consume in bits and pieces. A never-ending flow crosses the screen and we dip from one rivulet to another, often watching two or three different "programs" at once. The English call television "the two-minute culture"—the usual time they spend before changing channels. The golden section of our attention span is now measured in seconds, not minutes. Young watchers even have a "nesting channel" from which they start their diurnal migration. Programmers even refer to this activity as "video grazing" or "video surfing," while advertisers refer to it with more apocalyptic descriptions.

The reason? The bane of advertising is the remote-control wand. Invented in the 1950s as a wired remote called Lazy Bones (which should have been renamed Broken Bones since it resulted in hundreds of trips and falls), refined as the Flashmatic, which was cordless but could be set off by sunlight, and further polished by the installation of little tuning forks that could be triggered by a dog shaking his metal tags or the kid shaking the piggy bank, the clicker is now almost perfected using infrared and cheap microchips. Over one hundred million of these gizmos have created the couch potato and almost wrecked television advertising. Oddly enough, it has also influenced the transmission of shaming. Now with the voice-activated model, just a moan will render millions of dollars of creative advertising worthless. It comes as no surprise that some refer to the wand by the nickname "the power."

The current experience of watching television is like listening to the radio while driving a car. In the early days, one had to turn the station-selector knob, then in the 1960s press a preset button. Now you hit "scan" or "search" and wait for "your" feel-good entertainment to come forward. "Hurry up and choose," the machine says, but many of us just let it continually "search." The radio generation is a "one thing at a time" generation, a "you can't do two things at once" generation. The TV generation, by contrast, does "multitasking": homework, talk on the phone, watch a number of TV programs, and listen to the radio all at once.

As contrasted with reading, television almost requires us to do something else while we are choosing what to watch. You can eat, you can recline, you can walk around. An entire generation has raised its children with the machine on. You are still in perfect contact with the medium, still changing channels. Most of us use peripheral vision to consume most television. Television reads us to sleep, and reads us awake. Did I see that on television, or did I dream it?

The one thing television programming can't do is annoy you for long. The minute you feel bad, you change the channel. The producers of television flow know this. That is why so much is made of being the sleepy viewer's comforting friend. "Welcome to . . ." "Good evening, folks." "We'll be right back." "See you next week." "Stay tuned." "Don't touch that dial." "You wouldn't turn your back on a friend, would you?" the machine almost whines, aware that nothing will overcome the channel-turning impulse. "Stay with me a bit longer. By the way, did you hear the story of . . . ?" "Yep," we say, punching the key. "Already heard it."

Formula is the hallmark of television fare. Media reformers have found this out to their dismay. The availability of three channels or thirty channels does not change the lack of product differentiation. All networks ultimately behave as one, as do all shows inside a genre. We'll make you feel good, says one. We'll make you feel better, says the other. Count us in too, say the commercials.

THE POWER OF COMMERCIAL CULTURE

If Romantic art struggles for the condition of opera, and if Newtonian science aspires to pure mathematics, then television—all modern "free-market" commercial television—seeks the state of pure advertisement. Ideally the entertainment and the advertisement would melt into a seamless "advertainment." The power of television, however, is that it has drawn the rest of culture in behind it. All media are acting like television.

In fact, the media themselves are bundled up into huge conglomerates that own book and magazine publishers, movie studios, and television networks. So Disney, which owns a publishing house, two studios, magazines, and theme parks, buys CapCities, which owns ABC. Viacom owns a bundle of product producers and channels of distribution. So do Tele-Communications Inc., Sony, and News Corp. Time Warner, which also owns the requisite publishing houses, studios, and magazines, buys Turner Broadcasting to merge with its WB network. Westinghouse ditto with CBS, and General Electric with NBC.

But that's not the end of it. Here's why. The entire culture we live in is carried on the back of advertising. Now, I mean that almost literally. If you cannot find commercial support for what you have to say, it will not be transported. Much of what we share, and what we know, and even what we treasure, is carried to us each second in a plasma of electrons, pixels, and ink, underwritten by multinational advertising agencies dedicated to attracting our attention for entirely nonaltruistic reasons. These agencies, gathered up inside worldwide conglomerates with weird sci-fi names like WPP, Omnicom, Cordiant, True North, Interpublic, Dentsu, and Euro RSCG, are usually collections of established shops linked together to provide "full service" to their global clients. They essentially rent our concentration to other companies—sponsors—for the dubious purpose of informing us of something that we've longed for all our lives even though we've never heard of it before. Modern selling is not about trading information, as it was in the nineteenth century, as much as about creating an infotainment culture sufficiently alluring so that other messages—commercials—can get through.

This new culture is there when we blink, it's there when we listen, it's there when we touch, it's even there to be smelled in scent strips when we open a magazine. There is barely an empty space in our culture not already carrying commercial messages. Look anywhere: In schools there is Channel One; in movies there is product placement; ads are in urinals, played on telephone hold, in alphanumeric displays in taxis, sent unannounced to fax machines, inside catalogs, on the video in front of the StairMaster at the gym, on T-shirts, at the doctor's office, on grocery carts, on parking meters, on tees at golf holes, on inner-city basketball backboards, piped in along with Muzak . . . ad nauseam (and yes, even on airline vomit bags). We have to shake magazines like rag dolls to free up their pages from the "blow-in" inserts and then wrestle out the stapled or glued-in ones before reading can begin. We now have to fast-forward through the five minutes of advertising that open rental videotapes. President Clinton's 1992 inaugural parade featured a Budweiser float. At the Smithsonian, the Orkin Pest Control Company sponsored an exhibit on exactly what it advertises it kills: insects. No venue is safe. Is there a blockbuster museum show not decorated with corporate logos? Public Broadcasting is littered with "underwriting announcements" that look and sound almost exactly like what PBS claims they are not: commercials.

In order to hold our attention, these sponsors must make us feel good, but how can shame exist in a world in which feeling good is paramount? Alas, as much fun as the electronic media are to blame ("Kill Your Television Set" is a favorite bumper sticker) they themselves are only the surface explanation for the disappearance of shame. The deeper explanation is, I think, more economic in nature. Television is not the problem, *commercial* television is. Commercial television is simply too good at what it does—as the rest of the world is finding out. But such infotainment is delivered for a price. We have to pay for it, either by spending money or by spending time. Given a choice, most of us prefer to spend time. We spend our time paying attention to ads and in exchange are given excitement.

This trade is central to contemporary culture. Economists call this "cost externalization." If you want to see it at work, go to McDonald's. You order. You carry your food to the table. You clean up. You pay less. Want to see it elsewhere? Buy gas. Just as the "work" you do at the self-service gas station lowers the price of gas, so consuming ads is the "work" you do that lowers the price of delivering the infotainment. The trade is more complex. True, you are entertained at lower cost, but you are also encultured in the process.

So far so good. The quid pro quo of modern infotainment culture is that if you want it, you'll get it—no matter what it is—as long as there are enough of you who (1) are willing to spend some energy along the way hearing "a word from our sponsor" and (2) have sufficient disposable income possibly to buy some of the advertised goods. You pay twice: once with the ad and once with the product. So let's look back a step to examine these products because—strange as it may seem—they are at the center of removing shame from American culture.

Heroic Materialism and Unheroic Shame

Before all else, we must realize that modern advertising is primarily tied to things, and only secondarily to services. Manufacturing both things *and* their meanings is what American culture is all about. If Greece gave the world philosophy, Britain gave drama, Austria music, Germany politics, Italy art, then America gave mass-produced objects. "We bring good things to life" is no offhand claim. Most of these "good things" are machine-made and hence interchangeable. Such objects, called parity items, constitute most of the stuff that surrounds us, from bottled water to toothpaste to beer to cars to airlines. There is really no discernible difference between Evian and Mountain Spring, Colgate and Crest, Miller and Budweiser, Ford and Chevrolet, Delta and United. In fact, often the only difference is in the advertising.

For some reason, we like it this way. We don't consume the products as much as we consume the advertising. Logically, we should all read *Consumer Reports* and then all buy the most sensible product. But we don't. So why do we waste our energy (and billions of dollars) entertaining fraudulent choice? Perhaps just as we drink the advertising, not the beer, we prefer the illusion of choice to the reality of decision. Else how to explain the appearance of so much superfluous choice? A decade ago, grocery stores carried about nine thousand items; they now stock about twenty-four thousand. Revlon makes 158 shades of lipstick. Crest toothpaste comes in thirty-six sizes and shapes and flavors. We are even eager to be offered choice where there is none to speak of. AT&T offers "the right choice"; Wendy's, "there is no better choice"; Pepsi, "the choice of a new generation"; Coke, "the real choice"; "Taster's Choice is the choice for taste." Even advertisers don't understand the phenomenon. Is there a relationship between the number of soft drinks and television channels—about twenty-seven? What's going to happen when the information pipe carries five hundred?

I have no idea. But I do know this: Academic Marxists notwithstanding, human beings like things. We buy things. We like to exchange things. We steal things. We donate things. We live through things. We call these things "goods" as in "goods and services." We do not call them "bads." We like to feel good about them especially just after the moment of purchase. Postdecision dissonance is painful and we are often ashamed of the act of consumption. Here advertising can operate, reassuring us that the choice was a wise one. Who reads automobile ads, for instance? Most often they are read not by those about to buy, but by those who have just consummated the purchase.

All of this sounds simplistic, but it is crucial to understanding the power of advertiser-supported shame-free culture. As economist Stanley Lebergott has demonstrated in his *Pursuing Happiness: American Consumers in the Twentieth Century,* the still-going-strong industrial revolution produces more and more things, not because production is what machines do, and not because nasty capitalists twist their handlebar mustaches and mutter, "More slop for the pigs," but because we are powerfully attracted to the world of things. And we don't want to feel bad about it. Nor do the sponsors want us to. Advertising, when it's lucky, supercharges this attraction and removes some residual shame.

This attraction to the inanimate happens all over the world. Berlin Walls fall because people want things, and they want the culture created by things. China opens its doors not so much because it wants to get out, but because it wants to get things in. We were not suddenly transformed from customers to consumers by wily manufacturers eager to unload a surplus of crapular products. We have created a surfeit of things because we enjoy the process of "getting and spending." The consumption ethic may have started in the early 1900s, but the desire is ancient. Kings and princes once thought they could solve problems by amassing things. We now join them.

The balderdash of cloistered academics aside, human beings did not suddenly become materialistic. We have always been desirous of things. We have just not had many of them until quite recently, and in a few generations if some environmentalists are correct, we may return to having fewer and fewer. Still, while they last, we enjoy shopping for things and see both the humor and truth reflected in the aphoristic "Born to shop," "Shop till you drop," and "When the going gets tough, the tough go shopping." Department store windows, whether on the city street or inside a mall, did not appear by magic. We enjoy looking through them to another world. It is voyeurism for capitalists. Our love of things is the *cause* of the industrial revolution, not the consequence. Man is not only *Homo sapiens,* or *Homo ludens,* or *Homo faber,* but also *Homo emptor.*

Late-twentieth-century American culture is often criticized for being too materialistic. We should be ashamed of this reckless consumption, we are told, but we are not. Ironically, we are not too materialistic. We are not materialistic enough. If we craved objects *and* knew what they meant, there would be no need to add meaning through advertising. We would gather, use, toss out, or hoard based on some *inner* sense of value. But we don't. We don't know what to gather, we like to trade what we have gathered, and we need to know how to evaluate objects of little practical use.

Morris B. Holbrook, Dillard Professor of Marketing at Columbia University's Graduate School of Business, has argued that television shows like "The Price Is Right" (which has been a staple of television fare for almost forty years) celebrates what we know about merchandise—not necessarily value but price. "Every image, every detail, every nuance in the shopping-oriented game show moves toward the worship of possessions and toward the sanctification of materialism."[4] But Bob Barker aside, what is clear is that most things in and of themselves simply do not mean enough. In fact, what we finally crave may not be objects at all but their meaning.

For whatever else advertising "does," one thing is certain: By adding value to material, by adding meaning to objects, by branding things, advertising performs a role historically associated with religion. The Great Chain of Being, which for centuries located value above the horizon in the world Beyond, has been reforged to settle value into the objects of the Here and Now.

We are now closing in on the various but interconnected reasons why shame jumped the tracks so suddenly from American culture in the last thirty years. We are also closing in on why the big complainers about shamelessness tend to be fifty-year-olds. The people who want things the most and have good prospects to get them are the young. They are also the ones who have not decided which brands of objects they wish to consume. In addition, they have a surplus of two commodities: time and money, especially the former. If you can make a sale to these twentysomethings, if you can "brand" them with your product, you may have them for life. But to do this you have to be able to speak to them, you have to entertain them, and to do that you have to make sure you never make them feel bad.

In the chapters to come we will see the impact of an advertising-carried electronic culture on what used to be a hierarchical and institution-based print culture. We will see how entertain-me-now has transformed the great shame regulators, the church and the school. The current political correctness movement is a parody of how church and school used to behave. We will see how make-me-feel-good-now has revolutionized the shame-removal industry of psychology, giving prominence to twelve-step support groups, and the revival of the Romantic myth of the inner child. Hucksters like John Bradshaw have commandeered pop psychology, contending that you have nothing to be ashamed of because "they" (usually your so-called dysfunctional parents) made you feel bad. We will see how modern politics, thanks in part to negative advertising, has become more interested in slinging shame on others than on governing, and how the law, frightened by not being able to control shaming, often has made sentencing into a fiasco of fairness. Too much of our population now spends adolescence in jail. Finally, we will see how family life, irreparably changed by the deshaming of divorce and illegitimacy, has been in a state of free-fall since the 1960s. Fatherlessness has become the hallmark of the modern family, and we have already lived to regret not making it shameful.

But first, let's return to electronic popcult to trace the transformation of shame from Charles Van Doren in the 1950s, who was so ruined that he spent the rest of his life in self-imposed exile, to Madonna in the 1980s, who made behaving shamelessly into not just a source of a large income but into a role model for millions.

CHAPTER 5

THE FAME OF SHAME

How many times do I have to kill before I get a name in the paper or some national attention?
>—a serial killer in Kansas, in a letter to police

We should set up a special channel so killers could skip the serial murders and go straight to the studio.
>—CLIVE JAMES at a symposium on fame
>in the twentieth century in 1993

THE PECULIAR CASE OF CHARLES VAN DOREN

*I*T WAS ONE of my first memories from television and one of the most profound. There was lanky Charles Van Doren in that hot little glassed-in booth with the sweat pouring off him. He dabbed a folded white handkerchief to his brow as the seconds ticked away. He bit his lip and said, "I think—I guess . . ." Who knows who was in the other booth? Who cared? The show was called "Twenty-One," and it made no sense. An outrageously complicated question was asked. The microphone in the booth was turned off. Charles Van Doren was thinking. The music would start. That music was incredible. We knew it from the movies. It meant the monster was coming around the corner. The music would quit. His mike would come back on. He would answer the question with more nonsense. No monster came. Charles Van Doren was still alive.

It was just like school except that this guy was answering questions about things we had never heard of in a language only he spoke. Whatever he was saying, it was driving the teacher nuts. "You are correct!" Jack Barry kept crying in amazement. Now the sweat was on Mr.

Barry's face. He was going to have to pay up! Everything would explode and big numbers would flash across the screen. It could have been $64, or $640, or $64,000—it made no difference. What I enjoyed was seeing Jack Barry gasping for breath. I would have loved to do that to my teachers, especially Mr. Schutz and Miss Courtney.

When things turned out as they did and the subterfuge was uncovered, my parents were distraught. How could this be? Somebody far away did something wrong, and *they* were ashamed. They would bring down some book by Mark or Carl Van Doren from the shelf and display it like some precious relic. To them, books had to tell the truth, and if you wrote one of them, then your family was forever saved. To them, the Van Dorens were patrician intellectuals, university professors, "eggheads" and proud of it. To them, this was the man to defeat Elvis. To me, this guy was just a big kid who could outfox the teacher.

My parents didn't understand television. When the big red Zenith first came into the house, a professor friend of my father's taped a little black-edged note on the screen: "The printed word: RIP." They could have asked me. I knew from the beginning how it worked. I knew the emphasis in "quiz show" was all on the second word. This was *show* business. I knew television didn't tell the truth. Once I had tried to jump from the garage roof, just like Superman leaping off tall buildings, and once I had tried to jump on my bicycle, just as Wild Bill Hickock had done with his galloping horse. To understand television, you had to have tried what you saw there, and to have found that it wasn't real. You had to have jumped and fallen. It was all make-believe—that's why I loved it.

What happened next, however, I didn't understand. Charles Van Doren just disappeared. We never talked about him again. It was like a death in the family. Only later did I learn that he had gone into what would be lifelong seclusion. What was it Hawthorne had said, "Shame sets you apart"? Or, at least it used to. Meanwhile, the top part of Elvis, the wonderful and shameless Elvis, gyrated around the tiny screen, while over in the wings Ed Sullivan stood, index finger to lip, the last great gatekeeper in the age of pixels.

Much has been made of the quiz scandals as the end of American innocence. I think John Leo understood better when he wrote, "What really makes the period seem distant isn't innocence, but the moral outrage that all this lying provoked. Charles Van Doren may not have been our most egregious public sinner, but he was certainly the last one to lead a long life of shame and ignominy for what he did."[1]

That outrage was so fierce that all those around Van Doren were burned. Even in the wash of Robert Redford's 1994 movie *Quiz Show,* blame was still being passed around. The movie reignited some of that ancient heat because, as Redford told the *New York Times,* "The film raises the question of ethics. Are they going to keep the concept of ethics . . . or will it disappear from the language, like shame?"[2] Who was more culpable—the advertising agency, the contestants, the sponsor, the show's producers, the network? The son of the producer, Dan Enright, published a moving defense of his father. He wrote that his father "lived in his shame until the day he died, trying for years to make amends, haunted by his history in everything he did."[3]

"Twenty-one" was a central event of the 1950s; *Quiz Show* was a box-office disappointment in the 1990s. It did not tell the right story because the story had changed. The right story currently goes like this. You do something in public that gets attention. You are celebrated. Your picture is taken. Your image is shared, passed around. You are inflated. You get on television. A tabloid publication finds out something unsavory about you. Something shameful—say, you have spent a lot of time punching people, or had a child out of wedlock, or pictures of you doing something forbidden. They print it. Then the story makes its way to a television news show like "A Current Affair" or "American Journal." We *see* what you did. From there it may slide over into the prime-time interview shows, which are now the staples of the gasping networks, or to the syndicated talk shows. Your story might even make its way to the evening news shows, which now have special back-end stories of human interest. You should be deflated, but it's not working that way. Infamy and fame are merging. Your story, now notorious, moves back to print, maybe picked up by a wire service and from there by the national newspapers. Now you are no longer just well known, you are famous.

Clive James, in his witty and juicy book *Fame in the Twentieth Century*, points out that people used to be famous for what they did. Then, thanks to movies, they became famous for the lives they led while they were doing what they did. Now I would like to suggest that, thanks to television, you can become famous for doing something shameful while leading the life that is making you famous for doing something shameful.

In other words, in the modern version, Charles Van Doren would have been famous for being a Van Doren while performing the role of the enfant savant on television. Then he would have been found out by the *National Enquirer* under such a banner as "Enquiring Minds Scandalized by Enquiring Mind." The story would be picked up by a television cousin such as "Inside Edition," where we would have chatted with his landlady. Then, instead of heading out to the hills, Mr. Van Doren would have hired an agent, appeared on afternoon talk under the rubric, say, of Rotten Eggheads, and perhaps made a page in *People*. From there to a segment on one of the network magazine shows that, in the wake of "60 Minutes," air virtually every night. A made-for-television movie would reenact the entire sequence for those who weren't paying attention the first time around. Who knows what happens next? Perhaps a spot with Larry King, or a final triumphal return to print with mention in a newsmagazine and *USA Today*. After things had quieted down, Professor Van Doren might join the college lecture circuit where, like G. Gordon Liddy, John Bobbitt, Oliver North, Dick Morris, and doubtless someday soon O. J. Simpson, he would have been paid many thousands of dollars to tell all again and again.

The Rise of Celebrity, the Fall of Shame

If one is looking for the medium to blame for the initial detoxification of shame, one would have to start not with television but with the photograph. Oddly enough, losing face became less acute when faces could be passed around and examined. At the end of the nineteenth century we could for the first time stop human action, see it up close, put it down, and then look again. By far the most important kind of photo in the effacement of all emotions was the close-up, which allows the viewer to become nose-to-nose with the observed. The subject is god-like all right, but not all gods are good.

If not for the close-up, we might today live in a world where the only famous people are those who deserve to be on the basis of deeds. What was it after all that made Van Doren so powerful a figure but that the television camera was acting like the portrait camera of Matthew Brady? The image from the static television camera lingered at the end of Van Doren's nose, allowing us to see every pulsation.

Photography took the creation of imagery out of the exclusive hands of painters and engravers and made it available to everyone, especially newspaper and magazine editors. They could now illustrate stories with vivid, realistic images. The life of any stranger became personal in a moment. All television did was to put it into motion. Like it or not, a picture is worth more than a thousand words. It is also worth a fortune, as Alfred Harmsworth (later Lord Northcliffe), Joseph Pulitzer, and William Randolph Hearst all found out. Rupert Murdoch is just a Johnny-come-lately to this crowd. Very often what we like to see is what we can only dimly imagine doing. Much of what we can only imagine is just beyond the limits of toleration over there in Shameland.

The transformation of the newspapers and magazines into vehicles to carry such pictures came from the economic demands of the newly literate middle class. The old-line publishers fought first the engraved illustration and then the photo as debasing print. However, the adventures of the movies and especially television into the land of shame was fought by no one, at least no one who mattered to the producers. The various censoring agencies—from the Hays Office, to the Legion of Decency and the Catholic Film Office, to the FCC, and even the Supreme Court—only certified prurience, making it more attractive, albeit harder to get to. Print was consumed by the literate and was watched over by gatekeepers. But electronic images could be consumed by anyone, especially the young and unsophisticated. Profit and loss was the gatekeeper. No one in the business really cared as long as the sequences were not losing audience share.

The young audience is always the one most interested in scenes of shame and shamelessness, and no one ever went broke programming to them. By the 1970s, they controlled popular culture. After all, they were the ones with the disposable income and excess time to consume entertainment. More than that, they were the prime audience for advertisers, as they had not yet made up their minds about what brands to consume. Aside from makers of dietary supplements, denture adhesives, and Depends, no one really advertises to those over fifty because, even though they have most of the money, they have already decided what to smoke, drink, drive, and eat.

So the personalities favored by the young became important, they became stars, brands, by which consumers could know what story was being told. Those personalities were constructed inside consumer culture using photography, news services, movies, public relations, and television spots, all of which became linked inside huge conglomerates. The fanzines with names like *Photoplay* and *Starlife,* which used to orbit around Hollywood culture, have been pulled inside the information loop. Just look at Time Warner's magazines, for instance. Their two most popular recent introductions are *People,* founded in 1974 to "focus entirely on the active personalities of our time" and *Entertainment Weekly,* founded a decade later, dedicated to endless tidbits about youthful personalities and charts about movie/television/book sales. Both magazines have jumped loose from what used to be the single-page "People" section of *Time,* "The Weekly Newsmagazine." Meanwhile what has happened to *Time?* It's in the economic doldrums, over there grappling for advertising dollars with *Newsweek.*

The Connection of Celebrity to Shame: Joined at the Hip

In his 1964 book, *The Image: A Guide to Pseudo Events in America,* historian Daniel Boorstin defined modern fame in terms that hit home. "The hero was distinguished by his achievement, the celebrity by his image. The celebrity is a person well known for his well-knownness. We risk being the first people in history to have been able to make their illusions so vivid, so persuasive, so realistic that we can live in them."[4] And live in them, we have.

Movies were crucial in the fabrication of fame. During the gaudy 1920s, Hollywood stars were packaged as New World royalty. In the Depression they became deluxe New Deal editions of everyday people who liked fried potatoes, played baseball, and deferred respectfully to their fans. Myrna Loy is quoted as saying, "I daren't take any chances with Myrna Loy, for she isn't my property. I couldn't even go to the corner drugstore without looking 'right,' you see. Not because of personal vanity, but because the studio has spent millions of dollars on the personality known as Myrna Loy."[5]

She was right. The decisive change from being famous as a result of deeds done to achieving fame as a result of marketing was brought about by Hollywood as a way to sell product. The purposeful confusion of on-screen personalities with flesh-and-blood humans allowed a kind of morality play to be enacted, with humor characters acting out prescribed roles. Sometimes the results are bizarre. For instance, Marie

Curie was made famous by her deeds, but it was only Greer Garson's portrayal that gave her celebrity.

Television created a more potent version of celebrity that was even more immediate, but the bar code was harder to read. This celebrity moved between the entertainment and commercial worlds without causing a stir. These new nonthreatening characters came into our house free of charge and provided us endless entertainment. They became our personal friends. They were not gods like movie stars. There were few recognizable villains. Just folks. Perhaps a solecism is necessary here to describe this weird hybrid of advertising and entertainment personality—a telebrity.

The first such advertising telebrity was Gertrude Berg, who, in the 1960s, sold S.O.S. pads in the Yiddish-inflected language of her television character Molly Goldberg. "With soap, it's loaded," came from Molly, not Gertrude. Better known, however, were commercials in which Chris Robinson and Peter Bergman, actors who portrayed doctors on soap operas, sold cold medicine by admitting, "I am not a doctor, but I play one on TV." Best yet was Robert Young. A film star who played various roles to an earlier generation, to us he was a telebrity father—first as father/father on "Father Knows Best," then as father/doctor on "Marcus Welby, M.D." When he later prescribed decaf coffee for upset nerves, we got the patriarchal double whammy.

Sometimes the mix is so powerful that the ad creates its own reality. By the 1980s, James Garner and Mariette Hartley were so successful in a Polaroid campaign that many believed they were indeed husband and wife. And a few years later matters were so thoroughly confused that we had a political leader whom most of us knew not as an actor in B movies but as a telebrity employed by General Electric.

As we will see a few chapters hence, when Dan Quayle attempted to shame Murphy Brown for having a child out of wedlock, he succeeded—at least to some—because Murphy (Candice Bergen) was confused in the American mind with the spokeswoman for Sprint. This is the woman who tells you what kind of long-distance service to buy. According to market research done at the time, some viewers thought the Sprint woman was a wiseacre and needed instruction from the vice president. That both sitcom and ad characters were totally fictive was no problem. Sprint even released a commercial (July 1992) hoping to capitalize on the confusion. In the ad, fathers, mothers, and mothers-to-be all talk about whom to call with the news. Cut to Bergen/Brown, who looks skyward saying, "Gee, seems like everybody's having a baby these days."

I need now to add a new subcategory, which, for lack of a better word, I would like to call a shamelebrity. The shamelebrity is not a villain or even an antihero. He, or she, is simply someone who has done something wrong, often something shameful, and is able, with the help of press agents, tabloids, publicists, fanzines, and managers, to make the act into a sequence of images, a salable commodity. This sequence, soon called a scenario, results in a movie of the week shown on one of the major networks. Usually only after the movie can the shamelebrity become a telebrity and endorse products. If the character in question is female, she will most probably join Jessica Hahn, Donna Rice, Marla Maples, and Heidi Fleiss in endorsing No Excuses jeans.

Here, for instance, is Leona Helmsley. A crackerjack realtor, she became a celebrity by appearing in ads for her husband's hotel chain. She carefully crafted the image of a hands-on perfectionist who goes into a tizzy if the towels don't match, or if a dust bunny has crept under the bed. When you stayed at a Helmsley hotel you felt as if you were a guest of the queen, and the queen's personal servants would do your bidding. You would never have to complain; she would preemptively do it for you.

Then Leona was charged with tax evasion. Worse yet, she prated to one of those servants that only the little people pay taxes. Her comment

"Who said it's good to be the Queen?"

My ads tell you I'm the Queen of the Helmsley Palace, which suggests that all I have to do is march through the elegant lobby or down the grand staircase...I wish it were that simple...but it's not.

In order to make the Helmsley Hotels the most respected hotels in New York, I have to work harder than Cinderella (before the ball).

Because I care so much about the Helmsley reputation, I personally select the finest linens, hangers that do come out of the closet, the highest quality TVs, clock-radios, lamps, and furnishings. (Is that any way for a Queen to spend her day?)

Most importantly I have to be diligent about the people we hire. It is crucial that every one of my staff provides the kind of sincere, caring service my guests have come to expect.

When I'm not working with my staff, I'm answering letters from people all over the world. Most of them are letters of praise for the service at my hotels. Many are suggestions (I'm always open to good suggestions). This is a job I can't delegate. These letters were written to me, and they'll be answered by me.

And, just when I think I have a few minutes to sit down and polish the 5 diamonds awarded by the AAA to the Helmsley Palace (and never to any other hotel in New York), the phone rings.

Making sure that every guest receives royal treatment at every Helmsley Hotel takes a lot of work.

It's not easy being the Queen...but don't worry, I'm not abdicating.

Leona M. Helmsley

Leona M. Helmsley, President
Helmsley/Harley Hotels

The Helmsley Hotels of New York

THE HELMSLEY PALACE	PARK LANE	HARLEY OF NEW YORK	ST. MORITZ ON THE PARK	MIDDLETOWNE HARLEY	WINDSOR HARLEY
455 Madison Avenue	36 Central Park South	212 East 42nd Street	50 Central Park South	148 East 48th Street	100 West 58th Street

The Helmsley Palace is the only Hotel in New York ever to receive the ⬥ Five Diamond Award ♦♦♦♦♦
The finest Hotels in the World

For reservations call Toll-Free: 800/221-4982 or in New York, 212/888-1624. TELEX: 640-543. Or call your travel agent.

IN PALMIER TIMES: LEONA AS QUEEN OF THE HELMSLEY PALACE.

made its way into the tabloids. In the public mind she was remythologized as the no-longer-figurative but literal Queen Bitch. Not to be stymied by shame, however, once she was released from prison, she played this new persona to the hilt, using her very shamelessness to ad-

101

SHE KNOWS PEOPLE TALK ABOUT HER. SHE'LL EVEN SHOW YOU WHAT THEY SAY.

I recently suggested to my in-laws that they stay at The Helmsley Park Lane. They thoroughly enjoyed their stay and we had a delightful meal with them at the hotel. You truly epitomise perfection.

I appreciate the level of accommodations and try t…
Hotel whenever I travel. Thank you for …
little extras.

I will conti…

I was ecstatic that your chamber found my diamond and ruby earring. My grandfather gave it to my grandmoth… on their wedding day.

I will not soon forget my pleasant sur… when a very gracious employee saw his … And again, the night of the opera, your…

It was a very pleasurable dining exper… the whole family.

Thanks to you, I now have a magnifying mirror in ev… bathroom in my home and in my guest cottage.

Sincerely…

the hottest show on Broadway. I dropped my lipstick on my white mink — you had it cleaned before dinner.

Drop us a line to tell us what you love best about staying at a Helmsley Hotel. Or if there's something we can do to make your next stay even better. We promise it'll receive the personal attention of You-Know-Who.

The Helmsley Park Lane	The New York Helmsley	The Helmsley Middletowne		The Helmsley Carlton House	The Helmsley Windsor	For reservations and
36 Central Park South	212 East 42nd Street	148 East 48th Street		680 Madison Avenue	100 West 58th Street	information call (800)221-4982
New York, NY 10019	New York, NY 10017	New York, NY 10017		New York, NY 10021	New York, NY 10019	or in New York, (212)697-8300
(212)371-4000	(212)490-8900	(212)755-3000		(212)838-3000	(212)265-2100	or call your travel agent.

AFTER INCARCERATION: "SAY WHAT YOU WILL, SHE RUNS A HELLUVA HOTEL."

vantage. In a campaign called "Say What You Will, She Runs a Helluva Hotel," Leona proudly displays her personal correspondence. *She's ba-ack!*

The key characteristic of the shamelebrity is that he/she is a real person, not some figment of a press agent's imagination. She/he has crossed over into Shameland and returned . . . almost. Only after the media attention does this character become mythic, a figment of our popular imagination.

The initial shaming sequence does not have to be actual, but it has to be coherent. Tabloid print and television can fill in the outlines, provide a few close-ups, and chart the geographic terrain. We know what Joey Buttafuoco's boat looks like and we've been in his garage. We have seen the street corner where Hugh Grant propositioned Ms. Divine and we've seen the inside of his BMW. We have been to the 7-Eleven parking lot where John Wayne Bobbitt's penis was found and ditto the knife. We have visited the steps where Nancy Kerrigan's knee was whacked and we know all about Tonya, Shawn, and Jeff. We have seen the Menendez mansion, the gun, and the pool. We have been to the Regency Hotel with Frank Gifford and heard what he has had to say to the former airline stewardess. What is there about the Brentwood estate of O.J. that we do not know? For many of us it is almost as familiar as a second home.

The interminable made-for-TV movies and the overnight books that surround these events are for the slow learners. The rest of us already know the sordid details, whether we want to or not.

Have you noticed how most shamelebrities live on either coast? This is not from any deficiency of the Middle West; it's just that the tabloid maw from which they spew is in Manhattan and Los Angeles. Proximity breeds affection, and affection breeds addiction. Sometimes this immediacy can cause problems, as when *People* put Amy Fisher on the cover in 1992. The issue didn't sell in the heartland. Why? Because tabloid TV had not yet broadcast any of the Fisher/Buttafuoco snippets, so few people outside New York even knew who she was, let alone about her claim to fame.

A Taxonomy of Shamelebrity

There are many varieties and leagues of shamelebrity. Here are a few. The bottom fish are the wanna-bes of afternoon talk television. These are the barely literate trailer-park types who come forward to recount their own tales of egregious behavior. They are unique only in that they dig dirt on themselves. Shamelebrity for them is no longer a result of great or terrible deeds; it is an end in itself. It lasts a cultural finger-snap.

This phylum of shamelessness lives primarily in afternoon television. As with the soap operas, which they imitate and exaggerate by supplying real flesh and blood, the plot is almost always a family in distress. The initial consuming audience is young, predominantly female. But these shows are also rebroadcast in late prime time, around eleven o'clock, when a male audience joins in. This is an audience that used to follow the old-style attack-television shows of Joe Pyne, Alan Burke, and Morton Downey Jr., so the interview-as-professional wrestling is welcome and understood. This audience has patiently waited for its bread and circuses since the days of the Roman coliseum.

The ringleaders are Jerry Springer, Ricki Lake, Jenny Jones, and Montel Williams, among others. Whatever the topic, the format is generally as follows: One person—usually a woman, since women are most frequently cast in the role of powerless victim—comes out and tells all the couple's business. The story is welcomed by the apparently sympathetic host and a leering, jeering, cheering audience of her peers. This done, the other person—often a man—is brought on-stage, where he is confronted by his woman/women, booed or cheered by the audience, and gleefully encouraged by the host to confirm our worst suspicions. Someone has done something shameful, really shameful, and we have a chance to pass judgment. Although the audience passes the microphone around to excoriate the malfeasant, he is totally immune to shame and almost heroically unrepentant.

So what are the topics? Here is a week's sampling: "I Love a Serial Killer," "Two Women Pregnant by the Same Man," "Husbands Stolen from Their Wives by Neighbors," "Thirteen-Year-Old Mommies," "Same-Sex Lovers of Gang Members" and "You Dumped Me But Look at Me Now." We used to have to wait for the carnival to come to town; now it's every day, five times a day.

Higher up the food chain are the characters from the "real world" whose actual acts are less important than their attitudes. We used to see them only in *Police Gazette* or *Argosy*. Then they moved to the super-market tabloids. Now they are all over. What they share in common is that they have been caught doing something shameful. Often this act is something we might have considered doing too, but something stops us first. They continued.

They are unrepentant. That is part of their attraction. In fact, they seem slyly complacent. Why not? They have exchanged the income of notoriety for the loss of self-esteem. They may move from nonentity to infamous to famous in the matter of months, or they may just stay fa-mously infamous. It makes no difference. The line between fame and notoriety has been erased. We know this league of shamelebrity by their first names: Heidi, Tonya, Eric and Lyle, Joey, Leona, and all the others. No mea culpas here.

Although John Wayne Bobbitt is not typical, he is characteristic. An alleged wife-beater and convicted girlfriend batterer, Mr. Bobbitt appears completely unabashed, showing up on Howard Stern's New Year's Eve show to hawk T-shirts, and has even marketed a Bobbitt penis protector. For a time he was negotiating with *Playboy* for a photo spread in which his sometime-fiancée, a former topless dancer, ap-pears shirtless while he, with becoming shyness, keeps his on. Alas, this modern rendition of *Susanna and the Elders* never took place. They broke up before the photo shoot could occur. His rise, shine, evapora-tion, and fall was so brief that, although he tested for a game show called "Liars," he disappeared from public view before the pilot was made.

At the next level is what can only be called retroactive shamelebrity. Usually, unbeknownst to the celebrity in question, shame is applied by a third party for acts that are often independent of what the person did to become famous. The dismantling of fame is not new. "Formerly we used to canonize our heroes," Oscar Wilde wrote in 1891. "The modern method is to vulgarize them. Cheap editions of great books may be delightful, but cheap editions of great men are absolutely detestable."[6] He forgot to add, ". . . but very profitable."

Although this resettling of fame is the stuff of weekly television docudramas, look at the best-seller list and you will also see various examples of de-faming at work. So we have Kitty Kelley digging the dirt on Frank Sinatra and Nancy Reagan, or Albert Goldman vivisecting John Lennon. That is to be expected. Walter Winchell and the scandal sheet made the juicy tidbit into a full meal. No real harm done. After all, these people were well known for being well known, so knowing a little about the shameful stuff does no damage. That is part of show biz—the "warts" part of warts and all. And if the warts aren't in the right places, so what? It is difficult for public figures to sue for libel and slander.

It's also part of politics, so in a way, Joe McGinniss's *The Last Brother,* on Edward M. Kennedy, and Nigel Hamilton's *J.F.K.: Reckless Youth* are part of a tradition that stretches back to Lytton Strachey's wickedly ironic *Eminent Victorians.* Politicians have trouble suing too.

But what is surprising is the recent besmirching of those whose fame is solidly based not on *who* they were, but on *what* they did. Rifling through their locked closets is somehow not the same as dishing the dirt of those whose fame is based on being well known or being in the public arena. Here are just a few examples from the last few years: Jeffrey Meyers's *Scott Fitzgerald: A Biography,* Francine du Plessix Gray's *Rage and Fire,* on Flaubert, Ronald Hayman's *Tennessee*

Williams: Everyone Else Is an Audience, Joan Peyser's *Bernstein: A Biography,* Steven Naifeh and Gregory White Smith's *Jackson Pollock: An American Saga,* and Arianna Stassinopoulos Huffington's *Picasso: Creator and Destroyer.* In each of these examples shame is back-loaded onto someone who can neither defend himself nor profit from the notoriety.

Joyce Carol Oates has called this disturbing new subgenre "pathography." "Its motifs are dysfunction and disaster, illnesses and pratfalls, failed marriages and failed careers, alcoholism and breakdowns and outrageous conduct," she writes in the lead article of *The New York Times Book Review.* She named her baby Lourdes—clever, huh?

> Its scenes are sensational, wallowing in squalor and foolishness; its dominant images are physical and deflating; its shrill theme is "failed promise," if not outright "tragedy." That such biography often comes from the academy is to be expected from a group often obsessed with de-canonizing at any price.[7]

Right she is, but as we will see, that such stuff should come from the academy is no accident. The academy, currently informed as it is by relative values, political correctness, and revisionist history, is one of the major centers in the off-loading of ersatz shame in the modern world.

MADONNA: SHAMELEBRITY AS GODDESS

The pinnacle of shamelebrity is reserved for those whose sole claim to fame is their single-minded subversion of shame codes. Only one person has recently achieved this empyrean and as a consequence has received the highest tribute of fame. She has become a single-word eponym. The mere mention of Madonna is enough.

While it need not be mentioned that she is not the first to bear this single name, it should be noted that, in what is surely the prime post-modern subversion of values, the modern Madonna single-mindedly subverts almost all her predecessor's values. I say "almost all" because the one trait she maintained was partnerless sex. Until recently. When reproduction was inevitable, she did it the modern way—with her personal trainer outside any oppressive wed-lock. When she decided to "keep my baby," VH-1 threw her a "baby shower" by running a nine-hour loop of her videos.

Here is a woman who can't dance, can't sing, and can't act (or, at least by her own admission, can't do any of these very well), but what she can do is be shameless. "But that doesn't matter," she gleefully admits. "I want to push people's buttons. I want to be provocative. I want to be political."[8] What she calls being "political" has nothing to do with Washington, D.C., but whatever it is, it has made her one of the most powerful forces in American popular culture. In fact, for a while, Madonna was the most popular female entertainer in the world.

To understand how she has become such a force, as well as why she is now evaporating, we need to briefly revisit the late 1970s. Madonna was a creation of a startling new mutant medium—the music video—which was transmitted along a new pathway—the coaxial cable—to a previously unexploited market niche—the adolescent female. This new audience was the first to be informed by the concerns of feminism.

True, this audience had erupted in the 1940s with Frank Sinatra, then again with Elvis and the Beatles in the 1950s and 1960s. But in the 1980s it finally met a same-sex entertainer, and the combination was explosive. The combination was, just as Madonna says, political.

While boys have always had somebody to act out their fantasies of rebellion and stand in for their forbidden selves, girls have not. Until the mid-1970s, women rockers were basically submissive versions of Connie Francis. Admittedly, there were some exceptions: Ronnie Spector, Grace Slick, Janis Joplin, to name the obvious ones. But this changed with the Go-Gos, Siouxsie of Siouxsie and the Banshees, Joan

KEITH HARING, *MADONNA: I'M NOT ASHAMED* 1989 (ESTATE OF KEITH HARING).

Jett, Cyndi Lauper, and Chrissie Hynde of the Pretenders, who in varying degrees seized control of their careers and essentially asked, nay, demanded, to have lives of their own. They became the female side of the counterculture. But Madonna asked for more. In the "Burning Up" video, she attempts to separate herself by claiming new ground. She asserts she is not like the rest of the sisterhood for she has, in her proud words, "no shame."

But to be heard, she needed a new medium far enough away from the prying eyes and cocked ears of parents. In the mid-1970s Warner Amex Satellite Entertainment Company started Music Television, a nonstop, twenty-four-hour, commercial channel beamed via satellite across the United States. The content seemed harmless enough. Musicians had made performance films of their acts since the Vitaphone shorts of the 1920s and the soundies of the 1940s, so why not show them along with some advertising? Better yet, the videos themselves could be a kind of advertisement for the music itself, shunting the production costs to the music companies. The impact of this new delivery system was immediate, transforming not only the recording industry but show business as well. Performers who could sing as well as project a slightly outrageous persona (called "great visuals"), such as Boy George, Prince, Cyndi Lauper, Billy Idol, Tina Turner, and especially Michael Jackson, became "recording artists." On MTV commercial television achieved purity—the entertainment is the advertisement and the advertisement is the show.

MTV was an entire network dedicated to synthesizing this purity. Quick cutting, slow dissolves, computer-generated images, animation, wild angles, multiple-image montages, hallucinatory special effects, Chromakey, magnified close-ups, masked screens—everything that is implied in that portmanteau term "state of the art" is involved. Television must make everything visual, even music. Best yet, performers often never have to sing—it's all mime. When it is time to take the show on the road in the requisite "concert tour," similar technology allows the performer to reenact the video sequences with the jazzed-up recording studio music piped in over the sound system.

Old-fashioned purists, and even some legislators, were distraught that many of the most popular performers charged what seem to be outrageous prices for concert performances and then never sang a note.

They lip-synched instead. But the fans didn't care. The kids wanted to hear exactly what was on their $14 CD at home and to see a show that duplicated the video that they had memorized. Ironically, if the MTV performers really did sing in their concerts, the audience might have a legitimate grievance. Since the original was manufactured, shouldn't the "live" replica be likewise? "Is it live or is it Memorex?" Who cares?

This was the medium Madonna mastered—from video to concert to video to concert. For whatever else she may be, Madonna is an extraordinary mime. She has absolutely no fear of being seen. The camera, which so terrifies most of us, is nonexistent to her. In fact, as Warren Beatty says in *Truth or Dare*, Madonna's movie of her "concert" tour, "She has no life off-camera."

When you look at her early videos, everything falls into place. What she does so well is to pose. She assumes positions so effortlessly and so passionately that by the time you have made sense of what is being "said" in the scene, it's all over. So here we see Madonna as the "Material Girl" doing a better-than-fair imitation of Marilyn Monroe, as a Mexican hooker in "Borderline," as a pregnant teenager refusing to give up her baby in "Papa Don't Preach," as a porno-store dancer who skips off into the sunset with a preadolescent boy in "Open Your Heart." We see her being seduced by a black saint/priest in "Like a Prayer," groping at her crotch à la Michael Jackson while wearing a man's pinstripe business suit with torpedo brassiere in "Express Yourself," and feigning orgasm during "Like a Virgin."

Perhaps the video that best typifies this extraordinary talent is "Vogue," in which she "strikes the pose" of various moves in the black drag-queen subculture while marking it as her own manifesto: "Strike a pose; there's nothing to it."

Each video was dedicated to redirecting the energies of some shame event back on itself: masturbation, voyeurism, child sexuality, homosexuality, illegitimacy, prostitution, and religious sacrilege. In each, the fact that the music is highly emotive, rhythmic, danceable, and even sentimental makes the plot, so to speak, subservient. It's opera. And as the Italian Romantics knew, you can get away with anything in opera. In fact, the more outrageous the action, the less troubled we are. It's just a song, and songs, as we all know from childhood, are just fun. Lighten up. Or, to make the analogy more modern, the music video is a cartoon. No one complains about the outrageous violence in the endless "Road Runner" loop—it's just a drawing on celluloid.

In a bizarre legitimization of her own shamelebrity, Madonna was even fed by the hand that had pinched her. At the end of the 1980s came the Pepsi scandal. After paying $5 million for her promotional video, Pepsi yanked its "Like a Prayer" knockoff ad when the original video appeared. The MTV version was a too provocative commingling of sex and religion. When the Shameless One seduced a black saint and exposed her dripping stigmata in church, the salt-chip-and-sugar-water company said they wanted out. Pepsi left Madonna with $5 million and great press clippings.

This propitious act was soon followed by MTV's own refusal to air the "Justify My Love" video because of recently acquired standards. Now suddenly young adults in various sexual activities, polymorphous perversity, bisexuality, transvestism—all of which had been MTV's bread and butter—became spinach. But what could be a more certain sign of artistry than censure and exile? The avant-garde is not supposed to be liked, that's the whole point. Wasn't the Salon's refusal to display Manet's *Déjeuner sur l'herbe* a sure sign of its artistic merit? And didn't the famous critic Louis Etienne call the painting "shameless"? Well, said Madonna, that's what is happening to me too. I'm being censored. I am an artist, too. I'm a victim.

Alas, when Madonna attempted the same routines in her coffee-table book *Sex*, there were genuine howls of outrage. Books are not tunes; they don't evaporate into thin air. After 128 pages of Madonna indulging in everything from sadomasochism to lesbianism, pointing knives, whips, razors, and unsheathed stilettos at her genitals, and rhapsodizing about how being tied up is really "an act of love," most "readers" were exhausted.

And when Madonna attempted this a second time, the project was a complete dud. *The Girlie Show*, a "BoundSound" book that contained seventy pages of glossy photos and a brief but inane text (the latter written ALL IN CAPITAL LETTERS), along with a three-song "live" CD from Madonna's 1993 "Girlie Show" miniworld tour, rarely made it to the review desk, let alone many coffee tables. After all, how many times can you stand to see Madonna using a microphone stand as a phallus, being groped by bikini-clad female dancers, writhing against a scantily clad male dancer? Even shamelessness has limits.

When Madonna ties her videos together in a movie, however, the result is electrifying. Her *Truth or Dare* is worth looking at. As if to show the hyperreality of the music video, all the song-and-dance numbers are adaptations of their MTV originals and filmed in color. Reality is in black and white. But the reality pays off. We finally get a chance to see her audience (overwhelmingly young female), her publicity machine (including Alek Keshishian, who shot the film), her cast and crew, (young and often gay—the black dancers who are continually referred to as "my children"), and especially Madonna Louise Veronica Ciccone, a motherless Catholic girl from upstate Michigan, orchestrating Madonna, a machine made in MTV land.

As with cinema verité, the film is slices of real life. Much has been made of some of the slices. Here are some: In the title sequence, Madonna performs fellatio on a wine bottle as part of a dare. She demonstrates her indifferent behavior toward one of her "children," her makeup girl, who has been drugged, robbed, and sodomized, by saying that life in New York is really a "bummer." She pays a visit to her mother's grave (while brother Christopher cringes behind a tree), wondering aloud what she looks like now—"Probably just a bunch of dust." She invites one of her dancers, who clearly has no sexual interest in her, to play kissy-face with her in bed. She has lesbian come-ons with Sandra Bernhard and includes other show-business friends only to exclude them—Warren Beatty and Kevin Costner are patronized as if buffoons. When her embarrassed father comes to visit backstage, she shyly tells him that she has to change out of costume. She retreats to her dressing room, where, with fanfare, she shows her bare breasts to the camera and, of course, to us. Best yet, when Madonna is asked by the police in Toronto to tone the show down, she answers that she will never "compromise my artistic integrity." Whew!

As Executive Producer of *Truth or Dare*, Madonna is clearly choosing slices of her life that at first glance might embarrass any other celebrity. But when you realize her celebrity is based on shamelessness, there is a powerful coherence. This is not cinema verité but a very clever hagiography.

Madonna accomplishes in *Truth or Dare* what is only implied in the individual videos—an entire persona dedicated to life just over the margin. Raw and uncensored, she is sometimes engrossing, sometimes appalling, but always at the center of a shame-storm. She is, in fact, the very image of the modern adolescent female. She is caught between two worlds, as it were, one dead and the other struggling to be born. Where is her place? At home? On the job? In bed? Alone? With boys? With girls? Madonna is all about Mommy and Daddy, eroticism and romance, sexual politics and gender anxiety, peer pressure and individuality, sin and Catholicism. Where to go, what to do? She does not meet this borderline ambiguity with adolescent withdrawal, but just the opposite. She comes crashing over the line.

Madonna is the Portrait of the Young Woman as a Recording Artist, the distaff Stephen Dedalus for our times. She has made intense self-consciousness a way of life, an oeuvre, not in print but in pixels. While the French, who usually like this kind of thing, have labeled her "a woman without shame,"[9] American academics have made her part of the feminist curriculum.

For feminists, most notably Camille Paglia, Madonna is the ultimate

MADONNA, "STRIKING A POSE," 1990 (AP/WIDE WORLD PHOTOS).

liberated woman. She is in control of her body, her bank account, and, most important, her image. The very name of her tour, "Blond Ambition," says it all. She pulls her own strings, decides on her own hair color, and has her own ambition. Madonna's trademark torpedo bra, designed by Jean Paul Gaultier, is metaphorical armor against the monstrous regiment of men. If she wants to wear her underwear as outerwear, no one can stop her. Warren Beatty does her bidding, not vice versa. She wears the custom-made "Boy Toy" belt buckle, or "unchastity belt," because Madonna is doing the toying, not the boy. She is the woman in power, a dominatrix for GenXers.

That Madonna has achieved this power by exploiting a stereotype of the patriarchy—the shameless hussy—is not to be overlooked. Not by happenstance did she name one of her companies Slutco. The fact that she has achieved the highest respect of our culture—fame—by subverting its taboos is a nifty paradox. It has also proved her down-fall. For the cruelest words in American popular culture now obtain: been there, done that. Brazen became boring. Since the 1980s, she has been reduced to a parody, to bubble-gum videos, deluxe smooch music, and insulting David Letterman by using the F-word thirteen times while all the time facing the proper camera. She has become tame—even her Evita was domesticated—not because she has changed, but because our culture has. Thanks to Madonna herself, Madonna has now become not shocking but repetitious.

"I stand for the eighties," she told Jon Pareles of the *New York Times* in 1994, "and the eighties are over, so I'm over. I don't think about the eighties part of me and the nineties part of me, I am just doing what I want to do. And it just happens to be the nineties."[10] She was right; her time had past. As BBC commentator Clive James commented, she finally became "a mystery everybody knew about."[11] All that was left was to achieve the antimatter state of modern celebrityhood—known for being a celebrity who is no longer a celebrity. In the early 1990s, when Madonna graced *Esquire*'s cover in a dog collar and chain, she sealed her fate as, in the magazine's words, "The Most Boring Woman Who Used to Be Interesting." Almost all that was left was to find herself atop *Entertainment Weekly*'s 1993 "cold" list. The final indignity: Madonna on the cover of *Redbook* (January 1997) above the caption ". . . and the surprising plans she has for her daughter." You guessed it: no nose rings, no tattoos, no orange hair . . . at least not for a while.

Still, Madonna has had an extraordinary run. Most significant of all the many things she demonstrated was that the 1960s were indeed a demarcation line of American culture, the great divide, between the world of print and the electronic world, between a world controlled from above and one controlled from below, a culture of intellectual hierarchy and a carnival of entertainment. For whatever else Madonna may mean, she has shown that shame and shamelessness have profoundly and irrevocably changed.

CHAPTER 6

SHAME IN THE CULTURE OF RECOVERY

Toxic shame is far worse than the hungry dogs in the basement. It's like a herd of charging rhinos—a school of hungry man-eating sharks. You cannot let your guard down for one second.
   —JOHN BRADSHAW, *Healing the Shame That Binds You*

$\mathcal{I}$T IS AN instructive paradox that the culture that so prized rugged individualism should now be the culture that so willingly countenances victimology. Without fail, the shameless June bugs of popular tabloid culture, from Tonya Harding to John Wayne Bobbitt, from Leona Helmsley to the Menendez brothers, from Susan Smith to Joey Buttafuoco, have all claimed for themselves not innocence so much as blamelessness. Okay, they seem to say, I did wrong, but you should have seen what was done to *me*. If you think that what I did was bad, well, what about how I was treated? Now, *that's* really shameful. Would any of these miscreants have captured the spotlight of popular culture if they had said, "I did it. I was wrong. I'm ashamed"?

These characters are thrown up into shared popular culture not because they are unique, but because they are exaggerations of recognized types. They are quick-run cartoons, to be sure, but the underlying myth has been with us for a generation. In many ways theirs is the central story of our baby-boom times. On a thumbnail this classic chutzpah is that of the young man who, having murdered his parents, throws himself on the mercy of the court because he's an orphan. In our modern version he then asks for an annuity because their mistreatment made him do it. In addition, he tells first the *National Enquirer* and then Ricki Lake that he was only doing what others have

117

been doing all along. The only difference is that he got caught. He's honest about it. That should count for something. "After all," he says, "where do you think we poor orphans come from?"

In the cultural background of the 1990s, we are treated to a daily whine of this refrain on afternoon television. The libretto of trailer-park opera on afternoon talk shows, "I am shameless but still have my pride," is played out as carnival entertainment. Watch the gap-toothed geek get closer to the tabooed snake than you've ever imagined, says the nice young barker between commercials. Meanwhile, cycling in an endless loop over at MTV, performers like Madonna essentially franchise aspects of once shameful behavior in order to gather an audience for an advertiser. The grocery store checkout tabloid has spread through television like kudzu. Such stuff comprises the back end of the nightly news shows, spilling over into prime-time infotainment like "A Current Affair" and "Hard Copy."

Broadcasting the shameful acts of others is a major profit center. But simultaneously broadcasting the good news that the viewer has done nothing to be ashamed of is where the money is. Our little phosphorescent friend in the box in the corner speaks out of both sides of its mouth. And we love it. Madison Avenue, which sponsors the morality play of others in free-fall, reminds us of our own salvation—*if* we cooperate. "You, You're the One," "You Deserve a Break Today," "We Want to Be Your Company," "Your Happiness Is Our Reason for Being," "Grab for the Gusto," "You've Earned It," "We're Proud of You," soft-sell advertising tells us. The power of advertising-supported entertainment, an entertainment based on never having to say you're sorry and never having to admit responsibility for any act, is the power of a protection racket. This is the essence of television culture: They should be ashamed, you are in the clear. Stick with us. They are sinners, you are saved. This narco-narcissism mixed with a heady dollop of sadism has spilled over into other media.

Celluloid Stories and a Sense of Self

Although we've just taken a quick look at television in the last chapter, let's glance at the current status of storytelling from Hollywood. Is it possible to see a movie that makes *you* feel bad? Name one. Okay, a few sneak by, usually over studio objection, but even then they are rarely blockbusters. What studio exec would dare risk the box-office disaster and conglomerated opprobrium for unleashing such a dog? Most of us don't go to the movies to feel bad. Even *Entertainment Weekly* has recently (1996) thrown in the towel, saying that the term "summer movie" has become generic.

Yet, if you look at the movies of the generation before television, the post–World War II, pre–Korean War decades, what you see is a steady stream of melancholy people struggling to make sense of complexity and often finding disappointment. This angst permeated all genres. Go see *I Am a Fugitive from a Chain Gang*, or *The Grapes of Wrath*, or *Spartacus*, or *The Sand Pebbles*, or *Dr. Strangelove*, or any number of popular entertainments that denied audiences emotional pabulum, and you will see how much tastes have changed.

What is the *ciné noir,* for heaven's sake, but the bad medicine of life? Here indeed is the cinema of shame. Here we have a self-enclosed world in which a confused protagonist breaks a rule and *must* suffer. That's the whole point. We know punishment follows bad acts. The only question is, how is he going to endure it? The *mise en scène* is filled with venetian blinds, fog, and darkness because there is a world out there that shouldn't be seen. Secrets exist. Murder and mayhem are at its center. The plot revolves around someone doing something really naughty and then getting caught. Do it and pay, says the *ciné noir*. The hero does it. He pays. End of story.

Hollywood now seems determined, no matter how grim the yarn, to send audiences home laughing or, better yet, smiling through tears.

Although television has exacerbated this, it is hardly a new phenomenon. Back in 1939, producer Sam Goldwyn reacted to disappointing sneak screenings of *Wuthering Heights* by adding an epilogue in which Laurence Olivier and Merle Oberon are reunited in heaven. Needless to say, that scene is not to be found in Emily Brontë's famous novel, but it resulted in a big hit. Such lessons were not lost on the moguls. But they knew how to do much more than please—they took seriously their New World, first-generation responsibility to instruct. They were gatekeepers. They kept much out, but they let some shame in.

No longer. Movies are made today by companies that do not especially want to make movies. They want to make money. They are just as happy to string coaxial cable, publish a book or two, broadcast infotainment, or run a theme park. Movies are just part of the marketing "mix." So we do not express any consternation when told of the two endings of, say, *Fatal Attraction*. In the original cut of the film, the neurotic woman played by Glenn Close commits suicide to a recording of "Madame Butterfly," deliberately using a knife on which are the fingerprints of her one-weekend stand, Michael Douglas. The first movie ends with husband and father Douglas being arrested for her murder. Now, that's *ciné le plus noir!* Philandering husband gets framed.

Get me rewrite! In the second version the knife-wielding Ms. Close emerges from the bathtub to be shot by wife Anne Archer and all ends happily. Michael has learned his lesson with no pain. Hollywood did too. *Fatal Attraction* went on to become one of the year's biggest moneymakers. No more downers, please. Show me no shame.

How could we not continually be redefining shame downward in such an environment? Compare the print versions of *Schindler's List* or *Forrest Gump* to the movies and you will see the Disneyfication of mass-market entertainment. Feeling good, even when feeling good violates not only the integrity of the generating text or of reality as we know it, is paramount. Brush away your tears and smile for the camera. If what you want to make is money, and if blockbusters are the way to do it, and if relatively few people will see anything even tinged with shame, then you know what stories to tell.

I have mentioned television and the movies because, if feeling good is the crux of our shared national stories—be they in the fields of advertising or entertainment—then what about the story we tell ourselves? Each of us creates a fiction about ourself—a life script—that allows us to know how we are doing. Where am I? Relative to whom? Am I successful? Compared to what fictional grid? Am I happy? Well, let me check on what I think I should be feeling. We draw these fictions from the general pool of shared stories. Our grandparents drew them from print. We draw ours from television and the movies. No wonder we're anxious. We can't be that happy, regardless of what Hollywood and Madison Avenue say. Pass the Prozac.

The Doctor Will See You in the Health Section: Bibliotherapy

If you want to see the merchandising of the anxiety and relief of shame, go into any bookstore. What used to be a single shelf of self-help books by Dale Carnegie, Bishop Fulton J. Sheen, and Norman Vincent Peale has exploded into an entire subsection of books on building self-esteem. In the 1950s these books argued a variation of *The Little Engine That Could*. You can succeed. Just keep at it. I think I can. I think I can. I can. The modern version is dedicated to the concept of Recovery. Recovery is based on the Romantic story of The Child Is Father of the Man. Want success? Just relax. Let your inner child out. I feel okay. I feel okay. I am okay.

If you go into one of the national chains that have books divided into reading sectors, you often see a sign saying New Age, Health, Abuse, or Addiction. In large cities and in some small towns (university towns especially), the section has sprung loose to become an entire bookstore dedicated to self-esteem, to feeling good. These stores with names like Serenity (in San Diego), Miracles (in Wheaton, Maryland), and The Catbird Seat (in Portland), are part of the Recovery Store Network, an informal booksellers' network based, as you might have guessed, in Southern California.

Such boutique store owners estimate that about 80 percent of their sales are books.[1] In addition, they carry a selection of gift items relating to the various "anonymous" fellowships, support groups for overeaters, alcoholics, workaholics, sexaholics, anorexics, and the like. Just as the chain stores are divided into sections, so, too, are these stores. The sections are often very specific. You find your affiliation by your acronym. So the ACOA section is for Adult Children of Alcoholics, NA for Narcotics Anonymous, and CODA for Codependents Anonymous.

In addition to books, the stores stock anniversary medals and cards, commemorating a month, a year, or longer that a person has stayed "clean"; spoken-word tapes and musical tapes to use for relaxing and "getting in touch"; plaques (self-applied) announcing various victories; and T-shirts and posters with such slogans as "One Day at a Time," "How Am I?" (and the name of a treatment center), and "Easy Does It." You can even purchase Sponsor Bear, a cuddly stuffed animal that recites encouraging slogans when you pull a string in its neck.

Although the blush is now off the Recovery rose, one can see in these bookstores how powerful a movement it was. It was powerful because it romanticized shame. If anything, Recovery made shame a badge of deep feeling, a sign of sorrow, a mark of persecution. You were feeling the sorrows of Young Werther. As Shelley said, "I fall upon the thorns of life! I bleed!" Baby boomers, too, could capture that sense of Christ-like betrayal. You, too, were bleeding.

Every major New York publisher had a line of Recovery books by the 1980s. What had started just two decades earlier as regional houses publishing what were essentially manuals developed in detox hospitals suddenly became a major part of publishing. Why? Was it just that feeling downtrodden provided a comfortable sense of betrayal? D. H. Lawrence (*Fantasia of the Unconscious*) saw this. There is no more coherent way to observe life, he said, than from the vantage point of a victim. Nietzsche (*The Genealogy of Morals*) knew this too, well before it became an intellectual fashion. The economies of oppression can remove the dangers of self-assertion.

The very bookishness of the Recovery movement is an important part of its allure. To many people, seeing something treated in print, especially if it's your problem, testifies to its importance. You have this problem. There is a book on this problem. Ergo: the problem must be important. Some afflictions, like alcoholism and drug addiction, are truly debilitating, but some of them, like codependency and shopping a lot, are not. Additionally, in marketing Recovery books, the national houses were able to align their product with the stable territory of religious tracts. In fact, the concept of Recovery originally was religious, not psychological. It was once concerned with sin, shame, and redemption.

Even Freud never claimed any expertise with shame. Guilt, yes. Psychoanalysis might help you live with the tension of not measuring up, but it would not resolve it. For shame release, you went to the Church. You have sinned. You confessed your sins. You did penance. *You were forgiven.* Never mentioned was that the Church was also the prime shame provider. The Recovery movement, however, describes shame as an emotional state, a bad "lifestyle." The paradigm of "I was lost, but now I'm found," which had been the route to salvation, is now a central path to Emotional Wellville.

In the self-esteem movements of the 1960s like EST and the Esalen Institute, the religious and psychological views of shame essentially merged. The combination has proved synergistic as the self-esteem business became our secular religion: the Church as support group, the support group as Church.

The point where these two forces first touched, however, was not in some hot tub in Big Sur, but in the heartland, near wheat fields. The place was in Hazelden, a Minnesota-based chemical-dependency treatment center that integrated spiritual philosophy into a professional treatment program. In 1952, three years after its founding, Hazelden began its publishing program with *Twenty-Four Hours a Day,* a meditation book that has since sold more than seven million copies. Hazelden's publishing program remained modest until the mid-1970s, when addiction treatment started to become a legitimate part of the health care system. Hazelden soon became the Lourdes of Recovery.

By 1982 Hazelden changed the name of its publishing department to the Educational Materials division and launched a professional publishing program to serve the exploding treatment industry. Four years later the division was acquired by Harper San Francisco, the religious/spiritual publishing division of HarperCollins, a minor subsidiary of Rupert Murdoch's News Corp. Since then such houses as Bantam Books, Prentice-Hall, Villard Books, a unit of Random House, and Health Communications have all climbed aboard.

HarperCollins hit pay dirt with Melody Beattie's blockbuster *Codependent No More: How to Stop Controlling Others and Start Caring for Yourself.* The book coined a Recovery buzzword, defined a population (just about everyone), and made its author a superstar. Suddenly authors, not hospitals, were becoming an increasingly critical factor in the therapeutic equation. As the big New York houses knew, you don't sell the product, you sell the brand name. You don't market a gothic novel, you market a Stephen King novel. So, too, in Recovery Inc. the brand names were Melody Beattie and John Bradshaw, followed by Claudia Black, Anne Wilson Schaef, and Patrick Carnes. A canon of must-own classics was developing. *Healing the Shame That Binds You,* by John Bradshaw, and *Adult Children of Alcoholics,* by Janet Woititz, joined *Codependent No More,* and Son of Codependency, *Beyond Codependency: And Getting Better All the Time,* by Melody Beattie. Just as movies are described in terms of a few central blockbusters (*Thelma & Louise* was sold to MGM as a feminist *Butch Cassidy* mixed with *Easy Rider*), so the esteem-building, shame-depleting canon found its touchstones.

All through the 1980s television was continually churning up fresh oxygen-rich examples of new mutations of these central texts. All you had to do was watch Oprah and Phil. In fact, if you wanted to be with it, you needed an easily explained affliction. A surprising number of celebrities and other prominent Americans came forward to talk about the personal problems in their own lives. What would have been shameful a generation earlier now became a mark of humanity. We're just folks too, said the celebs. They often came lugging a book. So we had Betty Ford on her addiction to alcohol (*The Times of My Life*), Carol Burnett on growing up with abusive parents (*One More Time*), Suzanne Somers and Kitty Dukakis about life with an alcoholic father (*Keeping Secrets, Now You Know*). Following close behind was Elizabeth Taylor announcing her addiction to alcohol, painkillers, and bad love. And then there was Ali MacGraw, addicted to sex (with hunks like Steve McQueen and Bob Evans, for goodness' sake), and Patty Davis, President Reagan's daughter, a victim of family abuse. If they didn't have a manuscript in hand while making the talk-show circuit, they soon would.

If bibliotherapy is any gauge, there is almost no area of life exempt from the need to recover. Joining alcohol addiction is spousal/child/grandparent abuse, food addiction, sexual addiction, work addiction, money addiction (both getting and spending), shopaholism, and gambling. What is noteworthy is that while even children are now being provided with their redemptive texts helping them deal with Daddy the Workaholic and Mommy the Compulsive Shopper, nonwhite minorities seem almost totally unserved. Very little self-help about "soft" addictions is translated into Spanish, and nothing (that I could find) is written specifically for blacks or Native Americans. That baby-boom

Caucasians are so glutted with books about the afflictions of "adult (white) children" should tell us something. Are these Caucasians the only ones so victimized? Are they the only ones susceptible to the Cinderella or the Peter Pan complexes? Or are they the only ones susceptible to being susceptible?

It would be hard to take this seriously were it not for what it says about baby-boomer desire to get loose from shame. At times even the industry itself seems to recognize the nonsense. After all, how can a book entitled *I'm Not My Fault*, published by Safe Place Publishing, not meet with a small but audible howl? Can anyone seriously print, let alone read, what therapist Albert Ellis said as he started every day, "I will not should on myself today" and "I am not a worm for acting wormily."[2] Who cannot suspect just a hint of self-irony somewhere in the food chain? Andrews & McNeel even published *Codependent for Sure! An Original Jokebook*, and Ballantine issued Anne Wilson Schaef's *Laugh! I Thought I'd Die (If I Didn't)*. An example from the Recoveryland joke book: "We had one guy in the group who had a kid who was sniffing gasoline. He would come home and find him passed out on the lawn and he would say, That damned kid, I don't know whether he's dead or vapor-locked!" Another? "Two people are out in a canoe. One person falls overboard and as he's dying, sees the other guy's life flash before his eyes." All right, perhaps you have to have been there to think it's funny.

We don't need industry analysts to tell us that women are responsible for the vast majority of the total sales in Recovery books. What is unique, however, is that the books sell primarily by word of mouth. A "buzz" moves between various support groups and then jumps to other groups. In addition, from time to time a charismatic writer jumps loose to travel the hustings "giving seminars," which turbocharges the process.

So where are the men while the women are out "running with the wolves" or, perhaps more appropriately, attending a "workshop"? Perhaps no one has been a more eloquent or visible spokesman of the men's side of the shame-removal industry than poet, sweat-lodge leader, and PBS star Robert Bly. Bly's book *Iron John* made a lustrous appearance in the Recovery skies. Then poof! It disappeared. What happened? Why did Iron John rust?

Obviously, most men still live in a world where problem solving is a virtue, where discussion is seen as impediment to action, where getting well implies being sick. Stoicism is masculine; cooperation and commiseration are feminine. In a culture where independence is still prized by many, where the will to power is accepted, where self-reliance is central, there is little interest in forming new family surrogates. Women are more concerned with fitting in, men with breaking out. Hence "The squeaky wheel gets the grease" is the trope explaining problem resolution for men, while "The nail farthest out gets pounded first" is for women. As sociobiologists tell us, these strategies are in both their biological interests.

Also, the simple fact is that men are less often victimized than are women. In fact, men are often, at least in the Recovery world view, the problem. Hence the Successful Women Make Men Angry motif and the Why Good Women Hang Around with Nasty Men genre. To be codependent you need a partner, and more often than not that partner causing the trouble is a male, be he dad, hubby, or pal.

But men are not exempt from shame. Someone is buying such titles as *To Be a Man: Visions of Self, Views from Within*; *Silent Sons: A Book for and About Men*; *The Measure of a Man: Becoming the Father You Wish Your Father Had Been*; and *The Man in Me: Visions of the Male Experience*. Not surprisingly, many of the sales were made to women. In point of fact, men are not lining up to buy the latest tome by Manly Tuneful, nor are they heading out to the forest to pound the tom-toms with like-minded sensitive New Age guys (SNAGS). No, the fellows in the Recovery movement are over in the Unitarian basement trying to sober up. And in so doing, they are participating in the Ur-shame support group of this century: Alcoholics Anonymous.

What happened at Hazelden and at other Recovery centers in the 1950s was the adaptation of virulent Puritanism to a specific problem: addiction to booze. The tough spirit of Jonathan Edwards, filtered through the Oxford Group, informs the whole affair. Although now much watered down, the so-called twelve-step method was the rough-and-rugged philosophy of pragmatism applied to everyday life. And in this form, it is very masculine. You are an addict. You should be ashamed. You know what to do. Now, do it. Get this job done. Even the terms—twelve steps—a numbered and controlled progression from here to there, tells much about the mind-set. The shaming is direct and repeated.

Here is the AA process on a thumbnail. Get together with some guys. Sit on hard chairs. Admit your life is out of control. Accept that a greater power exists. Turn to that power. Look back to the self and admit the power from outside. Ask humbly. List all those who have been injured by your acts. Make amends. Go back and do the first steps again. And again.

What gives this sequence such power, and the reason it is often so much more powerful than individual counseling, is that it is done before a public. It is self-enforced shaming in front of a group of like-afflicted peers. Over and over the process goes: shaming, release of shame, shaming, release of shame. Wear the stigma, then take it off. It is almost like doing hand-squeezing exercises with the superego. In an earlier time it would have been called "professions of faith."

In a very weird way, AA works in exactly the same way that beer ads do, except in the reverse. In the standard beer ad the guys are all doing things together—hiking, fishing, camping—and then at the end they uncork a brewski and look meaningfully at each other. It doesn't get any better than this, they say as they hold up the bottle. In AA, they say it can't get much worse.

Like waves from a pebble thrown into a pool, the twelve-step recovery program—the "program," in AA parlance—led to an ever-widening circle of affiliated groups. Al Anon (started initially for the wives of men who comprised the fellowship of AA) and Alateen (for children from alcoholic families) and then the Adult Children of Alcoholics (ACOA) movement all used the same support-group method. Some fifteen million people now attend various support groups—virtually all victims in one way or another of (often self-diagnosed) posttraumatic stress disorder, or in the standard acronym, PTSD—which use variations of the AA technique.

The shame that these twelve-step groups tend to deal with best is not the core shame of a failed self, but the shame of addiction. Since shame is communicated from the outside, since it is essentially the result of our being observed by the Other, of not meeting some external standard, what these groups essentially do is to dissolve the privacy of the experience by making it the norm. Bring ten bulimics or a handful of shoplifters together and encourage them to talk *not* about the root causes of their affliction, but about the affliction itself, and chances are that part of the cloud will lift.

Certainly one of the by-products of the Alcoholics Anonymous approach is that when you reverse the force fields of shame, namely remove the behavior as being unique to the individual by having him confess it to a like-minded audience, the stigma dramatically lessens. No surprise that some addicts can become addicted to this process, and join serial support groups as a way of reaffirming identity. There are books for that too: *Breaking the Cycle of Support* is doubtless in the works.

Turn on, Tune in, Get Well: Dr. Bradshaw Will See You in the PBS Clinic

What separates the host of support groups in the Recovery movement from AA is that the power from without (it used to be called God) is regarded as the power from within (your inner self). The revival of Romanticism in the 1960s made such solipsistic assertions as "Let the Force Be with You" and "Trust Yourself" carry the weight of prayer. No matter. The key to Recovery is to believe that the self must trust the Other, no matter where it is located, to lower the threshold of shame and let us pass.

As with evangelical Christianity, with which it shares so many similarities, the Recovery movement is sometimes spread by charismatic ministers. They carry the changing dogma in much the same way itinerant preachers worked from town to town in the world before television. The campground reunion, the tent revival, is now conducted in the ballroom of your local Holiday Inn. Instead of a sermon on "Prepare to Meet Your Maker," there are workshops on "Finishing Your Business with Mom and Dad" or "Reclaiming Your Child Within." But the process is the same. Prepare yourself in your congregation/support group first, then gather together with others for a reassertion of the faith in front of the evangelist. Come loaded with the tools of comfort, be they relics of faith or a favorite stuffed animal. But be prepared to pay. The process of payment differs. Old-style Christian recovery asked for contributions by passing the plate. In the new-style Recovery version you pay up front and it's a bit more expensive— about $300 for a two-day session.

The current Shaman of Shameland is John Bradshaw from Houston, Texas. He has the proper credentials, which he elaborates with glee. On the vita: a broken family (his alcoholic father left when he was an adolescent), a failed career (he was never ordained by a Canadian seminary run by the Basilian Fathers), molestation (he was fondled by a priest), recurring addictions (first to alcohol, then pills), divorce (after twenty years of "marital warfare"), ripe family history (grandmother was an "incest survivor," mother a hypochondriac), currently afflicted (alas, he is still a rageaholic), and sexually dysfunctional ("sexually anorexic for nine and a half years" and only recently able to achieve sexual intimacy). He proudly, if humbly, describes himself as the product of five generations of alcoholism, four generations of male abandonment, and three generations of "emotional incest." This vita is continually invoked as "testimony." This man knows suffering the way Jimmy Swaggart knows the Devil. The Reverend Doctor Bradshaw has "been there."

After a life of preparation for victim stardom, Bradshaw found his way into counseling, from there to conducting "workshops," from there to televising these seminars, and from there to having as much as an annual one-million-dollar income. As with so much in American popular culture, the critical point was the step into the tube. For if ever there was a man loved by the television camera, here he is. Graying hair, piercing eyes, dulcet voice, animated face, he fits nicely into the corner of the living room. This man looks a lot like Fred Rogers, complete with the button-up cashmere sweater. What makes him especially good on the tiny screen is that he is a great hand actor. The concentrated energy of his delivery is in the pointing, chopping, grasping hands. Here he is slapping an imaginary child, now here embracing an imaginary lover. At the end of the show, his hands are open to us. He is waiting to receive us. He looks just like the picture of Christ in the Sunday school Bibles, only with the nice crew cut instead of the lustrous mane.

Bradshaw was discovered not in Schwab's delicatessen but in the pulpit of a Houston church. A staff producer of the local PBS affiliate saw him perform and asked if he would make videos of family counseling. When the videos were shown on Houston public television, they were an immediate success. The station was deluged with letters and phone calls. This man was the Sir Kenneth Clark of pop psychology, complete with flip cards, charts, and magic fingers. He made you feel intelligent about your ignorance. He had been in worse shape than you. There was hope. He made Recovery into Art. It had transcendent value. You did too.

PBS, forever searching for programming to use during its bimonthly begathons, hit the jackpot. For along with the letters and phone calls came the best kind of money—unsolicited checks. His show was picked up by some 140 stations, and by the late 1980s he was producing a regular flow of "Bradshaw On . . ." shows. Who has not seen him while channel-surfing, before an audience of teddy-bear-clutching, weeping adults hearing for what seems to be the first time: "It's okay to be you. I like you the way you are. You were hurt as a child and it was not your fault. You have nothing to be ashamed of. You are loved. You are loved. You are loved."

But it wasn't the weeping studio audience that was important to PBS, it was all the folks at home. Although the demographics of "Bradshaw On . . ." are nothing special, this audience has shown an incredible willingness to send in contributions. Best yet, you could show the same video over and over and no one seemed to mind. This stuff was addictive. However, ask this same audience what they think of televangelism and they will tell you it is dreadful. But they are seeing something very similar. You are saved, they are told by Bradshaw. Now save the station, says the program manager.

This is programming for the powerless, for those who feel betrayed by "the world," or who feel they deserve better. But it is also programming for those who fashion themselves intellectuals. Peppered throughout Bradshaw's presentations are the midcult names to conjure with: Ashley Montagu, Erik Erikson, Aristotle, Martin Buber, Robert Bly, Fritz Perls, Bruno Bettelheim, M. Scott Peck, Virginia Satir, Jung, Eric Berne, Jean Piaget, and, of course, Alice Miller. Every once in a while, to really deliver the whammy, we get a slug of Nietzsche. Academics sit bolt upright, eyes afire.

But it works. The "Homecoming" series alone has garnered more than $5 million for PBS outlets, and Bradshaw is often responsible for bringing in upwards of 10 percent of the affiliates' entire pledge goals.

Modern telemerchandizers like to synergize products. They build a pipeline from television tube to bookstore shelf and back. Videos spin off from the books, and books jump loose from the videos. We can see "Bradshaw On: Homecoming" or "Bradshaw On: The Family" while reading the literary adaptations. "Read the book, see the movie" has become "See the video, buy the book." Although never making it to the school lunch-box cover, for a while Bradshaw seemed all over the place. He was featured in *Newsweek, Time,* and even *Rolling Stone.* There he was on "Oprah," reducing the famous abuse survivor to tears. Check out his Web site (http://www.creativegrowth.com/Johnbio.htm) and you will see how much stuff he is merchandising. The Age of Bradshaw fit in nicely right between the Fall of Televangelism and the Rise of Home Shopping.

No matter what the configuration or the media, the touchstone is always the same: shame, toxic shame. So central is shame that an entire video/book was produced on the subject—*Healing the Shame That Binds You.* Although Bradshaw acknowledges that there are really two kinds of shame—tonic shame and toxic shame—the tonic variety is given little fizz. In fact, it is rarely, if ever, mentioned. Over and over in his various routines he points his finger at the Devil. He repeatedly names it in order to destroy its power. Toxic shame, toxic shame, toxic shame. Satan, stand aside. This demon is responsible for the 96 percent (not 95 or 97) of dysfunctional families. Shame causes addictions, codependency, abuse, eating disorders, divorce, abandonment. . . . You name it, this devil made you do it.

Here is Bradshaw at the calculator doing the math for us:

We have 60 million sexual abuse victims. Possibly 75 million lives are seriously affected by alcoholism, with no telling how many more through other drugs. We have no idea of the actual impact on our economy resulting from the billions of tax-free dollars that come from illegal drug traders. Over 15 million families are violent. Some 60% of women and 50% of men have eating disorders. We have no actual data on work addiction or sexual addictions. I saw a recent quotation that cited 13 million gambling addicts. If toxic shame is the fuel of addiction—we have a massive problem of shame in our society.[3]

How to solve this "massive problem"? Not easily. We need to do our "pain work," to reach down to our "lost child" and "recover it." We need to chose to "love this child" as our parents could, or would, not do, to "accept it unconditionally" and make time for its "revival." We need to "give back the hot potato of shame" to Mom and Dad by externalizing the "shaming voice" and then telling it to shut up. Then finally we will have the "life script" we are all entitled to. We will have a happy, happy life and know the "peace that passeth all understanding."

In his in-person presentation Bradshaw does what print and edited videos cannot do: he shows the deep evangelical roots of the circuit rider. Once the lights go down and the New Age lullaby music is turned up, and once the ballroom-filling audience has been properly launched into whimpering (this does not take long), Bradshaw hums and purrs like a Ferrari on his way to the salvation throughway. "I am toxic shame," he repeats, slowly, in cadences that exaggerate his soft evangelistic Texas accent. "I am what ruined your childhood, destroyed your self-esteem. I soiled your godliness." By now, people are sobbing, and not quietly. They are blubbering. Hundreds. The dozen or so therapists cruising the room have their hands full getting tissues, bending over the weeping, even ushering a few who have OD'd out of the room.

Like an accomplished preacher, Bradshaw does not stop. Nor does he acknowledge any of the crying. This is the background music of redemption. Some petitioners must not be able to stand the glory if others are to be saved. The old-time revivalists had to seed the audience with shills who would jump up and shout, "Hallelujah, I'm saved." Bradshaw doesn't need shills. These people have already paid at the door. They are primed, loaded, and fuse-lit when they walk in.

"It's too late to have a happy childhood, but it's not too late to repair the feelings," he repeats. There is hope. But where? Go back to that childhood. Do it again. Get it right. Be reborn. He even gives exercises to help. Wrap up in a blanket, have a friend feed you with a spoon, go to a playground and swing on the swings, finger-paint. In his own words now, the evangelistic crescendo:

See your little child. Take him by the hand [pause] Tell him you're the only person he's never going to lose [pause] Tell him to say, "If you stay here anymore, you'll die" [pause] Find your mom [pause] Find your daddy, if he's there [pause] Have your child tell them, "I can't carry your shame anymore" [pause] Leave the house [pause] Wave good-bye [pause] See your new family of affiliation up ahead [pause] They're waving to you [pause] Now go to them.[4]

Amen, brother. Just insert "Jesus" for "child" and you know what's really happening.

Of course, if you were to demur from these narcissistic assumptions, if you were to contend that happiness is more likely the result of achievement, if you were to say that playing nursemaid to one's child is guaranteed to render you still more infantile and dependent, if you were to contend that this view of self as victim is only a short-term narcotic, you would be said to be "in denial." Heathen. You have not given yourself permission to have feelings. You are a [pause, gasp!] Victorian! In a favorite bit of illogical thinking from the 1960s: If you are not part of the solution—you're the problem. Remember, Bradshaw says with singsong repetition, "we are called human beings, not 'human doings.' " Egad, responds the audience. Now, that's logical. Who cares if the middle ground is excluded?

What makes Bradshaw stew so tasty for so many is the concept of deserving grace. I was promised so much, so little has been delivered. This sense of betrayal is not surprising in a culture that continually assures us that "You, you're the one" and "We want to be your friend." But what is striking is the sense that getting back at Mom and Dad is The Way. They are the shaming devils. Bradshaw creates for his adherents a fantasy world in which their real-life failures won't ruin them. "Every time there's measurement and significance, there's shame," he says.[5] And who does that measurement in a God-free world? Why, wouldn't you know it, it's Mom and Dad who do that.

What Bradshaw offers is "lite" religion, free of a vengeful God, free of parental taboos, free of mystery, and, with the exception of daily communion with the inner child, free of demands. Just Be. In his warm-milk doctrine, there is no need to control or "shame" human desire; it will fall into place once we are healed/saved. Nor is hard discipline required to reach that inner peace. Just a few workshops. Bradshaw reads William Golding's *Lord of the Flies* from back to front. He reads *Candide* without the irony. He thinks Chateaubriand's *René* is about a deep thinker. Life gets better as you become infantile. Does this sound like a tie-dyed Christianity for the baby boomers? Junk food for superannuated hippies?

You bet. Should you have any doubts, just listen to the voice of hippiedom, oft cited by Bradshaw as his guru—Fritz Perls. Here the resident therapist of the ultimate recovery workshop—the Esalen Institute:

I have called shame and embarrassment Quislings of the organism. . . . As the Quislings identify themselves with the enemy and not with their own people, so shame, embarrassment, self-consciousness and fear restrict the individual's expressions. Expressions change into repressions.[6]

Let it all hang out—or else!

AND WHERE IS DR. FREUD IN THE AGE OF RECOVERY?

Shame was hijacked by pop psychology for a number of reasons. First, traditional psychoanalysis didn't know what to do with it. Freud pretty much overlooked shame, preferring to concentrate on guilt. Shame was just part of the galaxy of compulsions resulting from what he called "the common unhappiness." Shame is the discontent of civilization, part of the territory ceded by the id to the superego. It is the ineluctable result of having goals, of having a conscience, of having a raison d'être. You don't live up, you feel ashamed. No doubt original shame was part of the "reaction formation" resulting from the actions of the primal horde. In earliest times we had murdered the father and how could we ever expect to feel shame-free? The Oedipal Complex sees to that.

Carl Jung, Alfred Adler, and Karen Horney had a go at shame since much of what they investigated resulted from shame-related concepts (cultural status, inferiority, and self-hatred). But it was not until the work of Helen Block Lewis, an academic psychologist and a trained analyst at Yale, that the role of shame was studied as a diagnostic and therapeutic problem. What Dr. Lewis noticed was that a sense of shame led many patients to fare poorly in psychotherapy. In fact, many of them simply couldn't get loose from either shame *or* therapy. Studying transcripts from 180 psychotherapy sessions, Dr. Lewis found that therapists routinely failed to recognize a patient's feelings of shame. Or, if they did, they didn't know what to do. So they just continued on, expensive session after expensive session. She even coined a term *bypassed shame* to denote the phenomenon.

The real reason analysis has proved difficult is that the one-on-one, therapist-client interaction is ironically more conducive to generating shame than to lessening it. In fact, the entire experience of doctor-patient is predicated on a subtle shaming. "I'm sick, you're well" is what the analysand infers. The analyst can do little to change this. The familiar persona of the tweedy "shrink," puffing on his pipe in maddening silence, determined not to pass judgment, is just what is *not* needed. The patient has already confronted enough enigmas. Little wonder the support group and Bradshaw—potent in-your-face loving and accepting—are so successful. At least in the short run. Traditional analysis may ironically be yet another example of the iatrogenic syndrome of modern life: the professed expert is not helping to solve the problem but worsening it.

After years of study, Dr. Lewis finally concluded, "However good your reasons for going into treatment, so long as you are an adult speaking to another adult to whom you are telling the most intimate things, there is an undercurrent of shame in every session."[7] She wryly remarked that sometimes the only major evidence of previous analysis was an enriched language of self-debilitation. When you read that the famous analyst and author on shame Leon Wurmser *(The Mask of Shame)* had patients such as one who "abruptly" broke off analysis in the 1,172nd session, or another who remained in analysis for eleven years, or yet another who eventually killed herself by jumping off a bridge, you might well consider attending a John Bradshaw workshop, merging with a support group, and wearing a sweatshirt saying "Shame-free and Proud of It."

The reason the pop psychology of Bradshaw and the self-esteem section of Barnes & Noble have proven so successful is that they address the solution in the terms of the problem. Although we may think and feel that shame is deep to the core, actually it is micron-thin and—even though the microns are held together by superglue—it can be peeled off. The single most effective antidote to shame, many studies suggest, is a sense of self-irony, the ability of the thinking self to observe the feeling self and not judge harshly.

Ironically, this was Freud's prescription. The shame vaccination is not so much pride but acceptance. But to get to this point, one needs to have an audience. Feelings of shame can be alleviated if the person can admit them openly to others, feel respected instead of censured by them, and then be accepted. They accept you, you accept yourself. Hence the support group and the surprising success of the self-esteem movements. They are a virtual-reality therapy reversing the poles of the application process.

Shame has been hijacked by popcult in part because organized religion has given it up. Face it, shame is a downer. Who feels good about original sin? What we like is salvation, redemption, saturnalia, the weekend, and it is this idea that finds its way into Recovery. "Okay, okay, you fell into the slough of shame and bad feelings," says the Recovery movement, "but only because you were pushed. You can be born again, here, with us."

This synthesis of religion and psychology is hardly new; the influence of psychology on American religion starts with nineteenth-century communitarianism and was revived after World War II. Ralph Waldo Emerson can easily be heard behind the words of Norman Vincent Peale and Dale Carnegie. But since the 1960s, the religion that informs modern Christianity has been romantic paganism.

Whereas Emerson saw the manifestation of God in Nature, the current crop of ministers sees God in the Downtrodden Child Within. Where Thoreau would go into the woods in order to live deliberately and let the Outside in, we go down to the support group to get the Inside out. While Satan once lurked in the world around, now he has become a personality disorder. Sin has become what someone else has done to you. Self-esteem now carries the tradition of pietism. The fault lies not in ourselves, says the child of the 1960s, rephrasing Cassius in *Julius Caesar*, but in the others—especially our parents.

And this is the third reason why the various Recovery movements have had such success. What were the 1960s if not the great revival of Romantic interest in the natural condition of man? Since the Child Is Father of the Man and "a darling of a pygmy size," as Wordsworth said; since the noble savage is the ideal, as Rousseau said; since the preadolescent is "divine philosopher," as Coleridge said; then what better icon of baby boomdom than the images painted by Walter and Margaret Keane? These sentimental paintings of wide-eyed children who feel the truest of emotions, know the purest stream of truth, and understand the pathos of life, informed popular culture during the 1960s in a way still not fully appreciated. Their images hover in the imaginations of baby boomers, although the faces themselves have long since jumped loose to become the lingua franca of card companies, advertising campaigns, television programming, blockbuster movies, and the Recovery movement.

The pathetic child has become the keystone of our therapeutic culture. We see him/her everywhere. One of the few subjects we all find shameful is, according to a recent *Newsweek* poll (6 February 1995), any kind of child molestation. Real molestation is abominable, of course. But the power of the Recovered Memory movement is that real events need not occur. If you *feel* you were mistreated, violated, abused . . . then you were. This kind of impressionistic reality has more in common with a culture habituated to drugs and hallucinations than to "seeing life clearly and seeing it whole."

In this context, perhaps, it was predictable that the white middle class of the 1960s would have done what the first generation of Romantics did. They sought the redemptive experience through drugs. Whereas De Quincey, Coleridge, and Keats had only laudanum (an opium derivative), the baby boomers looked for the inner child using marijuana, LSD, and then prescription drugs like Quaaludes. Like their predecessors, few became really addicted to these drugs (the lower class would do that), but many became addicted to the myth.

You can hear this myth of childhood, of "splendor in the grass," in all the language of Recovery: growth, empowerment, worth, acting out, salvation, asking permission, affirmation, codependency, healing, serenity, to say nothing of the home metaphor: our inner child. You come to the support group/workshop with your teddy bear for a reason. Baby talk is not just encouraged, it is mandated. Little wonder that the diagnoses du jour in the 1990s are borderline personality and multiple personality disorder (MPD). Feel shame? Blame *them,* the Others—adults, especially parents. They tore you apart. They separated you from your buried self. In this narcissistic movement, confected nostalgia is an epistemology and the child within is the baby Christ.

CHAPTER 7

SHAME IN SHAMBLES:
THE PROFESSIONS OF SALVATION

....

In Adam's fall we sinn'd all.
—common Puritan sentiment

And just who are you to judge?
—common modern response

....

NTIL VERY RECENTLY, one of the reasons pop psychology has been so successful in off-loading shame is that the resistance has been so paltry. Habits have become addictions and personal values have elbowed aside general virtues because so few innocent observers to the parade of contemporary life have yelled out, "Stop! This king really has no clothes." Most of us would prefer to change the channel than confront the danger of trivializing shame.

In addition, the institutions responsible for maintaining the unarticulated rules of a culture have been having problems of their own. For instance, the political world, which historically served as the body politic of the constituent members, has become primarily concerned with reelection. Since the 1960s, a curious inversion has occurred. Joe Six-pack may have a higher threshold of shame than does his elected representative. The judiciary as well has been unavailable. Until recently, shaming has been not just ignored but actively avoided by the law. The reason is simple enough: Shame cannot be measured out accurately. The law often prefers measurement to justice.

Historically the great engine of shame has always been the Church, and as the Church started to share power in the nineteenth century, the school joined in. At that time these two institutions were often dove-tailed, if not at the altar, then in the vestry. They often shared person-nel, titles, canon, congregational space, and, most important, a calling to prescribe behavior. The clergy and the professoriat both came ex cathedra, wore black robes, spoke in a special language, and conferred various kinds of credentials. They controlled the rituals necessary to punish and could invoke the penalty of shame, namely, shunning. Ex-communication became denial of commencement. You flunked.

Until recently, matters were nicely divided into twos. Church and school were the teaching institutions: one concerned with sacred and the other with secular, one for the soul, the other for the soma, one preparing for tomorrow and the other for today.

These two capped and gowned arbiters had still more in common. Both callings have been for males, and males only—Caucasian males from the middle class, to be more exact. In both cases the calling came from beyond the pale—either from above or from the past. You had your choice: high church or high culture. And both have been more profoundly transformed in our lifetime than ever before.

On the surface, it is tempting to say these institutions have been transformed by a change in constituency—women and blacks have entered the ranks. It would be comforting to think that Church and school became more compassionate, kinder and gentler, more sensitive to the pain of others, because white males were forced aside. But the real upheaval has been in their relationship with their audience. Whereas once their parishioners came to them, now they have to go out to gather the audience. They have had to behave, in short, like com-mercial television.

The Church and school now make their case not by wielding the shame stick, but by promising the entertainment carrot. With some ex-ceptions, they now attempt to gather an audience by promising good feelings and fellowship, not fear and trepidation. No fire and brimstone, please. No harsh discipline. No shunning and no failure. Whereas they used to say, "You should be ashamed of yourself," they now say, "Be yourself, no matter what anyone thinks."

The Church fathers and the schoolmasters had no choice in changing their tune. They had to compete with a new institution—the advertising-supported worldwide electronic entertainment conglomerate—and they had to deal with a new congregation: the counterculture generation of the 1960s. Adapt or die is the Darwinian rule. Entertain or be turned off is the modern correlative.

Religious Shame: Rites of Reproduction

The major shaming events of the early twentieth century—out-of-wedlock births, homosexuality, adultery, abortion—came from the church. These taboos have to do with birth control and the social controls necessary to maintain stable family life. What is less obvious is that these "Thou shall nots"—complete with the shaming and shunning they invoked—separated Christianity from its earlier competitors. Ironically, perhaps, what was forbidden and shamed, as well as what was promised and valorized, made Christianity one of the longest-lasting and most stabilizing religions.

What is unique to Christianity is the deep sense of individual sin. We are conceived in it, born in it, live through it, and die drenched in it. More often than not, what is sinful has to do with sex. Far more than in other religions, sex is central to Christianity. In fact, at times the Church has seemed to care more for sex than for salvation. If you are a Christian, then God help you if you are not born in the proper heterosexual mold. Ditto with reproduction. You will need a loving God in the Beyond, for you will not find a forgiving brotherhood in the here and now. In other areas of Christian obedience you are allowed the occasional eccentricity—wealth, for instance, or usury, prevarication, or fighting, all things rather far from the spirit of Jesus of Nazareth—but sexually, you had better stay in line . . . or change religions.

Until the 1960s, you would have been wise to be heterosexual, because if you were not, you would have come in for a lot of unwanted "compassion" and blather about loving the sinner, hating the sin. Even if you were heterosexual, you were by no means in the clear. Masturbation was out, and so was premarital sex—and a lot of postmarital sex as well. Now it goes almost without saying that such sexual proscriptions were more honored in the breach than in the observance, but that's just the point. It's not whether you lie that is important; it's how you admit it. The Church even covered that by making confession a central aspect of the shaming process. Although (understandably) there are no empirical data, I daresay the most-confessed sins are sexual in nature.

We have only recently told the Church to mind its own business. In the modern world of cafeteria Christianity, we treat religion rather like the rest of the entertainment industry. We pick and choose. We may live to regret it. If our current failure with sex education is any indication, we may come to appreciate the intimate connection between hypocrisy, shame, and responsible reproduction.

For centuries, planned parenthood was in the Church's bailiwick. True, the Church was brutal, but is the reproduction roulette being played today any less horrendous? Since 1960 the incidence of single parenthood has more than tripled. Almost 30 percent of all American children are now born to unmarried mothers. In Harlem four out of five babies are now born to unwed teenage mothers who are barely able to care for themselves. In New Jersey in 1980, 67.6 percent of teenage births were to unmarried mothers; eleven years later the figure had increased to 84 percent.[1] The association of fatherlessness with poverty, welfare dependency, crime, and other pathologies points to a monstrous social problem—a problem religion used to address.

The Centrality of Western Sexual Shame

Sex started to be the Church's business as soon as it encountered the so-called pagan world. The Greco-Roman culture asserted the primacy of human sexuality, and sexual freedom was unquestioned—at least for some. Christianity introduced sexual fear and shame. No one was exempt. By tying the fall of Adam to erotic temptation in general, it made sexual relations the great fault line of humanity. Cross it and perish. More important than the promise of an afterlife, the concept of sexual sin was the basis for the incredible dominance and duration of the Christian world view.

The early Church did not pick and choose. All sex became shameful to the Church fathers. Coitus, even in the context of marriage, was only a temporary palliative to the disease of the flesh. The great codifier of sexual shame was Saint Augustine. He looked back on his life before his conversion to Christianity as one of enslavement to the lusts of the flesh. All of mankind, as Tertullian had said two centuries before Augustine, was inevitably infected with Adam's sin—his rebellion against God's will was our cross to bear. The taint of original sin passed through the very semen that gives life to human beings. The task of Christianity was repression of what makes us human: namely, sex.

The tradition of sexual denial was not new to Christianity, but it was revived with gusto. The idea of virginity as a desirable state grew and flourished. The oxymoron of the Virgin Birth was introduced as a mystery to prove a transcendent reality. Much was made of the fact that, despite the Bible's teachings, both Jesus and Paul had preferred celibacy to the ties of marriage and family. Continence became not just an ideal for the middle-aged after their childbearing years (a view that fit nicely with Roman civic virtue), but represented a move toward eventual renunciation and final salvation.

Sexual renunciation, a well-established albeit minor feature of most regions of the ancient world, was soon claimed as central to Christianity. Christianity owned it, marketed it, franchised it. In the late fourth century, Saint Ambrose and others even connected levels of perfection to sexual renunciation. Clement of Alexandria helped those who were confused by the grading system. He narrowed marital relations to the minimum interaction necessary for the procreation of children. If you were in doubt about the magnitude of your sins, just count your children. Coitus in excess of that number was sinful.

Perhaps the point of no return occurred in the fourth century. Jovianian, a monk from Bethlehem, took the position that celibacy was no holier than marriage and that those who had attributed pro-celibacy views to Jesus and Paul had invented a "novel dogma against nature." Jovianian was denounced for this view by such eminent figures as Jerome, Ambrose, and Augustine. He was subjected to shaming. He was excommunicated. Thus the dominant view was established. If you want sex, get married. If you want salvation, stay celibate. If you want to burn in hell, just be yourself, act natural. If there is one thing we learn from the saints' lives of the medieval *Legenda Sanctorum*, it is that the lives of the saved are lives that pervert the natural with an awesome single-mindedness. Sexual repression did not start with Puritanism or Victorianism, as we often assume. It is deep, deep in the heart of this religion.

I am not concerned with why sex became so dangerous—certainly there were economic, class, and medical reasons (finite food supplies, the rise of the clerisy, and sexually transmitted diseases, for starters). The simple fact is that by the Middle Ages the tracks connecting sex and shame had been well laid. They all led to the same place: the stable family. In numerous treatises of the thirteenth century we learn, "Man is naught but fetid sperm, a bag of excrement, and food for worms. . . . In life, he produces dung and vomit. In death, he will produce stench and decay." By the Renaissance things had been made a bit more scientific, but the gist remained. A seventeenth-century preacher,

Paul Beurrier, remarked, "Our bodies resemble glasses that break when they touch one another."[2] Little surprise then that natural love became so exciting, so erotic . . . and so shameful.

Thus did sex become the Christian version of Procrustes' bed. According to lore, Procrustes stopped hapless travelers on the road and compelled them to lie down on his bunk. Not very comfortable. If they were too short, he stretched them until they fitted, and if they were too big, he lopped off any overhanging bits. Procrustes, apart from his touching need for control, was unable to forgive anyone who did not fit his ideal. He was loony, of course, and his madness took the form of insisting that everyone must be alike, that they must fit his idea or he would do it for them. It is not an overstatement to say that, with regard to sexual behavior, Christianity is one of the most Procrustean of the major religions. In fact, no other major religion has been so obsessed about sexual conformity.

If Christianity was Procrustean toward heathens, and it most assuredly was, it was yet more brutal with its own. Celibacy, which seems so perverse to us today, was elevated to an apogee of purity—it was the paradoxical perfection of all sexuality. The only truly shame-free sex is no sex.

But why heterosexual renunciation for the entire priestly class? Homosexuality is too easy an answer. So, too, is a double standard in which the clergy is getting plenty of sex while denying it to hoi polloi. So, too, is the Marxist (and feminist) interpretation that writing the rules allows you to prove power by flaunting it. More likely, as religious historian E. P. Sanders has argued, are these two reasons. First, sexual renunciation is peculiarly well suited for the task of achieving social distinctiveness. Since the semiotics of sexual codes can be made to bear a heavy meaning, Christian militants of all kinds adopted their own (sometimes similar) sexual practices. Abstinence allowed them to stand out against society, to become eidolons of rectitude. Nothing is so compelling as a hunger strike. Second, on a more mundane level, as the

Church grew, its leaders came to exercise power and to control money. They were more to be trusted if they showed they could master carnal temptation. If you could control your glands, what could you not control?

For whatever reason, celibacy allowed the clergy to claim and hold the moral high ground. From here they were able to wave the shame stick at others without being questioned. After all, they were so *pure*. As the Political Correctness movement—an odd descendent of early Christianity—still shows, when you control the ideal, you define shame.

Looking at the Christian Church today, you can only see a dim pentimento of what was once painted in the boldest of colors. In the current patois, Christianity has simply lost *it*. It no longer articulates the ideal. Sex is on the loose. Shame days are over. The Devil has absconded with sin. Jesus Christ looks just the way Warner Sallman painted him in the 1940s, a Hollywood superstar bathed in the glory not of a celestial halo but of a klieg light. The priest is just a man, a friend, a pal. Individual choice is king. Do your own thing. Procrustes has folded up his bed.

As with so many other institutions under stress from the entertainment industry, the Church can no longer run the risk of losing its audience. Instead of speaking, it listens. "Judge not lest you be judged" has replaced "Go and sin no more." Every few years or so, each denomination convenes a committee with a name like the Special Committee on Human Sexuality and produces a lengthy report with a title like "Keeping Body and Soul Together." Almost invariably there is a call for radical change in traditional Christian attitudes toward sexual behavior. But who cares? The channel changer is hit before this program even starts.

American fundamentalism, an often ludicrous parody of early Christianity, is one of the few vestiges left. Characters like Rev. Donald Wildmon wage a feckless battle against the barbarians from Vulgaria who have taken over the airwaves. His American Family Association, a conservative Christian group based in Tupelo, Mississippi, is forever complaining that this most popular television show or that top-grossing movie is corrupting American youth. Few listen. He tries to shame Procter & Gamble or NBC, but with little impact.

Meanwhile down on the sidewalk in front of your local Planned Parenthood clinic, the only other church fanatics, who are acting like the ancient Church fathers, are making their pathetic and often violent attempts to be heard. That they are usually middle-aged males, that they are all eager to be martyred, and that they all practice an exquisite economy of thinking make them indeed the legitimate heirs of the ancient combative Church. Shame is central to them. But not to the rest of us.

If you want to see the disappearance of shame in Christianity, go to the fastest-growing segment—the so-called megachurch. Almost every town now has one. Where I live, it is called "The Rock." That's all. Just The Rock. These churches are constructed in what looks to be a mix between a shopping center and the local junior college architecture. There are no crosses, no steeples, no big doors, no arches anywhere—just lots of brick. Nothing soars. Signs out front say, Welcome to Joy or Experience the Fellowship of Excitement. Parking attendants are necessary, for the place is so full you have to walk a quarter mile to attend. These attendants have ear jacks and walkie-talkies. Instead of gray-haired deacons shuffling you to your seat, a perky teenager does the job. Each Sunday there are different services for different demographic target groups—grumpies, yuppies, teens, peewees—just like on TV.

Inside are upholstered theater seats or individual padded chairs, not hard wooden pews. What you hear is popular feel-good music, not dolorous hymns. There is no organ but an electronic synthesizer. It is not located in the apse (there is none) but smack in the middle of the floor, in the media center. From this command hub, images are projected to a series of screens.

Music is central. People sway and dance while singing. They are proud of this enthusiasm. Many comment on how this would never occur in their old church. They follow the words to the songs that are flashed on the wall above the pulpit—karaoke Christianity. The songs come from a distributor in Chicago and have the copyright message in big print down in one corner. The words are not really important. They all say the same thing. We're happy.

The pulpit has a TelePrompTer. A church choir is not dressed in robes but in street clothes and is backed up by a syncopated band. It is composed of twelve instruments. One of them is a sultry saxophone. There is no crucified Christ who died for your sins anywhere. And there is certainly no Satan. This is an icon-free zone. No one is watching your every move. You do all the watching, just like at home. Here is user-friendly religion. The minister smiles a lot and comments on how large the church is getting. "It's good to see so many new faces. Please be sure to fill out the visitor cards." You can almost feel your trigger finger reaching for the remote when things start to drag.

The *New York Times* ran a four-part front-page series on the megachurch in 1995. Their reporters went to the most famous megachurch in America, Willow Creek Community Church near Chicago. Thousands of people attend each week. Here is what the reporters heard from interviewing the staff. The worshipers are called "the clientele." Willow Creek has a marketing strategy and, the reporters were told, "the New Testament is part of that strategy." They were also told by a senior pastor, who did a demographic study, that the reason Willow Creek poached so many parishioners from nearby traditional churches was that "the pastors at those churches made them feel ignorant and guilty as opposed to lovingly giving them instruction." Another pastor had an epiphany while seeing *Batman*: "I made a flippant comment. Entertainment is really the medium of the day," he recalled.[3] He was able to take that insight back to his work and apply it. Reverend Lee Strobel, another one of Willow's many pastors, also took a fact-finding trip abroad. He visited Saint Paul's in London. He concluded, "It is not very user-friendly. The lighting is bad, you can't hear the guys up front, and it's uncomfortable."[4] A sign outside the chief pastor's office reads, "What is our business? Who is our customer? What does the customer consider value?"

These churches are not related to the television ministry of the 1980s. They are not smarmy, sleazy, or avaricious. But they are most definitely related to commercial television. They are simply in what William Dinges, a professor of Religious Studies at Catholic University of America, calls the "entertainment mode."[5] And as they themselves would say, they are "eating the lunch of other competitors."

They are so successful because they are being programmed from below, from the audience, just as with other media. Church officials check the pews just as executives from Time Warner examine the box-office receipts. In fact, they have found that mentioning the size of the congregation is a major part of the attraction. People like to see the top-grossing movie, they like to watch the show with the highest Nielsen rating, they like to read the book at the top of the best-seller list, they like belonging to the biggest church in the neighborhood. Belonging makes you feel good, successful, with the in group, on the winning side. During the service, much is made of how many juniors have attended youth fellowship, how many have attended the various workshops, the number of buses needed for a field trip, how full the parking lot is, how new parking attendants are needed.

In the old days churches were organized into sects and denominations. These groups then had upper-level headquarters located in the Vatican, London, New York, or even Nashville. The headquarters provided blueprints for everything from the building, to the service, to the Sunday school curriculum. No longer. The appropriate image for the megachurch is the independent production company. What they are producing is a good show, custom-fit for their clientele. The one thing they are not producing is anything private, anything sinful, anything shameful.

Traditional churches, although always the settings for the communal and public rituals of religious services, have been places for solitary contemplation. Wandering through the columns and chapels of Chartres can be as profound as any service. Such grand churches are dark on purpose. No such experience is possible in the megachurch, by design. There are no dark corners here. In fact, no corners at all. This is a site for conversation, not for communion, for fellowship, not self-examination. If you want privacy and darkness, go into your home entertainment center.

As with so much modern television-made culture, if you want to know what a company thinks of itself, check its advertising. For in commercial speech we see how the institution positions itself relative to what it perceives to be the demands of its audience and the offerings of competitors. We see, as they say in advertising lingo, what aspirational goal the company seeks to project, what it wishes to "own," what it wishes to trade with the consumer, its Unique Selling Proposition.

The Ad Project, based in Minnesota, supplies churches with promotional material. Church recruiters can order T-shirts, Christmas cards, "caring cards," posters, and all manner of books "focusing on welcoming ministry." The poster section of the catalog is divided into thematic groupings like *Ads with Challenging Thoughts* (over the Ten Commandments is the bold headline "For fast, fast, fast relief take two tablets," over a crucifix is "Comes with an after-lifetime guarantee") and *Ads for Today's Parents* (over a Renaissance painting of Madonna and child is the headline "Introduce your children to the original Madonna," over a movie still of Dracula cowering before a cross is "Are your kids learning about the power of the cross on the late, late show?").

My favorite poster ads are from the section *Targeting Young Adults.* The catalog explains that they "used a focus group of young adults, all in their twenties, to do our research for the latest ads." Here's what they came up with. Over a painting of Christ in robes is "We don't care what you wear to church. And considering he walked around in a sheet, Jesus probably won't either." Below the image the text continues, "Not everyone likes to dress up for church. And that's fine by us." In another, under the bold headline "If you think church is only for families, remember Jesus was single," is a picture of Christ standing atop an elaborately decorated wedding cake like the neglected but ever-patient groom.

In the modern world you buy a service from your church. The service is not hope for an eternity of salvation, but a next week free from bad feelings. Little wonder sex is rarely mentioned, and never as a source of damnation. Only the Pentecostals in the Bible Belt still care. Gary Trudeau drew the definitive cartoon strip of Christianity-by-demand. In the first frames, a young couple, prospective clients of the Church at Walden, are seen interviewing the pastor. They are told of the twelve-step Christianity offered. In the last frames they confess they are looking for a church where they can feel good, and while they certainly like the racquetball courts, they are not sure they'll be happy at Walden because of "the guilt thing." In the last frame the wife ends saying to the pastor that they'll shop around and "get back to you later."

ACADEMIC SHAME: THE STATUS OF HIGHER EDUCATION

It is not difficult to be cynical about the history of shame and the Church. From a certain perspective, it is so clear that here was the protection racket par excellence. The same institution that was hearing your confession and granting surcease was also loading shame into the social system, touching first this and that with the "Thou shalt not."

What are the seven deadly sins, what are the Ten Commandments, what are the endless reams of papal bulls and ecclesiastical edicts, but a continual resettling of the shameful on human behavior?

What the organized church did, as William Blake and his fellow Romantics never tired of reminding us, was to "bind with briars [our] joys & desires" (*The Garden of Love*). They did this by creating sin. *Sin* is a word rather like *weed, varmint,* or *predator.* Affixing the label allows the condemnation. Whoever fixes the words has the power.

The verifiability of science and the inevitable rise of reason as the epistemology of choice spelled doom for the world view of Christianity and its seemingly capricious placement of sin. There was no room left for the Devil. From Copernicus to Newton to Darwin, the pins were removed from scaffolding that had been so carefully placed around an understanding of the here and now. The Great Chain of Being, linking all that existed to divine power, was rent asunder.

The Church essentially had to spin off its secular concerns to an analogous institution, the school. Its knowledge monopoly had proved too unwieldy. The shifting of control lasted from the seventeenth to the nineteenth century in Western Europe and resulted in the great universities of Northern Italy, Germany, France, and England. These universities looked like their ecclesiastical cousins, but there was a difference. A machine was at the center, the printing press, and there was a new repository of precious icons, the library. By mid-nineteenth century, what to know about the natural world, how to know it, and the shame to be felt by knowing the wrong matters had been ceded from the pulpit to the podium, from the reliquary to the library.

Today students can't appreciate the anachronism of dons who wear robes, diplomas printed in Latin, fields of study with names like the Liberal Arts, the love of self-important titles such as dean, rector, and professor, breaks called "recesses," and even the various processions such as commencement and assembly. College students think education is just something made up yesterday. And why shouldn't they?

That's the way their history is being taught to them. There is a reason the selection of subject matter is called by the ecclesiastical name, the *canon.* The deep church nature of schooling is almost totally neglected, remembered, if at all, in such pettifoggery as debates over school prayer, the wearing of uniforms, and the choice of songs at holidays.

The great legacy of Victorianism—to make education independent of religious indoctrination—has proved the basis of a culture of unparalleled wealth and complexity. Instead of idealizing an afterlife of perfect forms, the industrial revolution and its apologists promised an improved here and now. Education means leading out of, and compulsory schooling was the path. Certain conditions must be met, however. You must learn, become fluent with certain information, to get, as we now say, properly credentialed. In the Church of Secular Capitalism, you can take the cash and let the credit go. But to get to that cash, you had to go through school.

To paraphrase Alice in Wonderland, this new religion of knowledge promised not jam yesterday or jam tomorrow, but jam today . . . well, maybe. Anyway, it was clear to all that some people got lots of jam, and most of them had gone to school. The contribution of thinkers like Thomas Carlyle, John Stuart Mill, Matthew Arnold, John Ruskin, Thomas Huxley, and John Henry Newman was to imbue that "here and now" with the deep values previously reserved for the hereafter. The "best that has been thought and known" became the liturgy, and progress became salvation.

Little wonder Victorianism was so earnest. Little wonder schooling was so important, and that shame became such an important pedagogical tool. The dunce cap was in the corner because the stakes were so high. Learn this stuff. The barbarians are at the gates. The philistines are coming. The professor is the priest. The critic is the bishop. The text is sacred. Ignorance is a sin.

One can see the sanctification of the secular in the subject matter of study. Take art, for instance. The study of art, especially Renaissance art, was a Victorian creation that came to carry transcendental importance. The construction of high culture became a replacement for the religious mysteries of earlier times. This aspect of Victorianism led directly to Modernism. And what was Modernism but the wholesale infusion of religious values to the productions of special men called artists? When James Joyce analogizes the process of human creation to the Eucharist, when he makes the "art" of writing into the consumption of the flesh and blood of Christ, you know that the paradigm of transubstantiation has been profoundly resettled into the secular world. When Yeats, Picasso, Eliot, Woolf, Mann, and Stravinsky, to name a few, made the case for redemption through art, it was only because the Victorians had paved the way. Little wonder that art appreciation became so important and that a new institution, the museum, became the new chapel.

Another great change is in the works. It is happening all around us. Again, a machine is at the center. It is television. Not just television, but advertiser-supported entertainment. It does not offer peace in the next world, nor does it promise a better life in this one. It promises pleasure right now, the minute you turn it on. The world split by Victorianism into Upper Aesthetica and Lower Vulgaria is rapidly coming back together as all the delivery systems of information are behaving as one. Books, movies, computer networks, newspapers, magazines, television networks, are owned by the same companies because they all program the same stuff, producing entertainment not just for the masses but for humans all over the globe. Jam, jam, jam. Now, now, now.

So what has happened to education and shame in this carnival culture? Since there is nothing we *need* to know, there is no need to blush with ignorance. In the last generation, we have essentially dumbed down what it means to be educated. Everyone is entitled not just to go to school but to have a degree. Under the guise of such cant as creativity, true understanding, relevancy, and cooperative learning, we have become culturally illiterate at the same time that everybody is a graduate of somewhere.

Canon? There is no canon. Have a look at any anthology of American literature, for instance. For decades this was the *vade mecum* of college students from coast to coast. Its contents varied only in choice of individual selections. But when you look at the most recent ones, an entire new list of artists appears. African-Americans, women, and Native Americans now make up a fifth of the contents. Nothing wrong with that except that these names keep changing as new political concerns shift.

A simple fact: most art and literature was created by middle-class white men living in Europe—the infamous DWEMs. There are many reasons for this, but just as the priesthood was male-oriented and wrote most of the theology, so, too, most literature has been created by men. This is not a race and gender problem; it is a supply problem. Most of the advances in mathematics have come from men because most of the people who practiced this trade have been males. In the modern world this is changing, to be sure. That there are few works of literature by African-American women writers of the eighteenth century is not surprising. Fabricating art retroactively to sell textbooks does no one a service.

Look at freshman texts. What are students reading in order to write? Advertisements. Popular songs. Manifestos. Again, nothing wrong with that, but the ads, songs, and manifestos keep changing. Here, have a look at a recent flyer for such a reader. Book publishers inundate professors with such advertising, as these books can be immensely profitable if adopted in large introductory classes. After the requisite introductory pages of puffery announcing the academic importance of the editors and the relevancy of the selections, a fold-out graph appears on the last page. Just as we have had audience-driven best-sellers, movies, television shows, and religion, here finally we have audience-driven "literature."

Comparison Chart

See how *The Winchester Reader* compares to other large thematic readers.

SELECTIONS	McQuade and Atwan THE WINCHESTER READER Bedford Books, 1991, 1,024 pages	Eastman et al. THE NORTON READER Seventh Edition Norton, 1988, 1,242 pages	Hunt THE DOLPHIN READER Second Edition Houghton Mifflin, 1990, 1,002 pages	Stubbs and Barnet THE LITTLE, BROWN READER Fifth Edition HarperCollins, 1989, 1,173 pages	Shrodes, Finestone and Shugrue THE CONSCIOUS READER Fourth Edition Macmillan, 1988, 1,146 pages
Number of Selections	124	206	105	165	193
Number of Selections by Women	54 (44%)	43 (21%)	37 (35%)	42 (25%)	53 (27%)
Number of Selections by Minority Writers	37 (30%)	15 (7%)	18 (17%)	15 (9%)	18 (9%)
Number of Selections by Non-western Writers	5 (4%)	1 (less than 1%)	2 (2%)	6 (4%)	4 (2%)
Number of Selections Written Since 1980	67 (54%)	48 (23%)	29 (28%)	45 (34%)	47 (24%)
Number of Writers also in *The Winchester Reader*	—	33	23	22	26
Number of Stories	12	1	10	10	28
Number of Poems	0	0	1	9	36
Number of Plays	0	0	1	0	2
Number of Chapters	41	13	9	12	10
Average Number of Selections per Chapter	3	16	12	14	20
Number of pages in Instructor's Manual	416	176	388	310	200

SELLING LITERATURE BY THE OUNCE (ADVERTISING CIRCULAR FOR *THE WINCHESTER READER*), 1991.

The column on the left announces the criteria and the shaded column under *The Winchester Reader* shows what is currently preferred. These criteria have nothing to do with complexity, profundity, or even application. Rather they involve gender, race, contemporaneity, and ease. Note that having no poetry is clearly an asset—it's too unpopular. The bottom category needs no gloss. The headline on the front page of this glossy flyer announces: "Like Nothing You've Seen—and Just What You'd Expect," and inside we are told that this "is the first of the next generation of large thematic readers, attuned to the needs of the nineties." Indeed.

Have a look at fields of endeavor inside English departments, for instance. The same dispersion of concentration has occurred. A new term is invoked to distinguish disciplines: "studies." Women's Studies, Film Studies, Studies in Popular Culture, African-American Studies, Queer Studies, Post-Colonial Studies, and You Name It Studies. You now major in English the way you play bingo. You pick one course from column A and one from column B and then shout, "Bingo, I'm educated."

This new curriculum is generated not from above, but from below. Here, have a look at the catalog description for a regularly taught introductory course at Wesleyan University (American Studies 180) and you will see the process unfolding in slow motion:

A collectively taught and student-organized course, it confronts the traditional character of teacher-student relations by rotating teaching responsibilities. The course challenges the hierarchy, oppression, and exploitation in modern American culture with a variety of critical analyses and alternative proposals. With the guidance of two student facilitators, groups of eight to 12 students will plan and read the course's agenda: They will educate themselves. Topics cover an introduction to current trends in leftist thought, including anarchism, ecology, feminism, Marxism, and ethnic perspectives. The class will deepen its understanding of these views with an analysis of sexuality, heterosexuality, gender, family, race, community, society, and liberalism. This course integrates the personal with the political. Projects have included guerrilla theater, community organizing, and campus activism.[6]

This course, once called "Towards a Socialist America," was not presided over by some callow graduate student but by the Benjamin L. Waite Professor of the English Language.

As the constitution of the student body has changed, as students have become more accustomed to education on demand, as the expectations for entertainment have increased, courses of study have to be continually revamped. The Curriculum Committee never stops meeting. When the department chair sees there is low enrollment in Chaucer and hordes signed up for guerrilla theater or for Studies in Lucy and Desi, and when the registrar rewards the department for the number of full-time students (FTEs), you can see what happens. The fingers on the remote-control wand of the curriculum belong not to the administrators but to the students.

The most interesting new field not based on race/class/gender has been Critical Studies. Some years ago this congealed into a short-lived movement called Deconstruction, which in itself was not particularly important but shows what was happening to intellectual shame. Deconstruction essentially held that since everything is interpretation, no one interpretation can be said to be better than any other. The concept of "privileging" becomes central. Can you say that English is better than French? No, all you can say is that they are different. So, too, with subjects of study. The back of a box of breakfast cereal is text enough. Bracket judgment. So just as the artist became priest in Modernism, so the critic dons the robes in postmodernism. And, *mirabile dictu*, everyone is a critic.

If no interpretation trumps another (although interpretations can vary in complexity and interest), then how can the instructor be asked to grade the interpretations of her students? If the NEA can't do it, how can the instructor? Grades used to be an evaluation and, as such, a shaming device for those who did poorly. Report cards were carried home to be signed by parents as a way of bringing parental pressure (shame) to bear on those who needed it. Do badly and your parents had to speak to your teacher. No longer. Report cards are for the student. They are no longer signed and returned. They are reminders of a performance relative to other members of a class as perceived by an observer chosen by happenstance. No wonder cheating is out of control.

At the college level, grade inflation continues this deshaming procedure. The percentage of students graduating with honors from the Ivy League has rendered the very concept meaningless. When the average grade is a high B, there is not much room for excellence or for distinguishing what there is of it with a higher grade. At least the "Gentleman's C" allowed for a range above and below. At some schools, like Stanford, the condition is now endemic especially in the Humanities. The president even writes to parents about the problem. He might better instruct his faculty. A sociology professor at Duke University has done the numbers. In twenty-five years, if grades continue to be inflated at the same rate as the last twenty-five, almost every student (98 percent) will have an A average. A colleague of mine has quipped that one of the current goals of higher education is "to succeed in having 90 percent of our students graduate in the top 10 percent of their class."

At the school where I teach, the administration attempted to solve grade inflation by simply removing all the minus grades so the student either gets an A, B+ or B, C+ or C, and so forth. Other institutions have found alphabet grades too shaming and have gone to Low Pass, Pass, Low High, and High. Meanwhile, the bottom grades have also been effectively removed through nonuse. It is impossible at most schools to flunk a course. At the eleventh hour, you drop. Or you take the course later and wash out the bad grade. If you have to take the course, there is always pass/fail to remove the stigma before it can be applied.

Between high school and college, between report cards emphasizing self-esteem and grade inflation removing mediocrity, lies the barrier, the hurdle that must be dealt with—the infamous SATs. Like it or not, the Scholastic Aptitude Tests are still one of the last shaming devices left in American education, and so what has happened to them recently is particularly instructive.

First, a few years ago, the testing service was accused of insensitivity to minority groups. They were hectored for having such words as *sonata* and *travelogue* on the verbal section. How insensitive. The testing service changed such examples. But then it was accused of being too difficult with the numbers, too harsh, too judgmental. Not only that, but test scores themselves were falling. No one feels good about that. So after decades of declining test scores, the proctors in Princeton, New Jersey, decided to rejigger not the system, but the grading. They call it "recentering," but the rest of us can only call it arbitrarily raising the score.

What is refreshing, however, is that no one makes any bones about the fact that the purpose is to neutralize a one-hundred-point drop in the national median SAT score over the past fifty years. Eighty points have been tacked on to individual scores on the verbal section, and scores on the math section have had thirty points added. As in the past, students now earn two hundred points on each test simply by showing up and signing their names. But what is new is that you can miss three answers and still get a "perfect score"—1600.

Indeed, it seems to me that no effect was intended or expected other than the removal of the shame of doing badly. The new scoring will not affect the difficulty of the test, students' performance, the ability of schools, colleges, and others to track score trends or standards used in college admissions and scholarship decisions. According to Bradley J.

Quin, the associate director of the Board's SAT program, "If a standard is at stake, it does not reside in the numbers chosen to express scores, but rather in the standards set by colleges and universities in admissions requirements."[7] Hum.

College admissions officers have already announced they will simply revise their standard of comparison upward. And the National Collegiate Athletic Association, which uses SATs to determine who is eligible to compete at Division I or II schools, has already raised the minimum required score for freshman athletes. So what's the purpose in this Orwellian exercise in double-think?

To remove the shame of admitting lower scores, Junior can now report home a higher number than did his older siblings. "Look, Ma, no cavities and an eight hundred in math!" This nonsense has been going on for some time. "Recentering" is only the most recent voodoo. The SAT, formerly called the Scholastic Aptitude Test, and the SAT II: Subject Tests, formerly known as achievement tests, have been jointly renamed the Scholastic Assessment Tests, so as to provide yet another boost to the self-esteem of our high school students. How many gold stars do they need? Or, perhaps more important, how many do their parents need?

This continual rejiggering is part of the same feel-good academic culture that allows seniors who have not finished the requirements for academic reasons to attend graduation and gather a blank piece of paper and a handshake lest they should feel left out of the ceremonies. As someone who stayed back a grade in high school, had a raging case of ADD, and barely got into college, I assure you that students—even the slow learners at the back of the class—know fraud when it's perpetrated. Recall as well that when these various training wheels are removed as they are in world-wide comparisons, our children, high in perceived self-worth, score near the bottom in mathematics, history, geography, and economics.

But the most shameful use of the SATs is by the colleges themselves. For as the *Wall Street Journal* reported in the fall of 1995, many colleges routinely inflate the average admission test scores of under-graduates as part of a marketing strategy to lure top-notch students.[8] If you want your school to appear more competitive, and thus be in a higher category in the *U.S. News and World Report* or Barron's rankings, then you drop the scores of those admitted in special categories like athletics or legacies (children of alums).

Even more problematic is the practice of early admission. For here, under the guise of cooperation with dedicated attendees, is another less admirable practice. By admitting students early, a college can re-duce the total number admitted during the normal process and thus lower its acceptance rate. A "selective" school can become "very selec-tive" by changing nothing but its time of admission. Since students and parents understandably assume that the quality of education is connected with the difficulty of getting in, playing the rating game becomes a central part of the college's marketing strategy.

Higher education is full of such shameful behavior. What about big-name professors who never teach? What about the rise of ethnic stud-ies that claim to "celebrate" difference and erase lines of prejudice, but often do just the opposite? What about how institutions overlook what they know to be fraudulent applications for government-backed stu-dent loans because they either don't want to lose choice recruits or be embarrassed by turning the kids' parents over to the Feds? What about departments producing a steady stream of unemployable Ph.D.s who are used by the institution for a few years to teach introductory classes and then discarded? What about the disappearance of not just the re-search paper but of the term paper as well? You can graduate from many universities and never have to write a paragraph.

What about big-time athletics in which so-called scholar-athletes never have to be students, let alone scholars? Many of these athletes at-tend an entirely different curriculum, getting graduation credits for passing specially fabricated courses. What about the fact that the administrative staff has increased more than 100 percent in the period 1960–1990 while the percentage of teaching staff has dropped? And, of course, what about tenure for the faculty? Here is a lifetime sinecure awarded not to protect freedom of speech, but to recompense a professoriat for what? For daring research? For low pay? For time to really think about matters? I honestly don't know.

By no means, however, is the often shameless academy exempt from shame. In fact, one of the most virulent shaming movements finds origin and support on college campuses. The Political Correctness movement, which often seeks to control the flow of conversation around certain ordained subjects, is often dependent on shaming. When the "outside" world howled in disbelief at the humiliations inflicted on certain students at Oberlin, or Stanford, or Penn, it was usually because the methods of shaming were so inappropriate and reckless, not because the social concerns were not legitimate. PC rituals often smack of Chinese re-education programs, complete with the mandatory trip to the counselor.

To a considerable extent, Shame on U education depended on shifting demographics and the island mentality of instructors. The professoriat, since the 1960s, has found itself composed of middle-class self-styled intellectuals, and so it is their concerns that are, in their rather dreadful term, privileged. Since they have very little to teach to a student body that considers college attendance a birthright and graduation a sine qua non, the instructor makes other nonacademic issues central. Roger Kimball caught the proper oxymoronic tone by calling them "tenured radicals." For them, not for their students, the university has become a "site of problematized discourse." For instance, a major concern of my professional organization, the Modern Language Association, is where to hold its convention. Certainly not in any state where incorrect legislation has been passed. That would be worse than a sentence fragment. So when California voted not to use tax dollars to educate illegal aliens, it was out. One disenchanted wag has commented that for one reason or another, the MLA cannot meet in forty-six of the fifty states.

The Ur-shaming movement was Marxism. One could never have found a more congenial world view for academics trained after the 1960s. Marxists explained both why they were unappreciated and why they were so important. For a while in the 1970s hardly a day went by when one did not hear in the halls such jargon as Antonio Gramsci's "ideological hegemony," Adorno and Horkheimer's "culture industry," Enzensberger's "consciousness industry," Schiller's "mind managers," Real's "mass-mediated culture," the old standby, Marcuse's "systematic moronization," and the best balderdash yet, his "repressive tolerance." Little wonder they were "marginalized" by the workaday world they pretended to understand so well. They always called Western culture Late Capitalism. What they were was Very Late Marxism.

Everyone in higher education had to become a specialist. You can't just be a Marxist, you have to be a Derridean, or a Post-Colonialist, or some other subvariety. Some years ago at a tenure vote in my department we were told every department needed a Foucaudrian (whatever they are). Then last year, for the first time in a decade, I overheard one of my graduate students ask, "What's a Foucaudrian?" Here today, soon passé. Cultural studies has become an endless belt, bringing employment to a lucky few who step on it at the right time, but helping the students little. The big problem of higher education is, can Johnny read? The big problem of secondary education is, can Johnny stay in school? The two are linked, but we never talk about it.

My favorite tale of academia happened at The Dalton School, a tony private school in Manhattan. Some years ago the school was given a $2 million grant by an alum to treat "learning disabilities" among the youngest students. The first three grades had four hundred students and twenty teachers. With the grant money, fourteen full- and part-time disability specialists were added. Within a few years, more than half of the school's fourth graders had been referred for special disability education.[9] There was an epidemic, all right, but was it of disability or of educational specialists?

Colleges are now harvesting that crop. In a 1994 survey by the American Council on Education, 3 percent of full-time college freshmen identified themselves as learning-disabled. Reading disorders like dyslexia have been joined by auditory processing disability, attention deficit disorder, and, my personal favorite, dysrationalia. Dysrationalia is "the inability to think and behave rationally despite adequate intelligence." More interesting than the edu-jargon is that most of the disabilities are appearing at better schools. The smarter the students, the more likely they are to be learning-disabled. Take Brown University, for instance, a very selective school for high achievers. Robert Shaw, a dean responsible for helping learning-disabled students, told the *New York Times*, "Ten years ago there were six people on my list [of the learning-disabled]. Now I've got 175 undergraduates and 25 graduate students." He goes on to wonder not whether the school should provide extra time on exams—that's a given—but "whether we're supposed to provide alternate forms of exams." Different exams, he says, is "still up in the air."[10] Needless to say, many of these disabilities are diagnosed by experts on the college's counseling staff.

The problem is not naive administrators and nest-feathering specialists, although they helped; it is that higher education, like the Church before it, has lost importance in the entertain-me-now world. Additionally, since everyone can be certified in some form or other (even community colleges, renamed "junior colleges," got renamed again and made into members of state university college systems), since the government helps pay the way (with guaranteed loans from Washington), and since universities prefer to grow bigger instead of better, "higher" education has become just an extension of your local high school.

As comforting as explanations offered by the likes of Allan Bloom, E. D. Hirsh, and William Bennett may be, the academic gatekeeper disappeared not because he was negligent, not because he was elbowed aside by boisterous PC nitwits, not because he smoked reefer or was drenched in Marxist hogwash. He got rendered obsolete by an audience that simply did not need what he had to communicate. A century earlier the Church fathers did not let down their guard and let the heathen enter because they were inattentive. Their parishioners simply had other matters on their minds. The canon got thrown out because nobody much cared for it. It had no protectors. It was hard to understand and, worse yet, often shaming. Electronic entertainment is pleasurable, and the number one rule about shame is that it is not entertaining. Alas, as we are now seeing, the results of such entertainment are proving hardly entertaining.

CHAPTER 8

THE PUBLIC FACE OF SHAME

Have you no shame?
—JOSEPH WELCH to Senator Joe McCarthy

I am not a crook.
—RICHARD NIXON to the American people

You should be ashamed of yourselves.
—NEWT GINGRICH to welfare mothers

*B*Y NOW YOU know I believe something happened to shame in the 1960s. As I write this, I am in my fifties, just about the proper age necessary for the rigor mortis of misplaced memory syndrome to have set in. Doesn't every fifty-year-old believe that something profound happened just as he was growing up? "When I was a kid . . ." is the inevitable beginning of a sentence that invariably points to some massive shift in culture. What a coincidence! Every fifty-year-old scold was an adolescent just when some really important decline in standards was occurring. I should change my first names to J. Alfred, part my hair in back, and dare to eat a peach.

Having confessed the tendency to distort that goes with this age, let me reassert that something moved along the tectonic plates of shame, and that commercial television had a lot to do with it. In fact, I think that generations hence, whatever is now called Victorianism will be seen as lasting, in popular culture at least, well into the mid-twentieth century. Nobody in the trenches much cared for Modernism; it was a dud.

Advertiser-supported television tells different stories than those you hear in a print-based culture. Since shame is a social construct, it has to be communicated. Without a steady supply of shame-based stories, our susceptibility to the sensation has lessened. Ironically, our willingness to shame others has increased. Of course, their susceptibility has been lessened, and so the stakes must be made higher if the shaming is to succeed.

As we have seen, there are many other venues where we can observe this phenomenon. I will investigate two very public ones: politics and the law. In the former I will examine the Velcro-to-Teflon transformation from Joseph McCarthy to Newt Gingrich, and in the latter I will chart the progressive uneasiness of jurists in using public shaming as a punishment, an uneasiness that may now be waning.

POLITICS AND SHAME

There is no dearth of examples of shameless politicians milling around both sides of the beltway. There was Oliver North, who was knee-deep in Iran-Contra and convicted in the scandal only to have the jury's decision set aside on a technical point. He won the Virginia Republican Party's nomination for a U.S. Senate seat. Then there was former Washington, D.C., Mayor Marion Barry. Convicted of cocaine possession and sentenced to prison, Barry was barely out from behind bars before beginning his political comeback. First he won a city council seat, then he recaptured his old job at City Hall. What about Senator Bob Packwood of Oregon? Faced with more than a dozen women's accusations that he made unwanted sexual advances to them, the senator denied the charges, looked for dirt on his accusers, and then blamed his problems on drink. He quit to save others embarrassment, so he said, but his own pension may have been what he had in mind. A recent member of this ignoble club has to be Benjamin Chavis, who was fired as executive director of the National Association for the Advancement of Colored People after failing to inform his board of directors that he had committed the group's money to pay a settlement of a sex discrimination lawsuit filed against him. Was Chavis ashamed over being caught doing something so stupid? Not on your life. Instead, he noted that he had been hired on Good Friday. "Now there has been a crucifixion," he said.[1] In 1995 he went on to help Minister Farrakhan lead the Million Man March to atone for the past and restore dignity to the present. After he became a minister of the Nation of Islam, Chavis petitioned to remain in the clergy of the United Church of Christ. The Church recommended that he leave. As I write this, our president has just stopped renting out rooms in the White House. Camp David, however, is still up for grabs.

Have these guys been watching too much of Jenny Jones, Ricki Lake, and Jerry Springer? Have they been spending too much time at Madonna concerts? Have they pressed their ears too close to Howard Stern? Have their inner children been liberated by John Bradshaw? Nope. They've just been practicing their trade in the kinder, gentler world of modern politics. Thanks to advertising-supported campaigning and a general debasement of public service, in one generation the political world has become almost a parody of itself.

To show how quickly this happened, follow the path of well-known politicians from Joseph McCarthy to Richard Nixon to Dan Quayle to Newt Gingrich—a kind of Tinkers to Evers to Chance (plus one) of increasing shamelessness. That they happen to be Republicans is only for reasons of symmetry; they could have been Democrats (almost) as easily.

Senator Joseph McCarthy of Wisconsin burst on the national scene in 1950. To public approval, he cited numerous alleged Communists who had infiltrated the government. Ahead of his time, he even attacked the entertainment industry. Though Mr. McCarthy's charges were largely reckless and unfounded, he wasn't sent packing until the viciousness of his attacks was exposed during the famous Army-McCarthy hearings of 1954. As the public watched the meanness of Mr.

McCarthy and his sidekick, Roy Cohn, on television, the senator's popularity plummeted and even Republicans were emboldened to criticize his tactics.

But what brought McCarthy to his knees was just a quip of anger from a patrician lawyer from Boston, Joseph Welch. After the senator had proved particularly obstreperous and bullheaded about insisting that someone or other confess his affiliation with the Communist party, Welch had had enough. "Have you no shame, Senator?" he politely hissed. That was all, and that was enough. McCarthy had no retort. The gallery erupted in spontaneous applause. The senator just sat there harrumphing at first, then growing calm. Looking at the kinescope today, you can see his confusion. He turns to Roy Cohn as if to say, "What's going on? Why are they clapping?" If anyone knew the dynamics of shame, it was Cohn. But too late. McCarthy senses something is amiss and struggles to call the next witness. You could see the sweat gather all over his pudgy face and then his eyes drop down behind his heavy black glasses. His head tilts slightly forward.

A few years later, Charles Van Doren would experience the same painful deflation. Both he and McCarthy were being evaporated in what was one of the most powerful meltdowns of human life. They were held up to public scorn and allowed to—in a metaphor to come a generation later—twist slowly in the wind. They must have felt as if they were being lynched, as if they were suffocating, as if they were gasping for air. They did not know what to do, and so they did what we all do when shamed: they passed out. McCarthy went back to refuge in Wisconsin, and Van Doren went into hiding in Connecticut.

Now fast-forward a decade or so. Television, the seeing eye of the Other, is being absorbed. The CBS logo, the actual eyeball, is omnipresent. The show that transformed public culture into television culture was hosted by Edward R. Murrow. It was called "See It Now," and we could. We went to different places. Then in "Person to Person" we could actually go into people's private space and observe them like armchair anthropologists. We even went to visit McCarthy out in Wisconsin, and Morrow showed what a drunken husk the senator had become. Then Morrow did a special show called "Harvest of Shame" (1960) about the treatment of migrant workers, and we felt a national sense of communal embarrassment. Television could go inside not just houses and individuals, but inside groups of people as well. We sat there and watched. Adapt to this or die, was the political imperative. Look right into the eye, our eye, and don't flinch, became the first rule of political survival.

This was the genius of Richard Nixon. In his legislative investigations, in his campaigns, in his "Checkers" speech, in his "secret plans" for this or that, Nixon showed himself the new public man. He didn't just have a veneer, he had an integument as thick as an elephant's hide. He didn't dodge shaming, he withstood it. Occasionally he even seemed to invite it as a way of proving himself. I can't be shamed, therefore I am.

Although Watergate was indeed a "third-rate burglary," as he so accurately characterized it, it set into play a series of events that led eventually to articles of impeachment and his resignation. Nothing since has come close to generating the fears for the nation evoked by the Saturday Night Massacre. In the space of one evening, Nixon fired Attorney General Elliott Richardson and his deputy, William Ruckelshaus. Both had refused Nixon's order to fire special prosecutor Archibald Cox, who was leading the Watergate investigation. It was Solicitor General Robert Bork who finally relieved Cox of his duties.

For months afterward, "what did he know and when did he know it" became almost a wink-wink joke. Nixon knew a lot, and he had known it for a long time. We knew it, he knew it, and he knew that we knew he knew. So was he going to be shamed by admitting this?

No way. Instead, he quit. We have all seen him about to enter the air force helicopter, his eyes up, his hands high above his head. We may even remember his farewell speech. He nearly wept as he sum-

A RESIGNED NIXON SAYS A SHAME-FREE GOOD-BYE, 1974 (AP/WIDE WORLD PHOTOS).

moned the memory of his dead mother—a "saint," he called her—and then suggested that Watergate was nothing more than a test of his greatness.

We think sometimes when things don't go the right way, when we suffer a defeat, that all has ended. Not true. It is only a beginning, always. Greatness comes not when things always go good for you, but the greatness comes when you are really tested, when you take some knocks, some disappointments, when sadness comes. Because only if you have been in the deepest valley can you ever know how magnificent it is to be on the highest mountain (9 August 1974).

Then he adds, "Never be petty. Always remember others may hate you, but those who hate you don't win unless you hate them, and then you destroy yourself." What extraordinary advice for a man whose downfall was precipitated by exactly this action. Would that he could have heard his own words as the first plumber was dispatched to repair the first leak.

This man was brazen. He was solid brass. He couldn't be shamed in public. He had circumvented the Constitution and grossly abused the powers of the Oval Office to punish his multitude of perceived enemies. Worse, he destroyed Americans' faith and trust in the presidency. But he wouldn't say "uncle." When President Ford issued Nixon an unconditional pardon, it was unsatisfying to many because Nixon couldn't have cared less. Or so it appeared. In the twenty or so years before his death, he never blinked. He never looked down. That was his genius. And that was his legacy. The ultimate Stonewall. Shame-proof.

The *Random House Historical Dictionary of American Slang* (1994) notes that Watergate gave birth to a seemingly never-ending series of scandals that are called "gates." The usage is not limited to the United States, as Winegate, Volgagate, and Labourgate all attest. The dictionary goes on to say that Watergate has led to an "enormously productive combining form."[2] Even advertisers now use it. "Has your business been Rategated by promises of savings?" asks AT&T in a recent print ad.

But gate-o-mania also signaled a new approach to politics. If you were to survive in the public arena, you were going to have to be vaccinated against shame. Your -gate would come, be it Iran-Contragate or Whitewatergate, and Nixon showed what to do. Politicians would have to turn from being seen as golden retrievers to being pit bulls.

The next transformation in public shaming occurred as politicians realized the power of *delivering* shame as a risk-free method of doing business. Spiro Agnew had attempted this with his William Safire–written speeches about antiwar protesters and left-leaning liberals ("nattering nabobs of negativism"), but it was in political campaigning, especially in television ads, that this method could really "work."

The prototype of the negative ad was the most famous, or infamous, political commercial ever made. It was the 1964 "daisy" spot for Lyndon Johnson in his presidential battle against Barry Goldwater. The ad showed a little girl pulling the petals off a daisy, accompanied by quotations from LBJ about peace in a nuclear world. In the background we heard a sonorous voice tick off, "Ten . . . nine . . . eight . . . seven . . ." and so on, until, *boom!* the atom bomb went off, presumably taking the damsel and her daisy with it.

Goldwater's name was never mentioned; it didn't have to be. The commercial was withdrawn after one showing. According to Bill Moyers, then LBJ's press secretary, there were never plans to show it more than once anyway. Moyers now admits that "it was good advertising and bad politics."[3] Just the attack suffices. Explanations are unnecessary. The negative commercial was born.

One sees a variation of this in the shaming attacks made by Vice President Quayle on the entertainment media. In the spring of 1992, Los Angeles erupted in riots after the Rodney King verdict. Fifty-eight people died. Vice President Quayle made a speech to the Commonwealth Club of California in San Francisco. It was a stump speech, as the California presidential primary was taking place. The subject was the breakdown of family values, an appropriate topic given what was happening to the south.

Near the end of his speech Quayle called for "social sanctions" against women who bear children "irresponsibly." The audience knew what he meant. As an aside, he lashed out against a popular television program, "Murphy Brown," in which the title character, a single woman played by Candice Bergen, has a child out of wedlock. "It doesn't help matters when prime-time TV has Murphy Brown—a character who supposedly epitomizes today's intelligent, highly paid, professional woman—mocking the importance of fathers by bearing a child alone and calling it just another 'lifestyle choice,' " he said.

For that comment he received the political equivalent of gas splashed on flames. For the next six months everyone had at him. He was such a clean-faced innocent, and here he was flinging shame. Remember clearly: had you ever heard of Dan Quayle before he was chosen as vice president? Yet who can forget his "What a waste it is to lose one's mind, or not to have a mind"? or the added *e* in potato? But this time Quayle had hit pay dirt, ironically, not for himself, but for others. He had attempted to shame not televison producers, but a totally fictional character. After all, we knew who Murphy Brown really was. She was not really Candice Bergen. Murphy was the spokeswoman for Sprint long-distance service and a wise-cracking sardonic television reporter.

What Quayle learned was that it didn't matter who Murphy Brown really was, what mattered was that we all knew she couldn't answer back. The show's creator and longtime producer, Diane English, issued this sensible enough statement from her Hollywood office. "If the vice president thinks it's disgraceful for an unmarried woman to bear a child, and if he believes that a woman cannot adequately raise a child without a father, then he'd better make sure abortion remains safe and legal."[4] No one listened to this argument. Candice Bergen and various editorial writers also tried to retort, but in the modern television world, unless Murphy Brown took to the airwaves herself, Quayle was home free.

When, years later, Dan Quayle claimed vindication in his appropriately self-serving memoir, *Standing Firm*, by saying that the world has come around to his way of thinking, he got it half-right. Murphy Brown would have little trouble raising a child out of wedlock; in fact, once we met the father (Murphy's ex-husband), we might well think she should do it alone. But raising a child is no hassle for the "haves"— they can hire surrogate parents. Murphy Brown had it even better. She got little Avery Brown essentially written out of the show. Raising a child for the "have-nots" is a different story, and, alas, one too often told. A harsher reality writes their scripts. Their kids don't conveniently disappear.

What the political world really learned from Quayle's example had less to do with family values than with the power of attacking figments of popular imagination. Quayle had stumbled into what would become known as the Culture Wars. To wage them successfully you needed to be able to isolate some pastime, and then harpoon it as the great menace plaguing our shores. What was it in the early 1990s? Murphy Brown. What is it today? Gangsta rap? Violent movies? Pornography? The National Endowment for the Arts? Trash TV? The Smithsonian's view of the bombing of Japan? The NEH-supported "National Standards for U.S. History"?

From Pat Buchanan's speech at the 1992 Republican convention in Houston when he gleefully used the term "culture war," to Robert Dole's broadsides against Time Warner, whenever Washington goes up against Hollywood, the pot and the kettle have at it. No matter. Dan Quayle can take comfort, and even pride, in the fact that his Murphy Brown address is the best-remembered speech of the Bush presidency. Who remembers anything George Bush himself ever said, aside from a thousand points of something?

The next wave of public shaming came in the Republican Congress after the elections of 1994. With a change of leadership in the House of Representatives to Newt Gingrich, the shame spotlight moved yet again. This time it settled on a collective image of "have-nots," most specifically, the welfare mothers, leaching the resources of the "haves." The term "welfare mother" tracks, albeit in nicer language, Ronald Reagan's infamous denunciation of black mothers as "welfare queens." It reflects the chill, abstract view that the true enemy is not poverty, but poor people—especially poor women. That is what made Speaker Gingrich's shaming so powerful. Unlike Quayle, Gingrich didn't aim at TV or at a fictional mother. He aimed at the real thing. He implied that what poor women most need is moral fiber. More powerfully, he implied they are living shamelessly on purpose.

Why are the fathers not also held culpable, and isn't what the poor are doing exactly what the middle class is doing too? "I'm all with Newt," said Barbara Ehrenreich, dyed-in-the-wool Democrat who now writes essays for *Time* magazine. "Let's bring on the shame . . . let's point the finger of shame at employers who don't pay a living wage or husbands who batter wives and force them to flee."[5] True enough. She has a point. Still, what is interesting is that this is one of the rare occasions in recent memory in which shame is being revived as a way to change antisocial behavior.

There are certain irrefutable facts about the welfare debate with which all sides agree. First, antipoverty programs have not reduced the number of poor people any more than building more prisons has reduced crime. Second, the welfare system as currently administered has created a permanent underclass that largely lacks motivation and role models for escaping poverty. Third, for many, welfare has become a "career" that is passed down from one generation to the next.

Aid to Families with Dependent Children has been in operation for decades. It is a colossal failure, producing generations of dependents. Continuing to spend almost $200 billion a year—much of which never trickles down to the poor but is consumed by bureaucrats, caseworkers, service providers, and vendors who administer poverty programs in the private sector—is a waste of money and lives. It is as

WHAT GOES AROUND COMES AROUND: GINGRICH BEING SHAMED FOR PROPOSED MEDICARE CUTS, 1995 (AP/WIDE WORLD PHOTOS).

compassionate as continuing to provide crack to an addict because he might feel bad if he doesn't get it. So why not try shame? But shaming won't work unless it is administered fairly.

Gingrich has been unambiguous about his willingness to do exactly that. In a speech to the National League of Cities in 1995 he pointed to the social changes wrought a century ago by a culture willing and able to wield social opprobrium in public:

The Victorians reduced the number of children born out of wedlock almost by 50 percent. They changed the whole momentum of their society. They didn't do it through a new bureaucracy. They did it by reestablishing values, by moral leadership, and by being willing to look at people in the face and say, "You should be ashamed when you get drunk in public. You ought to be ashamed if you're a drug addict" (20 March 1995).

Such shaming works, however, only if you also shame the middle-class recreational drug user as well, even though that user can usually "get away with it." Shaming works only if you point out to the middle-class serial parent that he is doing a poor job fathering his children and behaving just like his counterpart in the ghetto. Getting married and divorced in between families doesn't change the result. Fatherless families are a danger to everyone. If you are going to use shaming, it must be applied across the board just as it usually was in Victorian days. Middle-class people should be ashamed of not maintaining family values not for themselves alone, but because they are examples for those who are striving to be like them. Is this hypocrisy? You bet. But recall La Rochefoucauld's "Hypocrisy is the tribute vice pays to virtue." It is hypocrisy for a reason, and as such, goes by a different name: it is a social value, what William Bennett calls "constructive hypocrisy."

In the main, Gingrich is correct. Poverty and addiction are not caused by a lack of money or willpower. They are caused by a loss of shared aspirations, a lack of shared goals. This is not a ghetto problem, it is an American problem. Ghetto life exaggerates urban life; it is not a separate world. A society that ignores or opposes a set of core standards that motivates people to work, stay married, exercise self-control, and be honest exhibits a poverty of the spirit that no amount of money can enrich. Those core values are maintained by carrots and sticks. Carrots don't always work.

The irony of modern politics is that to be a successful politician in the post-Nixon era, you need to be shame-proof, yet to address many modern problems, you need to be willing to use shaming. Newt Gingrich is not helped by his own behavior in his personal life. Nor has he been helped by skirting one House rule after another, in preparing his first book, in preparing his college course, in responding to the House Ethics Committee about its financing and content, in his plan to pay his fine to Congress, or in repeatedly flouting IRS regulations in pursuit of political gain.

So here on a thumbnail is the paradox of political shaming as currently practiced: to be able to walk quietly and carry the stick, you need to be shame-proof. But the minute you lift that stick, you demonstrate exactly the qualities you should be ashamed of. Hence in our desire to shame others while remaining shame-proof ourselves, we have lost touch with the intimate and legitimate link between shame and politics. As Walter Berns, a law professor at Georgetown, has observed, "There is a connection between self-restraint and shame, and therefore a connection between shame and self-government or democracy."[6] The Victorians knew this. Colin Powell knew it and indicated that it would have been a central part of his domestic program. Many of the rest of us seem to have forgotten.

THE LAW AND SHAME

What the law does not forbid let shame forbid.
—Seneca, *Troades*

Breakin' rocks in the hot sun. I fought the law and the law won.
—Bobby Fuller Four (1965)

The word *stigma* means blot or blemish and is a signifier of inflicted shame. The word comes to us from Latin, as the Romans literally branded unruly slaves and criminals. These brands were lightly burnt onto the skin and disappeared within a few years. Many of those branded were Christians. In a provocative bit of cultural jujitsu, early Christianity picked up the concept and applied it retroactively to the wounds of Christ. His wounds received on the cross would miraculously appear on the hands of a true penitent: the stigmata.

A stigma is different from a "mark," which is deep within the body. The mark of Cain, for instance, is forever embedded in an entire race.

Or a witch's mark is impossible to remove. You should temporarily shun someone with a stigma. But you should avoid forever someone with a mark. What stigma is to mark, humiliation is to banishment.

All cultures apply stigmas. In many parts of the world some kind of face or body paint is used. The system used to allocate stigmas is called the law. Stigmas have to be applied with great caution lest they become subverted, as the Romans learned. The key to their effective use is not their application, but the willingness of those who see them to respond by shunning. Wrongly applied, they become "badges."

In American history the best-known use of stigmas was by the Puritans. Who does not know of Hester Prynne's scarlet letter? What we don't realize is that an entire alphabet was used. So in Maryland, for instance, county justices could brand *H* for hog stealer, *R* for runaway slave, or *T* for thief. Colonial America was an ideal culture for such shaming. Here was an isolated community with real danger around the edges. Being cast out, if only temporarily, meant confronting genuine peril. There was great safety in conformity, in circling the wagons, in living close. In addition, being incarcerated meant social and financial expense for the group. How much more efficient to use the pillory, dunking stools, stocks, or even branding, and let public opprobrium bring the miscreant back into line. Tar and a few feathers did the work of jail.

Oh mercy! we say. How cruel and heartless were our colonial ancestors. We prefer to use small, costly iron boxes far from public view. We forget that the rise of imprisonment was an aspect of the great social transformation of Romanticism. Assuming man to be naturally good (Rousseau's noble savage, Wordsworth's "Mighty Prophet! Seer Blest!" and all that), putting misfits in jail was thought to literally give them a chance to re-form. Like liquids of different density shaken up, the natural goodness would float to the top. *Penitentiary* originally meant a place to do penance, to get "in touch" with your better self. That sentimental view is long past. Today many people seem to spend their entire lives going into and out of the cages. In fact, a considerable percentage of our population now believes that a little prison time is part of standard maturation. Many of the rest of us seem willing to let this occur. So when the demand for boxes outstrips the supply, we just build more of them. What an irony! The less effective prisons are in reducing crime, the higher the demand for still more imprisonment.

Not everyone, however, agrees. In recent years the dispensers of the law are finally realizing that shame has a place in punishment. Stigma, judiciously applied, can be a far more efficient method of behavioral modification than cage time. In one of the best overviews of the legal situation, Dan Kahan, a professor in the University of Chicago Law School, concludes "What Do Alternative Sanctions Mean?" by contending that shaming can be an equitable method of punishment. Properly administered, degradation ceremonies are inexpensive, efficient, fair, and an effective deterrent.

So we find judges in Florida insisting that, after repeated offenses, drunk drivers apply a neon sticker or special license plates to their cars, alerting all of danger. A slumlord is sentenced to house arrest in one of his rat-infested tenements. He is greeted with this sign: Welcome Reptile! In other cases, this time in Rhode Island, child molesters have been forced to pay for their pictures inserted in a local newspaper with the caption "I was convicted for child molestation. If you are a child molester, get professional help immediately, or you may find your picture and name in the paper and your life under control of the state." "Megan's Law" in New Jersey gives county prosecutors the right to inform neighbors of a relocating offender. A repeat offender has been required to post signs with letters at least three inches high around his residence and car: DANGEROUS SEX OFFENDER—NO CHILDREN ALLOWED.

Shaming works best in a population sensitive to social degradation. Ask an adolescent male which he prefers—suspension from school for a week or having to wear a frilly bonnet for an hour in gym class—and

BILLBOARD IN LA MESA, CALIFORNIA, 1995.

you'll find out. A purse snatcher in high school is forced to put taps in his shoes. In the *New York Times* of March 24, 1996, is a photograph of a young man whose punishment was to stand for a weekend in front of the gas station where he had skimmed cash, holding a sign saying "I am a thief."

In my estimation, ten minutes under the dunce cap may have done more than vials of Ritalin for those suffering from attention deficit disorder, dysrationalia, or whatever affliction du jour is conjured up by counselors and drug companies, accepted by gullible parents, and haltingly paid for by insurance companies.

One of the most efficient ways of collecting unpaid student loans has been for the collection agency to send a list of truants to the local newspapers. This has worked wonders, especially with doctors and lawyers. The most efficient way to collect past-due land taxes is often to insert a flyer in the newspaper with the names of debtors. So, too, in Miami and other cities, the posting of the names of "johns" on freeway billboards seems to deter prostitution.

One of the more interesting uses of shaming is the "perp walk" per-

Tell these people to stop drinking and driving.
(They obviously won't listen to us.)

The 1994 Minnesota DWI Hall of Shame.
Mothers Against Drunk Driving.

Print ad from Minnesota Mothers Against Drunk Driving, 1994.

formed daily in many big cities. It is a standard scene on the evening news, captured every day in the city's papers, the brief moment when the alleged perpetrator of whatever latest atrocity is walked by police out the door of a station house. We watch as an accused murderer or mobster, helplessly handcuffed, is dragged through a horde of screaming reporters and jostling photographers. You naturally assume you're seeing a barbaric mob wreaking random havoc. What we don't see is that this is a choreographed ritual for shaming, all parties participating for the camera.

In New York, for instance, the perp walk is a vital part of the criminal justice system, with its own etiquette and traditions. It depends on the collusion of police, photographers, and editors. When time is short, the walk is from one door of the courthouse to another, just long enough for the pictures to be taken. This is called a "perp parade" and it has to be done well before the evening news deadlines. In the old days, the perp was allowed a coat to hide behind, but in the modern version he has only his hands. Sometimes the perp refuses to cooperate, as with John Gotti, who was unfailingly polite and chatted up the reporters.

The most recent revival of a shaming ritual long out of fashion is the chain gang. The once common sight of felons in chains breaking rocks, or road crews in groups of five linked with eight-foot chains, disappeared about thirty years ago. After the 1932 film classic *I Am a Fugitive from a Chain Gang* portrayed brutal conditions for prisoners, states removed leg irons from work crews. Now public opinion has changed again. *Cool Hand Luke* is already a generation old, long forgotten. When revoking an inmate's television privileges is the commonest form of discipline (or so the public believes), something else must be done. So the chain gangs are now reappearing, and with much hoopla.

First in Alabama (which prides itself on this kind of thing), then Florida, and then in southwestern states like Arizona, men in specially colored garb (not the broad black-and-white stripes of yore) are linked together to pound pebbles out of rocks. This is occurring in full public view; in fact, the press is encouraged to cover it. Although the prisoners voluntarily choose the work details, the predictable criticism has resulted, along with the expected euphemisms. In press releases the Florida Department of Corrections, confusing purpose with its own PR, calls it the Restricted Labor Squad.

In the *New York Times Magazine* of September 17, 1995, under a

NEVER LOOK DOWN: JOHN GOTTI, THE DEFIANT "PERP," 1990 (AP/WIDE WORLD PHOTOS).

two-page full-color photo showing just the legs of inmates (all African-Americans, incidentally and most unfortunately; the article later went on to point out that the five-man groups are usually "racially correct"—three blacks and two whites apiece), is this caption:

> Roadside Attraction—The fiction is that chain-gang work is rehabilitating. The reality is that it is pure spectacle. Above: An eyeful for motorists on Interstate 65 near Huntsville, Ala. Opposite: Handcuffs are removed so a prisoner can perform the useless task of breaking rocks.

Brent Staples, who usually writes for the editorial page, continues the caption's sentiment in the text below:

Any animal with teeth enough will chew off its leg to escape a trap. Human beings behaved similarly when chain gang imprisonment—a successor to slavery—swept through the labor-starved South during Reconstruction. Beaten and driven like maltreated beasts, shackled to one another around the clock, prisoners turned to self-mutilation to make themselves useless for work. They slashed their bodies, broke their own legs, crippled themselves by cutting their tendons.[7]

Staples goes on to reiterate that the work the gangs do is valueless, that this represents a resurgence of spectacle into American life, that "the men in shackles and white suits are medium-security prisoners—not quite the ax murderers, assassins and sundry death-row candidates that onlookers might wish to imagine. The gangs are made up of nonviolent criminals only—check forgers, deadbeat dads, safe crackers, parole violators," and that people pass by the carful to gawk.

All this that Mr. Staples condemns is, of course, exactly the point. Public punishment, something long lost in our culture, should be directed to work of no value. What you did in the stocks is just sit there. You lost face. You were degraded. The act is a "spectacle" on purpose. It needs to be watched by others if it is to have the desired effect. And, perhaps most important, shame will not affect ax murderers and "sundry death-row candidates." Who wants to shame them? Check forgers, deadbeat dads, all manner of bullies, and parole violators are another matter.

How degenerate, how Southern, and how barbaric, says the ever urbane Mr. Staples, mindful of the world view of his more usual habitat. Do a Nexis search of the use of shame on the editorial page of the *Times* and you will see it is one of their favorite invocations. Shame on this, shame on that, they say about once a month. How much of *their* shaming sticks?

Often modern shaming depends on the proper use of media. A generation ago the editorial page might have worked. Shame worked in pre-electronic cultures wherever people couldn't get away from their communications environment—a neighborhood, a town, a village. Once people began to wander away, shame didn't work as well. The malfeasant could escape the hot blush by ducking into a corner for a while. You need to know that you are known to be shamed.

For most of us, the speed of communication has changed to 186,000 miles a second. So it means that you can reach anyone anywhere in the country in less than a sixtieth of a second. Everyone, everywhere. But alas, not in your backyard. This makes shame one of the most powerful means of social control again—if you know how to use it.

Advertisers have become especially susceptible to countrywide shaming. Large corporations that produce essentially interchangeable products like toothpaste or automobiles know that an annoyed customer is often far more potent that a satisfied one. You may not switch brands because one is better than another (rarely the case), but you may switch because you don't like something the company is doing elsewhere. Even worse than a dissatisfied customer is an outraged one who complains not about the product but about your entire way of doing business. Sears Roebuck and Unilever reduced their advertising budgets for trash TV as the direct result of bad press and fears of alienating customers.

Avoiding public shaming is one reason why cigarette companies like RJR-Nabisco and Philip Morris attempt to keep their nasty products away from their other brands. This is also why they are so skittish about what entertainment they sponsor lest they disturb a small, vociferous audience. It is also why they are finally willing to 'fess up to their past subterfuges. For instance, the shaming of large corporations that sponsor violence on television such as General Motors and the U.S. Army has proven one of the few predictable ways to temper content. Calvin Klein pulled ads featuring pubescents in their underwear because of public outrage. Time Warner got rid of its highly profitable

interest in gangsta rap because it was publicly humiliated by the un-
likely team of William Bennett of Empower America, C. Delores
Tucker of the National Congress of Black Women, and countless editorial writers.

Many cities are finding that their local-access television station,
made possible by the coaxial cable, is also a powerful tool. So in Seattle
a list of those convicted of soliciting prostitution and of repeated drunk
driving is regularly scrolled down the screen. For six months the city
of Miami flashed names and addresses of sex buyers on the city's cable
channel, Met 9. Cable officials said the program attracts a big audience,
but legal problems put an end to the practice as the names of some innocent people were accidentally included. Although prostitutes continue to ply their trade, officials say that embarrassing sex customers
has worked.

There is no doubt that using shame as punishment is dangerous.
Shaming is very volatile and must be used with extreme caution. True,
we may not be the ideal culture in which shaming can function. Island
communities are most sensitive. We are not the Japanese, Eskimos,
Easter Islanders, or the colonial Puritans. But even so, we are filled
with social islands. Internet users, for instance, are susceptible to "flam-
ing" or criticism on the screen. Why not use it to shame virus-
spreading hackers? Adolescents, who cause much of modern crime,
are island dwellers. Gangs, football teams, and fraternities depend on
shame, often brutally delivered. Why not try to leach some of that
power in the name of social harmony?

To many of the have-nots in our culture, the threat of social degradation as currently delivered is hollow. But to conclude that inhab-
itants of the inner cities can't respond to shame is as ridiculous as
the nineteenth-century idea that nonwhites could not blush and
hence were shameless. Quite the opposite, as Sheldon Zhang has argued in "Measuring Shame in an Ethnic Context." As with other
discriminated-against groups like Gypsies, blacks are probably more

susceptible to shame than their white inner-city counterparts. The thesis of Fox Butterfield's recent *All God's Children* is that the roots of black violence lie in the internalizing of antebellum white codes of honor and shame.

Much of ghetto organization is based on boundaries drawn by shaming. The power of being disrespected, of being "dissed," shows the shame fields are indeed electrified. The law should work with that community to find out what is appropriate. We may need to be equal *before* the law, but not necessarily punished in exactly the same way. Punishments need to fit the crime, the criminal, and the community.

In my state of Florida, for instance, the police have protected marchers who chant at drug dealers, "Drug dealer, drug dealer, you ain't cool—you're just acting like a fool" and "If you keep selling that crack, we'll be back." The police have stepped aside while the marchers have drawn chalk arrows in the street pointing at a drug dealer's house. The best part of such shaming is that residents see themselves as enforcing their own standards. They chant to their neighbors, "Neighbor, neighbor, don't you hide—come on out and join our side" and "If you can't join the fight, turn on your porch light." The lights, as Mireya Navarro reports for the *New York Times* of August 30, 1996, flicker on.

The main problem with shame is that, once applied, it can't be controlled. In the science of modern punishment, perhaps too much has been made of maintaining control. Classical penology isolated four ends of punishment: retribution, rehabilitation, deterrence, and incapacitation. Only incapacitation can be controlled with any predictability. Even that is hardly precise. At least three million people now pass through state and federal cages each year, costing billions of dollars (at $20,000 per young prisoner and $69,000 for those over age sixty) and doing untold damage (8 to 16 percent are victims of sexual assault while in prison). Our current incarceration rate of 519 per 100,000 is five times greater than most industrial nations. The figures for Mexico and Japan are 97 and 36 respectively. If the rates of recidivism are correct, many of these dollars are being inefficiently spent. Rehabilitation has not occurred; it is often not even attempted. The risk/reward ratios may be moving in favor of shaming, if only because other methods have proven so wasteful, so spiteful, and so—dare I say it?—racist. Does anyone really doubt that the high percentage of blacks in the prison population mutes the public reaction to an unsatisfactory penal situation?

In addition, we need to restore shaming as a legitimate topic of cultural conversation. Although it is not politically correct or easy to discuss, stigmatizing behavior is not always so dangerous as its alternatives. Not demeaning certain behavior is sometimes worse. Look at it in reverse. Behavior once stigmatized as deviant is now tolerated and even sanctioned. Divorce and illegitimacy, once seen as betokening the breakdown of the family, are now viewed benignly. Illegitimacy has been officially rebaptised as "nonmarital childbearing," and divorced and unmarried mothers and fathers are lumped together in the category of "single-parent families." Addiction has become not a function of willpower but of genetic determinism. Violence is often considered an economic strategy, not a reckless disregard for the rights of others. Are we better off for having removed the stigma that surrounded these events? While it may be comforting to think the stifling oppression of Victorian shame is lifting, what is underneath may be worse.

CHAPTER 9

SHAME, SHAME, COME BACK SHAME: AMERICAN CULTURE SINCE THE 1960s

....

It's the rich wot get the pleasure.
It's the poor wot get the pain.
It's the same the whole world over.
Ain't it all a bloomin' shame?
                    —popular Victorian music hall song

....

*D*OES ANY OF this matter? Is this all just a Dennis Milleresque rant from someone paid by the state to complain? And isn't shame always in shambles at century's end? Isn't that the transgressive nature of the *fin-de-siècle*? Perhaps so. But one needs to distinguish saturnalia, or the temporary lifting of taboos, from decadence, or the effacement of the standards. The carnival that used to spring up alongside the Church, sometimes literally nestled in an external corner, now stands on its own. A problem of American culture is that Mardi Gras is no longer connected to Lent.

If history is any guide, where a culture draws its invisible lines of shame, and how it communicates its rules of passage around certain events, are of central importance. Have too few "Thou shalt nots" in your moral ecology and society can become a jungle. Have too many and you get a desert. What is human history but a continual cycling between these extremes? What explains cultural extinction but when the cycles go too far in either direction?

The Roman Empire saw a huge influx of shameless, decadent, and hedonistic behavior after the frugal ideals of the Roman Republic. Even at the time, historians and moralists warned that this selfish acceptance of individual freedom and promotion of individual pleasure at the expense of the group's well-being would end in blood and tears. It did.

France in the late eighteenth century was notorious for its looseness of morals and the blatant sexuality of its court. As in imperial Rome, the upper classes were immodest and haughty. "Let them eat cake" was not a dietary instruction but an arrogant assertion of separateness, a shameless indulgence in a double standard of values. One of the professed goals of the French Revolution was to return to a unified system of values. One of the actual results of the revolution was the rise of Napoleon.

Weimar Germany in the 1920s and 1930s also witnessed unparalleled lack of self-censorship and restraint. Look at its theaters and cabarets. Great entertainment, lousy art. A neopagan cult of the body beautiful was widespread and focused sybaritic concentration on the self. The Nazis later exploited what they regarded as a breakdown of standards by exaggerating conformity. Yet the cult of solipsism and the idealizing of blood were nevertheless very much part of Nazi practice.

I am not arguing that modern-day America is going the way of these earlier cultures, but only that ruthless violence and lawlessness often follow public acceptance of immodesty and shamelessness. Extremes breed each other. Romanticism follows neoclassicism and precedes Victorianism as a matter of course. One generation attempts to apply taboos, the next attempts to remove them, and so on in an endless Viconian cycle. Squeeze, release, squeeze.

At the extremes, however, any of these cycles can turn chaotic. When the waves become too elongated, the culture becomes not shameless so much as ashamed of the trivial. Deviancy gets defined down not just too far, but too far away from the accepted norms. Euphemisms appear not to cover the dirty, but to hide the unattractive. Wrong becomes inappropriate. *Shocking* becomes not a term of opprobrium but of praise.

From a historical perspective, a sense of modesty and restraint— what used to be called civility or politeness but what is now often called

Victorian prudery—can mediate these extremes and protect the general weal. Such modesty is dependent on keeping certain activity hidden from the young and the uninitiated, on keeping secrets. What is kept hidden is often quite superficial, like the sexual act, and often it is quite profound, like religious mysteries. But the point is that as the youngster grows through various stages, she is introduced to these secrets, these shared codes of socialization.

Shame is the public modesty that keeps these secrets until the truth is ready to be understood and assimilated. Thus is shame central to restraint, the beginnings of self-control, and rise of a decent and fair society.

Essentially this is why advertiser-supported television is so important to understand. Such entertainment *tells* secrets. It can't help it. Its lack of restraint is what makes television so attractive. The best way to gather an audience is to tell secrets. No one can resist "Pssst, have you heard this?" This was not the case in early television, in what is now grandly called the Golden Age of Television. When the only people who could afford sets were middle-class, a daylong standard of programming was possible. Programs were standardized and predictable because control was exerted from above. Sponsors were proud to announce their affiliation: "Texaco Theater," "U.S. Steel Hour," "Kraft Television Theater," "Philco Television Playhouse," "Firestone Hour," to name just a few.

But no more. Once 97 percent of homes had a medium that is dependent on finding the largest possible audience for each day-part, programmers willy-nilly transmit what is titillating to each discrete audience. What is titillating is what is usually just over the edge of modesty. Each "day-part"—late afternoon, early prime, prime time, late night—must promise something different for each audience segment. After all, that promise and predictability are exactly what makes television viewing exciting. The only gatekeeper is the one who reads the Nielsen daily numbers.

Television takes nothing but an eye to consume. You need no language. Children love it. What they see by surfing the channels is what they used to have to grow into—they see the rituals of mature life. They see Secrets writ large. A teenager today watching late night television sees things only adults would have known of in a pre-electronic world. In the pre-electronic world, secrets came into your house as your parents monitored them. Or else they appeared in brown envelopes with no return addresses. What you once saw in private in your closet you now see in early prime time. A generation ago few people knew that FDR was paralyzed from the waist down. Who today does not know that John F. Kennedy wasn't?

It is no happenstance that in countless studies (the most recent being the October 1995 report of the Carnegie Council on Adolescent Development), behavior such as smoking, drinking, coitus, profanity, and homicide has been committed by younger and younger children. What would you expect? By the time they are eighteen, adolescents will have sat in front of a television more hours than they will have spent in a classroom. It is no surprise that they have an inflated sense of themselves and their ability to handle complex experience. You would, too, if you had been repeatedly told that "You're the one," "You're worth it," "You are special," "You deserve a break," and, well, you know the rest.

Television can't be stopped. "Kill your television set" makes a better bumper sticker than a reality. The oxymoronic television culture *is* our culture. *Circus Americanus.* The carnival used to come to town once a year. "Step right up and see what was once only imagined," said the barker. Now it stops every day in your living room. "Stay tuned. Don't touch that dial," says its successor. The carnival told secrets for a price, and so, too, does television. Watch the commercial, see the show, learn the secret, watch the commercial, see the show . . .

Of course, *you* don't watch television for secrets, but your children do. And like it or not, as they watch they are being inoculated with a kind of homeopathic antidote for shame. They are watching things being uncovered. They see careless mating behavior, they see children raised out of wedlock, they see Madonna and Michael Jackson, they see sanitized violence and death, they see endless sitcoms based on subverting social norms. Of the many shifts in popular culture that commercial entertainment can be held partly responsible for, here are two: the rise of gambling and the fall of the nuclear family.

TELEVISION ADVERTISING AT WORK:
THE REMOVAL OF SHAME FROM GAMBLING

Lead us not into temptation . . .

—The Lord's Prayer

This could be your ticket out . . .

—Illinois Lotto billboard in south Chicago

If you want to see how lightning-fast advertiser-supported television can remove shame, pause to consider the case of gambling. A generation ago gambling was illegal, except in a few places like Las Vegas. How fast has it grown? Only computer software and on-line technology have grown faster. How big is gambling today? Bigger than the gross national product of China. In the past decade the industry has more than doubled to a whopping $482 billion, making it by far our most popular form of entertainment in terms of dollars spent. The movie industry, by comparison, brought in less than $6 billion at the box office in 1994.[1]

Every state except Hawaii and Utah has changed its laws to allow some form of gambling, whether on riverboats, at casinos on Indian reservations (thanks to a 1988 Indian Gaming Regulatory Act that allowed first bingo, then casino gambling), or in a state lottery. Unlike Communion wine leading to a jug-a-day habit, there is clear evidence that lottery participation leads to other forms of gambling.

There is nothing intrinsically shameful about the lottery. Lotteries were important in our earlier history, helping to finance the American Revolution, the French and Indian War, and even to fund the universities of Harvard, Princeton, and Dartmouth. A French national lottery even helped finance the Statue of Liberty, for goodness' sake. But these lotteries were discontinued in the 1880s, when gambling was stigmatized as affecting those least able to afford it.

Then in the 1960s, with new methods of computing bets and payouts, the lottery was revived. Usually it was done in the name of helping education, an irony simply too depressing for comment. The excess monies might have been better earmarked to plaster posters of Joe Camel all over Mr. Rogers's neighborhood and to litter Sesame Street with empty beer cans.

Be that as it may, this exquisitely regressive tax has flourished thanks to omnipresent advertising on television. And this is the shameful part of the current situation. We are continually told: "You deserve to strike it rich." "What are you going to do with your millions?" "We've created two hundred millionaires in ten years. Now it's your turn." "Life is short. Don't miss your chance." "One lucky number is worth a lifetime of hard work." "All you need is a dollar and a dream." "Somebody's gonna win . . . it might as well be you." Never once are we told that our chances of winning the Big Jackpot are slightly less possible than drawing four royal flushes in a row, all in spades, then getting up and meeting four strangers in a row with the same birthdays.

Admittedly, gambling is hardly new. Various number games have siphoned off millions, especially in urban areas, but the process was done on the sly. It was a secret. The numbers racket was run by the mob. Knowing this might not have deterred participants, but at least they knew the government disapproved. Now gambling is sponsored by the state and called "gaming."

Of course, such betting affects the poor. A 1987 Duke University study calculated that the lottery is the most regressive tax currently sponsored by the state. Another study, this one in Iowa in 1986, showed that a dollar from the poorest segment of have-nots was five times more likely to be spent on the lottery than a dollar from any other income group.[2] Analogize the lottery to investing in equities, if you must, but the economic characteristics of the participants are totally different. And so, too, is the professed purpose. Patronizing? You bet. That is exactly what shaming does in a culture, any culture.

ENTERTAINMENT AT WORK: THE REMOVAL
OF SHAME FROM DIVORCE

Men are like pinch hitters. So what's the deal? . . . I don't want
some guy in my life forever who's going to be driving me nuts.
—Michelle Pfeiffer on why she chose
to raise a child without a father

When one sees how quickly shame was effaced from gambling, it is no surprise that the aspirational images of family life have changed so dramatically since the 1960s. The family went from no-laughing-matter to the butt of jokes in a wink. Just mention Ozzie and Harriet to a thirtysomething and you will see what I mean. Marriage has become, if not a joke, then a joking matter.

This transformation was especially rapid in the middle class, where the social costs of continually blending families was minimal. Just look at the cartoons in any issue of *The New Yorker*. In a recent example two youngish adults are saying to each other, "It's only marriage I'm proposing after all, not a lifetime commitment." In another cartoon a fatherly type is explaining to some rapt Wall Street twentysomethings, "Life was primitive. Both bankruptcy and divorce were still no-nos." And in a third, one elderly couple to another: "It is unbelievable how time flies: all *our* children are divorced, too."

Indeed, divorce has become a minor bump on the suburban beltway of life. Ellen Goodman, syndicated columnist for the *Boston Globe*, writes (12 April 1995) that this used to be a joke of the 1960s:

> Have you heard the one about the 95-year-old couple who went to divorce court after 70 unhappy years of marriage? The judge asked them why they hadn't split long ago. The couple said, "We were waiting for the children to die."

Goodman relates that when she tells the joke today, no one can understand the humor. People no longer stay together "for the sake of the children."

If you really want to access the temper of our times, check the Hallmark card rack down at your local stationery store. We have come to depend on these cards to convey our deepest feelings. Here's one for someone recently divorced. On the outside of the card we are told to consider your broken marriage like a "record album." On the inside you are comforted by being assured that you are now a new "release" and will have plenty of play. And here's one for the kids to give to "released" Mom's new husband or boyfriend for Father's Day. The card thanks the surrogate for doing all the dad stuff even though this dad is not the biological parent. As with all serious cards, the surface text is un-ironic and compassionate. On a deeper level, however, what is being said is that, while the adult can and should enjoy the liberation, the kid had better learn to accept the loss and start anew.

I dare say that in one generation the shared sense of what a family is has changed more than ever before in modern times. Hallmark knows. After all, Hallmark is where you go When You Care Enough to Send the Very Best®. Hallmark is a company understandably protective of its "intellectual" property. When I asked if I could quote these card lines verbatim I was politely, but firmly, discouraged. Their "public affairs and communications" specialist went further, insisting that I be sure to capitalize the trademarked motto and follow it with the trademark symbol. More intriguing, however, was this point from the same letter:

> Divorce is a serious and usually stressful life event. Remarriages can create treacherous interpersonal dynamics. In other times, war, fatal disease and byzantine legal forms governing inheritance created stresses and strained family relations. Uplifting and/or healing messages have been bound into culture and religion for centuries.

Please don't get me wrong. It is not that divorce is not traumatic; it surely is. Rather it is that divorce has become a right of self-fulfillment, not an admission of failure—albeit a perfectly human one. Unlike war, pestilence, and "byzantine legal forms" (like insisting on all caps and the trademark symbol?), nobody made you say those vows or make those promises. We still assume marriage is an act of free will.

And what of the kids? With about half of all marriages in the U.S. nowadays proving temporary, with more than a million babies born each year to women who never wed in the first place, and with estimates that half of today's American children will spend at least a portion of their childhood in a single-parent family, it is hardly surprising that children's issues have soared up the charts of problems that worry us. It is hardly surprising that so many kids are confused. We may not know what to do, but Hallmark, at least, knows: the nuclear family is going through meltdown and uplifting messages are in order for the adults.

One obvious reason for our sense of a deserved "restoration" is that we are no longer ashamed when families fall apart. War, pestilence, and the legal system are all matters over which most individuals have no control. We are subtly encouraged to see ourselves as innocent victims of divorce disease, divorce war, and divorce lawyers. Hallmark may speak the cultural truth. We're off the hook. After all, counselors tell us not to take divorce personally; ministers say it's okay by them;

lawyers call it no-fault; feminists say that women need to be free of oppressive male domination; sociologists say the old patriarchy is worn out; and the entertainment industry says, what the hey, it's all for show anyway.

Take the recent blockbuster *Mrs. Doubtfire*, for instance. In this 1994 movie, Robin Williams plays the ineffectual but loving Daniel, husband to the hard-charging Miranda. He spends so much time as the sensitive New Age father that he is never "there" for his wife. He loves to play with his kids, not with her. She asks him to move out. He does. But he misses the kids so badly that he returns in disguise as Mrs. Doubtfire, a Scottish nanny who brings order and discipline to the house. Now things go splendidly. "Who needs a husband when I've got you?" Miranda confesses to Mrs. Doubtfire.

The problem is, of course, that Miranda is correct. She doesn't need a husband who is just another kid. She has it all. She has come a long way, baby. She can bring home the bacon and Mrs. Doubtfire can fry it up in a pan. The film ends not by reintegrating Daniel into the family but by allowing him to split off, playing with the kids daily, having his own job and apartment, and doing his own socially responsible thing. The one thing he is not doing, however, is being much of a father. That's okay, says the movie at the end, there are many different kinds of families. Go for it. Do it your own way. Nothing to be ashamed of. Was this movie put together by studio executives poring over the demographics of "blended" families, of separated parents taking their offspring from various partners to the movies? You bet. It's a feel-good movie for those who feel bad.

If you want to access the rapidity of changes in shame and family life, compare *Mrs. Doubtfire* to the 1942 box-office smash *Now Voyager*. To be sure, these movies are from different genres—sitcom and melodrama—and appeal to different audiences—children and adults—but they are still instructive. In *Now Voyager,* Bette Davis also transforms, as does Robin Williams, but she metamorphoses from a dowdy spinster (Aunt Charlotte) to a stunning woman of the world (Camille Beauchamp). She makes this transformation from ugly duckling to gorgeous swan because she has fallen in love with a man, Jerry, played by Paul Henreid. Only problem is that Jerry is married and has a young daughter, Tina. In between clouds of then-shame-free cigarette smoke, Bette realizes that she must never disturb Tina's home life, bad as it may be. The subject is not even discussed. It is sacred. We never even meet Jerry's wife. We don't have to.

Bette, having turned her back on marriage proposals from other men (for which her mother says she should be "ashamed") and having become fabulously wealthy after her mother's death, decides on a separate peace. She will live her life as Tina's surrogate mom and Jerry's lifelong companion. How she intends to carry this off is not entirely clear. But no matter. At the movie's end, she and Jerry look up to the skies (again through a miasma of cigarette smoke), and Bette says the immortal lines "Oh, Jerry, don't ask for the moon. We have the stars."

Now, we all know what is going on here. We know what it is to ask for the moon. What we don't know is what it means to ask for the stars. We soon find out. Asking for the stars is settling for less than you want because to do more would be to unsettle a family, albeit an unhappy family.

Now Voyager is high camp to us today. Who is concerned with unsettling families, happy or otherwise? We don't grab the hankie and softly weep. We go for the gusto. To hell with the kids. *We* deserve a break today, not them.

Is there any need to recite the dreary statistics that result from this attitude? Is there any doubt about how well children from single-parent families fare relative to those from a more stable environment? In a 1987 study of 171 cities, University of Chicago sociologist Robert Sampson found the "strongest predictor" of violent juvenile crime, specifically murder and robbery, was that the child grew up in a female-headed household.[3] Already, by the mid-1990s, 40 percent of the nation's children are not living with their fathers. Fully half of them will be separated from their dads for at least some of the time while they are growing up. No one disputes any longer that these fatherless children are far more vulnerable to the poverty, violence, lawbreaking, drugs, school failure, and other social pathologies that any civilized culture abhors.

So why do we spend so little time attempting to shame fathers into doing their jobs? The ending of *Mrs. Doubtfire* is happy, *Now Voyager* is sad. In real life—at least as far as the children are concerned—it is just the reverse. This is the story that needs to be told.

Knowing the importance of fathers, why does the Christian right spend so much energy excoriating homosexuals? Why are the only groups of men trying to shame their fellows into accepting responsibility—groups like Promise Keepers and the Million Man March—doing it in the service of weary chauvinism? Why are liberals so frightened of passing judgment, of name-calling, and of forcing what were once natural consequences onto careless actions? Why does the Republican party go after such phony targets as welfare mothers when they clearly know better? Meanwhile, the culpable dad trips merrily on his way, fiddling while the family burns.

There are many reasons that we do not, as Dr. Seuss suggested, "hop on pop." The myth of the need of masculine independence, the frontier promise of starting over, and the belief that kids can survive better in a fractured family than in a fractious one are a few. True enough. But one important explanation has to do with the trivializing of shame. Fathers used to shame their children and, in so doing, were themselves caught up in the ethos of obligation. It wasn't called "shaming," it was called "disciplining," and before that it was called "restraining." Fathers thought that was their job. The old cliché that mothers loved unconditionally, but a father's love had to be earned, was treated as a truism. It was. Mothers said they loved you for just being you. Fathers asked, what have you done for me recently. The relationship was reciprocal as fathers had obligations too. Father surrogates were all over the place saying the same thing to males, be they children or adults, rich or poor. These gray eminences were in the pulpit, they were behind the podium, they were behind the bench. They were always looking down at you, singing the same refrain. You want my approval, you earn it. And you earn it the old-fashioned way—you work for it, you behave.

Of all the responses to such shaming, one is immediate. It makes you feel bad. It's humiliating. And if there was one thing the TV-fed baby boomers of the 1960s did not care much for, it was feeling bad. "Turn on, tune in [and if this makes you feel bad], drop out." In retrospect, this generation may have been strangled by its own love beads.

Another explanation is that with the rise of feminism, consciousness-raising, and greater opportunity in the workplace, women assumed many of the responsibilities of the men—except shaming. Go into any bookstore and look in the Gender section. Pick up any book on feminism. Look in the index. See what you find under "children" or "family." Not much. Usually nothing. Meanwhile, the male was supposed to lighten up, be less domineering, be more sensitive, and, well, let his repressed feminine side loose. Stop withholding love and quit being judgmental, he was told. He did. So who was laying down the electric fence? No one.

As David Blankenhorn and Barbara Dafoe Whitehead, both of the Institute of American Values, have recently argued (he in *Fatherless America: Confronting Our Most Urgent Social Problem*, she in a widely noted *Atlantic Monthly* article entitled "The Failure of Sex Education"), this new view of family roles took hold with a vengeance. Although we have spent much cultural time discussing the role of women in the workplace, ask men to define their job at home and they show the degree to which the "new father" (nurturing, sharing, nonjudgmental, androgynous) has displaced the "old father" (strong, egotistic, harsh, breadwinning, shaming). We are now seeing the result of the new father being enacted daily. The new father, for all his sensitive New Age ways, is redundant. He has been given his walking papers. All too often, he walks.

Blankenhorn discloses the great gulf between such largely traditional, morally grounded convictions about what fathers should be and do and what he terms "contemporary elite discourse on fatherhood." In his words:

> In today's dominant cultural conversation probably the central prescription regarding fatherhood is to lower our standards. Expect and accept less. Instead of good fathers, settle for child-support payments, divorce reform, and other attempts to salvage something from the wreckage. Don't get too preachy. Focus more on rights than on responsibilities. Search for adequate substitutes for fathers.[4]

If this is what the "haves" are willing to accept, is it any wonder the "have-nots" have given up on fatherhood? When the middle class accepts divorce and serial partnerhood as a standard, is it any wonder that the lower class does it too? All that differs is that the poor simply remove the stumbling blocks of marriage and divorce from the process. If you think that poor men are going to "stay together for the sake of the children" when they see what their affluent brothers are doing elsewhere, you've got to be kidding.

No wonder child-support payments from absent fathers are low. A more interesting question is, why are they as high as they are? No wonder the divorce revolution—the steady displacement of a marriage culture by a culture of divorce and unwed parenthood—has been so successful. No wonder dads have disappeared. No shame in that. But plenty of harm. In 1979 the fatherless rate was 21.6 percent. In 1990 about ten million American families—27.5 percent of homes with mothers and children—had no father present.[5] The rates are increasing daily. If this continues, we will reach a point at the turn of the century when half of the children in this country live in fatherless families. Some millennium.

That the destigmatizing of divorce has been no help to children is indubitable. The feminization of fatherhood (for lack of better words) also did no great service to men. It removed, or at least lessened, a fundamental and historic role in society—protector, nurturer, mentor, guide, and shame instructor for their children *and for each other*. Many who oppose tougher divorce laws for families with children fear that such laws will only restore the bad old days when women were trapped in abusive marriages, dominated by oppressive men.

Our anxiety about patriarchial suffocation is still so intense that often low-level and predictable dissatisfaction is expressed through the clarion call of spouse abuse. The gist of these pressures is that men are not to be stern—which is all to the good—but this is often understood by men as not having to be responsible to a family—which is bad. Ramifications of the resettling of paternal roles abound. The rise of sperm banks, abortion on request, and the willingness to extend matrimonial and social benefits to same-sex partners have all been part of the recalibration of fatherhood.

The debate over unwed mothers has drowned out the much broader cultural debate unfolding over fatherless America. Assuming that fatherhood, more than any other male activity, helps boys to become good men, and assuming that fathers do a better job of directing male aggression toward prosocial ends than do their surrogates such as stepfathers, moms-as-dads, and the old favorite, the gang—then what to do? How can the constructive, protective, and liberating force of fatherly shame be reintroduced?

Blankenhorn has some ideas about what to do. He urges that men take a fatherhood pledge, that public housing favor married couples, that sports stars and religious leaders speak up for marriage and fatherhood, that a parenting-impact analysis of all proposed federal legislation be required, that more textbooks for high school students stress marriage and family responsibility, that the White House issue an annual report on the state of fatherhood in America, and that men of goodwill gather together to create Fathers' Clubs in their local communities.

Fiddlesticks! Not bad ideas, well-meaning, but they are not likely to accomplish much. If we were to get truly serious about fatherlessness, we would not only be paying attention to reforming welfare and "restigmatizing" illegitimacy, we would also be devising ways to make divorce and separation for families with small children shameful FOR THE MIDDLE CLASS. We would quit using the term *no-fault,* especially when children were involved. We would give tax advantages to families who stay together, or adopt, and we would reward them increasingly over time spent together. Most of all, we would attempt to make the Deadbeat Dad into a national symbolic villain like the Child Molester or the Racist. His name would be in your newspaper. The missing child would have to step aside; Deadbeat Dad's picture would be on the milk carton.

It may well be that the lottery and the deadbeat dad are the appropriate tropes for our time. How to earn a living and how to provide for the family have become—to many among us—games of chance. Will I win the jackpot? Will I become a dad? These questions can be treated with whimsy for those with plenty of disposable time and money. After all, they can recover by redeploying assets. But for the poor, with nothing to fall back on, such magical thinking as getting rich quick or parenting without planning can only exacerbate a sense of hopelessness. After all, the odds are not in their favor.

Although experiencing the painful blush of shame is hardly a long-term palliative, removing shame from gambling and careless procreation is a guaranteed short-term and long-term disaster. That the resettling of shame thresholds in the areas of work and reproduction has been not just countenanced but also at times encouraged by the state is a paradox almost too demoralizing to contemplate.

CONCLUSION

$\mathcal{C}$LEARLY HUMAN BIOLOGY and evolution have hardwired us to experience the jolt of shame for a purpose. Shame shocks in every culture, and in every culture this frisson is painful—especially to the young. Although the sensation may be pan-cultural, individual cultures write the operating instructions for these shame programs, and they can inscribe wildly different protocols. Sometimes the codes appear to make no sense whatsoever. They often seem gibberish from both inside and outside a culture. Why can't I say that word? It's just a bunch of phonemes. The very illogic of much shame may account for part of its power. Give up personal control, it demands, do this, don't question it, don't do that, get in line, conform. The lesson from history is not so much what lasting cultures forbid as it is that they forbid certain acts and then apply shame continually and fairly to the violators.

In other words, if the jolt of shame is used to encourage cooperation—regardless of the task at hand—it produces a sense of community and hence stability. The group can now get on to matters of more import; the bond has been made. However, if shaming is used to intimidate and exclude legitimate members of the society, then it only undermines the sense of unity. Shame becomes not unifying but fractious. Tell the "haves" they can behave one way, tell the "have-nots" they must behave differently, and trouble is on the way. You can set your watch by it. The dustbin of history is filled with such erstwhile cultures and has room for plenty more.

Knowing this, we might do well to consider that shame is no enemy and shamelessness no friend. The object is not to be free of shame but to be ashamed of behavior that is dangerous to the community. In fact, we might do well to admit that using shame is nothing to be ashamed of; rather, it shows an understanding that feeling bad often has a central purpose. Using shame to oppress, however, is not only cruel but ultimately counterproductive.

We had better learn how to invoke shame, because so many of our current problems can't be solved by clicking the remote control. The only way they will be solved is if certain people feel bad—not that they go to jail, pay a fine, do community service, but that they *feel* bad. When they break a code, they need to feel a hot blush passing over their faces. In a weird kind of homeopathic voodoo, they need to feel a little death lest a bigger one ensue.

Since the relatively recent replacement of a hierarchical culture, controlled from above, with a carnival culture, controlled from below, our temptation has been to think that feeling bad is just not "right." Bad feelings, we think, must be a sign of some disturbance, some churning of otherwise still waters, some flaw in the personality or in a relationship. Losing face hurts and it is often not fair. In our typically adolescent response to painful anxiety, we say to the shamer, "Don't be a downer. Quit laying this trip on me. Leave me alone. Don't pass judgment." This is the language of child to parent, and it has become the baby boomer's lingua franca. I'm okay, you're okay, we're okay. We rarely consider that feeling bad, feeling the blush of shame, may indeed be culture's way, the family's way, and even the individual's way of maintaining social balance and purpose. Sometimes you are not okay. Me too.

For instance, here are some problems for which public policies must depend on shame to succeed. In each case, since the 1960s, our well-intentioned but overly solicitous government has done just the opposite. Shame has been effectively removed as the feds have come in to pay the short-term price.

- **Population:** We need to make people feel very bad for careless reproduction habits. You certainly don't need to call the offspring bastards, but you should consider calling *both* parents something derogatory regardless of race, sex, or class. In the antediluvian days of my youth, pregnant teens were placed in special classes or schools. This raised the ire of many who thought this was discriminatory. It was. The government has since insisted that unwed mothers be "mainstreamed" or else the schools would be prohibited from receiving federal funds. Ask teenage girls today if they would consider having a baby out of wedlock and 55 percent say they would.[1] Why not put the unwed fathers in special classes? Someone should be discriminated against. Illegitimacy should not be considered a birthright. If we are as concerned about child abuse as we claim, then we might consider that giving subsidies (about half of all AFDC spending goes to families formed by unwed teens) and special legal protection to children having children is a particularly virulent (because it seems so compassionate) form of mistreating our children.

- **Violence:** We need to make the use of force into something shameful. When gunfire is the second leading cause of death among Americans ages ten to nineteen,[2] you know that the codes of repression have unraveled early. Perhaps in addition to the V-chip, which will shunt violent programming past the impressionable young, we need an S-chip to do just the opposite with shame. A great deal of Western literature does precisely that. We had best not lose it.

- **Education:** A series of level playing fields is necessary for an equitable society. School is one of them. Schools are not where noble social experiments take place, nor are they places to redress wrongs committed elsewhere. They are rooms in which fundamental skills necessary to make one's way to a better future are taught. You don't go to school to feel good, nor to be warehoused. You go into those rooms to learn how to read, write, do math, and think clearly. The lower grades should be funded the way we fund prestigious universities: overpay and underwork teachers. Then get out of the way. Shutter all graduate schools of education. Quarantine all their graduates. My worst students go into K–12 teaching; that's shameful. My best go to law school; that's even worse. Ironically, many of the budding law students would much prefer to go into teaching, but that job has been made intolerable by low pay, lower prestige, a bingo curriculum, wacky administrators, and incessant government meddling. Few adolescents need a Harvard education, but every child should have a public Phillips Andover available.

• **Race and gender:** We need to make such well-meaning but ill-conceived programs as race norming, affirmative action, minority set-asides, and quotas shameful (to many they already are) by providing equitable rewards for hard work, and special help for the genuinely disadvantaged.

• **Addiction:** We need to quit explaining bad habits in terms of chemical or genetic addictions. You should be ashamed of being an alcoholic even if your genes "predispose" you to drink too much. Willpower trumps predilection. The current vogue of "medicalizing character" undermines our sense of personal responsibility and shame.

• **Values:** Evil is not relative, the Devil is not just a misunderstood fellow, Jesus was not a matinee idol, certain principles are better than others, and some are downright shameful.

But how do we do this? One thing is to bring back the penalty of public shame, namely, shunning. This is a legitimate part of our Western heritage. The Puritans did it. The Quakers did it. We do it during war. It used to be a major part of education. Not every problem has a legislative or judicial solution. Way back when, this was effective: Socrates chose death over shunning by his beloved Atheneans. Michael Milken feels worse losing his seat on the stock exchange than in doing jail time. Joe Six-pack, dumped by the Elks, is distraught. Deadbeat

Dad doesn't want his neighbors to know about his callous behavior, let alone his kids. A gang member "dissed" in Harlem feels it too.

Ostracism—expulsion from the group—can be harsh on the individual but beneficial to the group. It works best when loss of status can be easily observed by peers. Wherever you find an ideal of respectability, however dim, you find sensitivity to shame. Ironically, having the law send certain lawbreakers off to jail can be counterproductive when incarceration carries no humiliation. All too often, jail time has become the enemy of shame rather than its ally. Some debts are not so easily (and privately) paid. So, too, having public programs to remedy problems individuals must confront removes stigmas that ought to be applied not just for the individual but for the group. How else do the young learn responsible behavior? Welfare, as Charles Murray has argued in *Losing Ground*, can become "insidious" when it protects recipients—and onlookers—from the results of shameful actions. Reticence, a crucial component of social responsibility, is very often based on the fear of feeling shame. Very often that fear is acquired secondhand by watching others suffer.

We don't need to force adulterers to wear a scarlet letter, but it wouldn't hurt to send a stronger signal that such dangerous and reckless behavior is more than . . . inappropriate. We can't condemn illegitimacy while condoning divorce in families with young children. We can't control the shameless content of much television entertainment, but we can embarrass the advertisers who sponsor it. While Madonna may be oblivious to the danger of flaunting single parenthood, Gerald Levin, CEO of Time Warner, who writes some of her checks, is not. No one wants to get into the classroom, but it does no harm to remind instructors that no one is helped when all students get A's, or when poor students are simply passed on to graduation rather than held back to learn. Ministers can be praised for matters other than gathering a large flock and building bigger buildings. Psychologists and social workers who pride themselves on always supporting their "clients" regardless of the damage done to others might rethink their positions. They may have profited from the shame-removal industry, but have the rest of us? The feisty Laura Schlessinger, of the *Ask Dr. Laura* radio show, should not be the only counselor willing to discuss publicly the redemptive powers of shame. And, finally, while we can't make parents of youngsters stay together, we can hold them publicly accountable for the damage caused to their offspring.

If we are going to speak the language of morality, we are going to have to use the S-word not on the distant others, but on the group near at hand. On us. We need to let the sensation do its work, even if it feels bad. We need to be willing to say, "Shame on you" to miscreants; to "put to shame" those who act carelessly; to criticize those who "know no shame"; and to say, "I'm sorry. I'm ashamed of myself" when we are wrong. Being "for shame" means being intolerant of behaviors that ultimately injure us all. Restoring shame requires not just being judgmental, but being willing to articulate that judgment to those who may simply not know how irresponsible they are being. We need always to remember, however, that the goal is not to shun but to educate. The final emphasis must always be on reintegration.

Most of all we need to quit being so frightened and ashamed of shame. It holds a central position in all lasting cultures for a reason. Shame is not the disease; properly used, it is the cure. As a social construction, it is how we communicate certain key virtues, how a sense of decency is developed. We are not born with an on-board governor of actions; morality has to be installed. Conformity to certain baseline standards is not a luxury, but a necessity. Like it or not, inflicting the sting of shame is how successful cultures have protected the group from the dangers of individual excess. Feeling bad is often the basis of a general good. Civilization is not without its discontents. The alternative is, as the Victorians knew and we have recently forgotten, worse, much worse.

END NOTES

CHAPTER 1
1. Steinhauer, 1995:C1.
2. Friend, 1994:28.
3. Stacks, 1995:26.

CHAPTER 2
1. McNatt, 1995:A6.
2. Smith, 1995:C1.
3. Burgess, 1839:30.
4. Hitchens, 1996:70.
5. Schneider, 1977:24 and Taylor, 1985:60.
6. Heller, 1974:23.

CHAPTER 3
1. Heller, 1974:29.
2. Himmelfarb, 1994:35.
3. Gladstone, 1982:163.
4. Gauldie, 1994:22.
5. Lasch, 1995:34.
6. Magnet, 1993:19.
7. ————, 1993:36.

CHAPTER 4
1. Hoffman, 1996:B3.
2. Fox, 1984:29.
3. Lewis, 1995:A17.
4. Holbrook, 1993:41.

CHAPTER 5
1. Leo, 1994:24.
2. Wakefield, 1994:26.
3. Abcarian, 1994:3.
4. Boorstin, 1964:38.
5. Gamson, 1994:35.

6. Kakutani, 1994:C1.
7. Oates, 1988:3.
8. Conniff, 1993:211.
9. Reuters News Service, 26 November 1992.
10. Pareles, 1994:1.
11. Marin, 1993:1.

CHAPTER 6
1. Rivkin, 1990:27.
2. Karen, 1992:53.
3. Bradshaw, 1988:67.
4. Sandomir, 1991:36.
5. Lord, 1992:42.
6. Perls, 1969:178.
7. Karen, 1992:50.

CHAPTER 7
1. Whitehead, 1994:70.
2. Doniger, 1990:27.
3. Niebuhr, 18 April 1995:A1.
4. Goldberger, 1995:B4.
5. Niebuhr, 16 April 1995:A1.
6. Waite, 1995:43.
7. Innerst, 1995:A3.
8. Manno, 1995:A12.
9. Adelson, 1995:A10.
10. Lewin, 1996:12.

CHAPTER 8
1. Head, 1994:7.
2. Lighter, 1994:870.
3. Shales, 1983:C1.
4. Rosenthal, 1992:A1.
5. Wetzstein, 1995:A2.
6. Berns, 1971:127.
7. Staples, 1995:62.

CHAPTER 9
1. Sack, 1995:4.
2. Gould, 1995:40.
3. McLeod, 1995:A1.

END NOTES

4. Blankenhorn, 1995:211.
5. Jay, 1995:A17.

CONCLUSION
1. Gallagher, 1996:A14.
2. Children's Defense Fund Report, 5 April 1996.

WORKS CITED

Abrarian, Robin. "Whatever Happened to Good Old-Fashioned Shame?" *Los Angeles Times*, September 25, 1994, E1.

Ackerman, Robert J. *Silent Sons: A Book For and About Men*. New York: Simon & Schuster, 1993.

Adelson, Joseph. "It's 1995 and Johnny Still Can't Read." *Wall Street Journal*, October 20, 1995, A10.

Alter, Jonathan, and Pat Wingert. "The Return of Shame." *Newsweek*, February 6, 1995, 21–26.

Bauml, Betty and Franz. *A Dictionary of Gestures*. Metuchen, NJ: Scarecrow Press, 1975.

Beattie, Melody. *Beyond Codependency: And Getting Better All the Time*. New York: Harper & Row, 1989.

—————. *Codependent No More: How to Stop Controlling Others and Start Caring for Yourself*. New York: Harper & Row, 1987.

Bellafante, Ginia. "Playing 'Get the Guest.' " *Time*, March 27, 1995, 77.

Benedict, Ruth. *The Chrysanthemum and the Sword: Patterns of Japanese Culture*. Boston: Houghton Mifflin, 1946.

Berns, Walter. "Pornography vs. Democracy—A Case for Censorship." *The Public Interest* (1971), 22:3–44.

Blankenhorn, David. *Fatherless America: Confronting Our Most Urgent Problem*. New York: Basic Books, 1995.

Bly, Robert. *Iron John: A Book About Men*. Reading, MA: Addison-Wesley, 1990.

Boorstin, Daniel. *The Image: A Guide to Pseudo Events in America*. New York: Harper & Row, 1964.

Bradshaw, John. *Healing the Shame That Binds You*. Deerfield Beach, FL: Health Communication, 1988.

Braithwaite, John. *Crime, Shame and Reintegration*. New York: Cambridge University Press, 1989.

Broucek, Francis. *Shame and the Self*. New York: Guilford Press, 1991.

Brown, Peter. *The Body and Society: Men, Women, and Sexual Renunciation in Early Christianity*. New York: Columbia University Press, 1988.

Browne, Thomas. *Religio Medici*. 1642 reprint. New York: Cambridge University Press, 1953.

Burgess, Thomas. *The Physiology or Mechanism of Blushing*. London: John Churchill, 1839.

Burke, Edmund. *Reflections on the Revolution in France*. 1790 reprint. Edited by William Todd. New York: Rinehart, 1959.

Burnett, Carol. *One More Time*. New York: Random House, 1986.

Buruma, Ian. *The Wages of Guilt: Memories of War in Germany and Japan*. New York: Farrar, Straus & Giroux, 1994.

Butterfield, Fox. *All God's Children: The Bosket Family and the American Tradition of Violence*. New York: Knopf, 1995.

Cohen, Jane R. *Charles Dickens and His Original Illustrators*. Columbus, OH: Ohio State University Press, 1980.

Conniff, Ruth. "Politics in a Post-Feminist Age." In Adam Sexton, ed., *Desperately Seeking Madonna,* 210–213. New York: Dell Publishing, 1993.

Cotton, John. *Milk for Babes*. 1646 reprint. Northhampton, MA: John Metcalf, 1836.

Darwin, Charles. *The Expression of the Emotions in Man and Animals*. 1872 reprint. Chicago: University of Chicago Press, 1965.

Debenport, Ellen. "In Japan Being Wrong Means Having to Say You're Sorry." *St. Petersburg Times*, February 7, 1993, A12.

Delbanco, Andrew. *The Death of Satan: How Americans Have Lost the Sense of Evil*. New York: Farrar, Strauss & Giroux, 1995.

Dickens, Charles, *The Personal History of David Copperfield*. 1849–50 reprint. New York: Oxford University Press, 1966.

————. *Oliver Twist*. 1837–39 reprint. New York: Oxford University Press, 1966.

Doniger, Wendy. "Why the Body Is Disgusting." *New York Times Book Review*, September 23, 1990, 27.

Dostoyevsky, Fyodor. *Notes from Underground*. 1864 reprint. Translated by Ralph E. Matlaw. New York: E.P. Dutton, 1960.

Douglas, Mary. *Purity and Danger: An Analysis of Concepts of Pollution and Taboo*. New York: Praeger, 1966.

Dukakis, Kitty. *Now You Know*. New York: Simon & Schuster, 1990.

Dunlap, Albert J. *Mean Business: How I Save Bad Companies and Make Good Ones Great*. New York: Random House, 1996.

Edgerton, Samuel Y. *Pictures and Punishment: Art and Criminal Prosecution during the Florentine Renaissance*. Ithaca, NY: Cornell University Press, 1985.

Elias, Norbert. *Power and Civility from the Civilizing Process*. Translated by Edmund Jephcott. New York: Pantheon, 1982.

Ellis, Havelock. "The Evolution of Modesty." Part 1 of *Studies in the Psychology of Sex*. Vol. 1. New York: Random House, 1936.

Ellis, Walter. "Whatever Happened to Shame and Remorse?" *Sunday Times of London*, October 24, 1993, feature section, 1.

Erasmus, Desiderius. *On the Manners of Children*. 1530 reprint. London: John Tisdale, 1560.

Eschenbach, Wolfram von. *Parzival*. Translated by H. M. Mustard and C. E. Passage. New York: Vintage, 1961.

Fields, Suzanne. "The Speaker's Lagging Indicators: Why Shame and Respectability Are Making a Comeback." *Atlanta Constitution,* March 20, 1995, A8.

Firestone, Ross, ed., *The Man in Me: Visions of the Male Experience*. New York: HarperPerennial, 1992.

Ford, Betty. *The Times of My Life*. New York: Harper & Row, 1978.

Fowler, James W. "Review of *Shame, Exposure and Privacy*." *The Christian Century* (1993), 110(24):816–19.

Fox, Stephen. *The Mirror Makers: A History of American Advertising*. New York: William Morrow, 1984.

Friend, Tad, and Anya Sacharow. "White Hot Trash." *New York Magazine*, August 22, 1994, 22 ff.

Gallagher, Maggie. "Why Murphy Brown Is Winning." *Wall Street Journal*, June 3, 1996, A14.

Gamson, Joshua. *Claims to Fame: Celebrity in Contemporary America*. Berkeley, CA: University of California Press, 1994.

Gangelh, Bonnie. "Shame Needs Some Respect." *Houston Post*, February 8, 1995, D1.

Garner, Lesley. "Goodbye to Shame and Hello! to Blighted Lives." *The Daily Telegraph*, February, 2, 1994, 18.

Gauldie, Enid. *Cruel Habitations: A History of Working-Class Housing, 1780–1918*. New York: Barnes & Noble, 1974.

Gladstone, William. *Diaries*. Edited by H. C. G. Matthew. Oxford: Clarendon Press, 1982.

Goffman, Erving. *Asylums: Essays on the Social Situation of Mental Patients and Other Inmates*. Garden City, NJ: Anchor, 1961.

Goldberger, Paul. "The Gospel of Church Architecture, Revisited." *New York Times*, April 20, 1995, B1.

Goldman, Albert. *Lives of John Lennon*. New York: William Morrow, 1988.

Goldsmith, Oliver. *The Vicar of Wakefield*. 1766 reprint. New York: Oxford University Press, 1974.

Goodman, Ellen. "Divorce Revisionism: The Sake of the Kids Is Central But Don't Neglect Unhappy Parents." *Pittsburgh Post-Gazette*, April 12, 1995, C3.

Gould, Louis. "Ticket to Trouble." *New York Times Magazine*, April 23, 1995, 38 ff.

Gray, Francine du Plessix. *Rage and Fire: A Life of Louise Colet, Flaubert's Muse*. New York: Simon & Schuster, 1994.

Hamilton, Nigel. *J.F.K.: Reckless Youth*. New York: Random House, 1992.

Harrington, Michael. *The Other America: Poverty in the United States*. New York: Macmillian, 1962.

WORKS CITED

WORKS CITED

Haury, Don. *I'm Not My Fault*. New York: Safe Place Publishing, 1995.

Hawthorne, Nathaniel. "The Haunted Mind." In *Twice-Told Tales,* 222–26. New York: Dutton, 1967.

Hayman, Ronald. *Tennessee Williams: Everyone Else Is an Audience*. New Haven, CT: Yale University Press, 1993.

Head, John. "Shame Is Not a '90s Thing." *Atlanta Constitution,* August 29, 1994, 7.

Heller, Erich. "Man Ashamed." *Encounter* (1974), 64(2):23–30.

Himmelfarb, Gertrude. "Clinton & Congress: The Victorians Get a Bad Rap." *New York Times*, January 9, 1995, A15.

———. "Queen Victoria Was Right. She Succeeded by Tying Moral Principles to Social Policy." *USA Today*, March, 13, 1995, A15.

———. "Re-Moralizing America." *Wall Street Journal*, February 7, 1995, A22.

———. *The Demoralization of Society: From Victorian Virtues to Modern Values*. New York: Knopf, 1994.

Hitchens, Christopher. "The Death of Shame." *Vanity Fair*, March 1996, 68 ff.

Hoffman, Jan. "Pass the Tissues: Collins Is Accused of Having No Shame." *New York Times*, February 9, 1996, B3.

Holbrook, Morris B. *Daytime Television Game Shows and the Celebration of Merchandise: The Price Is Right*. Bowling Green, OH: Bowling Green State University Popular Press, 1993.

Huffington, Arianna Stassinopoulos. *Picasso: Creator and Destroyer*. New York: Simon & Schuster, 1988.

Innerst, Carol. "College Board Halts Slide." *Washington Times*, April 1, 1995, A3.

———. "Renaissance of 'Shame' Rebuilds Values." *Washington Times*, March 26, 1995, A1.

James, Clive. *Fame in the Twentieth Century*. New York: Random House, 1993.

Janeway, James. *A Token for Children*. Philadelphia: J. Pounder, 1813.

Jay, Peter. "Suddenly, Fathers Are Important." *Baltimore Sun*, March 23, 1995, A17.

Johnson, Sheila. "Can Japan Muster an Apology?" *Toronto Star*, August 26, 1992, A19.

Kahan, Dan M. "It's a Shame We Have None." *Wall Street Journal,* January 15, 1997, A16.

———. "What Do Alternative Sanctions Mean?" *University of Chicago Law Journal* (1996), 62:591–653.

Kakutani, Michiko. "Biography Becomes a Blood Sport." *New York Times*, May, 20, 1994, C1.

Karen, Robert. "Shame as a Cause of Emotional Problems." *Atlantic Monthly*, February 1992, 40–70.

Kaufman, Daniel. *To Be a Man: Visions of Self, Views from Within*. New York: Simon & Schuster, 1994.

Kaufman, Gershen. *Coming Out of Shame: Transforming Gay and Lesbian Lives*. New York: Doubleday, 1996.

———. *The Psychology of Shame: Theory and Treatment*. New York: Springer, 1989.

Kaus, Mickey. *The End of Equality*. New York: Basic Books, 1992.

Kelley, Kitty. *His Way: The Unauthorized Biography of Frank Sinatra*. New York: Bantam Books, 1986.

———. *Nancy Reagan: The Unauthorized Biography*. New York: Simon & Schuster, 1991.

Kesey, Ken. *One Flew Over the Cuckoo's Nest*. New York: New American Library, 1962.

Kimball, Roger. *Tenured Radicals: How Politics Corrupted Our Higher Education*. New York: Harper & Row, 1990.

Kington, Miles. "A Rough Kind of Justice Set to Music." *The Independent* (England), November 14, 1991, 28.

Kohn, Moshe. "In the Beginning There Was . . . Shame." *Jerusalem Post*, September 17, 1991, feature section, 1.

Kolbert, Elizabeth. "Wages of Deceit: Untrue Confessions." *New York Times*, June 11, 1995, B1.

Krauthammer, Charles. "Defining Deviancy Up: Deviancy and Normality in America." *The New Republic*, November 1993, 20–5.

———. "History Hijacked." *Washington Post*, November 4, 1994, A25.

Laing, R. D. *The Politics of Experience*. New York: Pantheon Books, 1967.

Lapham, Lewis. *The Wish for Kings: Democracy at Bay*. New York: Grove Press, 1993.

Lasch, Christopher. "For Shame: Why Americans Should Be Wary of Self-Esteem." *The New Republic*, August 10, 1992, 29–34

———. *The Culture of Narcissism*. New York: Norton, 1979.

———. *The Revolt of the Elites and the Betrayal of Democracy*. New York: Norton, 1995.

Lawrence, D. H. *Fantasia of the Unconscious*. Harmondsworth, England: Penguin, 1971.

Lebergott, Stanley. *Pursuing Happiness: American Consumers in the Twentieth Century*. Princeton, NJ: Princeton University Press, 1993.

Leo, John. "Faking It in *Quiz Show*." *U.S. News & World Report*, October 17, 1994, 24.

Leslie, Ann. "The Terrible Penalty of Betraying Our Family Values." *Daily Mail*, March 11, 1995, 8 ff.

Lewin, Tamar. "College Toughens Its Stance on Learning-Disabilities Aid." *New York Times*, February 13, 1996, A1.

Lewis, Anthony. "Abroad at Home: An Anatomized America." *New York Times,* December 8, 1995, A17.

Lewis, Michael. *Shame: The Exposed Self*. New York: Free Press, 1992.

Lighter, J. E., ed., *Historical Dictionary of American Slang*. Vol 1. New York: Random House, 1994.

Lord, M. G. "That Inner Child Is Just a Big Baby." *Newsday*, October 25, 1992, 36.

Lowenfeld, Henry. "Notes on Shamelessness." *Psychoanalytic Quarterly* (1976), 45(1):62–72.

WORKS CITED

Lynd, Helen Merrell. *On Shame and the Search of Identity*. New York: Harcourt Brace, 1958.

Mackenzie, Henry. *The Man of Feeling*. 1771 reprint. New York: Garland Press, 1974.

Magnet, Myron. *The Dream and the Nightmare: The Sixties Legacy to the Underclass*. New York: William Morrow, 1993.

Manno, Bruno. "The Real Score on the SATs." *Wall Street Journal*, September 13, 1995, A12.

Marin, Rich. "They're Hot! (They're Not)." *New York Times*, August 1, 1993, B1.

Massaro, Toni M. "Shame, Culture, and American Criminal Law." *Michigan Law Review* (1991), 89:1881–1944.

McGinniss, Joe. *The Last Brother*. New York: Simon & Schuster, 1993.

McGuffey School. *McGuffey Reader*. 1836 reprint. Charlottesville, VA: McGuffey School, 1937.

McLeod, Ramon G. "New Evidence that Quayle Was Right." *San Francisco Chronicle*, December 9, 1994, A1.

McNatt, Glenn. "Sleaze TV." *Baltimore Sun*, March 25, 1955, A6.

Meyers, Jeffrey. *Scott Fitzgerald: A Biography*. New York: HarperCollins, 1994.

Miller, William Ian. *Humiliation: And Other Essays on Honor, Social Discomfort and Violence*. Ithaca, NY: Cornell University Press, 1993.

Mitchell, Jann. *Codependent for Sure! An Original Jokebook*. Kansas City, MO: Andrews & McNeel, 1995.

More, Thomas. *Utopia*. 1516 reprint. New Haven, CT: Yale University Press, 1974.

Morrison, Andrew. *Shame: The Underside of Narcissism*. Hillsdale, NJ: Analytic Press, 1989.

Moynihan, Daniel Patrick. "Defining Deviancy Down." *The American Scholar*, Winter 1993, 17–30.

Murray, Charles. "The Coming White Underclass." *Wall Street Journal*, October 29, 1993, A14.

————. "Underclass: The Crisis Deepens." *Sunday Times of London*, May 22, 1994, feature section, 1.

————. *Losing Ground: American Social Policy*. New York: Basic Books, 1984.

Naifeh, Steven, and Gregory White Smith. *Jackson Pollock: An American Saga*. New York: C. N. Potter, 1989.

Nathanson, Donald L. *Shame and Pride: Affect, Sex, and the Birth of the Self*. New York: Norton, 1992.

————. *The Many Faces of Shame*. New York: Guilford Press, 1987.

Navarro, Mireya. "Residents Disrupting Drug Trade." *New York Times,* August 30, 1996, A12.

Newsom, Robert. "The Hero's Shame." *Dickens Studies* (1983), 11:1–24.

Niebuhr, Gustav. "Power Shift in Protestantism Toward a New Church Model." *New York Times*, April 29, 1995, A1.

————. "Religion Goes to Market to Expand Congregations." *New York Times*, April 18, 1995, A1.

————. "Where Shopping-Mall Culture Gets a Big Dose of Religion." *New York Times*, April 16, 1995, A1.

Nietzsche, Friedrich. *The Birth of Tragedy and the Genealogy of Morals*. 1872 reprint. Garden City, NY: Doubleday, 1956.

O'Heath, Anthony. "The Death of Modesty." *Daily Mail*, October 15, 1994, 8–9.

Oates, Joyce Carol. "Adventures in Abandonment." *New York Times Book Review*, August 28, 1988, 3.

Olasky, Marvin. *The Tragedy of American Compassion*. Washington, DC: Regency, 1992.

Pareles, Jon. "Madonna's Return to Innocence." *New York Times*, October 3, 1994, section 2; 1.

Perls, Fritz. *Ego, Hunger and Aggression*. New York: Random House, 1969.

Peyser, Joan. *Bernstein: A Biography*. New York: Beech Tree Books, 1987.

Piers, Gerhart, and Milton B. Singer. *Shame and Guilt: A Psychoanalytic and a Cultural Study*. Springfield, IL: Charles C. Thomas, 1953.

Pinkerton, James. "Society's Ride from Babbittry to Bobbittry." *Los Angeles Times*, January 21, 1994, B1.

Pocaterra, Annibale. *Dua Dialogi della Vergogna (Two Dialogues on Shame)* Ferrara, Italy: Appresso B. Mammarella, 1592.

Postman, Neil. *Amusing Ourselves to Death: Public Discourse in the Age of Show Business*. New York: Viking, 1985.

Pruden, Wesley. "Trying to Survive in the Era of Shame." *Washington Times*, March 17, 1995, A4.

Quayle, Dan. *Standing Firm: A Vice-Presidential Memoir*. New York: Harper-Collins, 1994.

Rawls, John. *A Theory of Justice*. Cambridge, MA: Harvard University Press, 1971.

Reuters News Service. "French Media Watchdog to Sue 'Shameless' Madonna." November 26, 1992, Thursday, A.M. cycle.

Rich, Frank. "Gingrich Family Values." *New York Times*, May 14, 1995, D15.

Ricks, Christopher. *Keats and Embarrassment*. New York: Oxford University Press, 1974.

Rivkin, Jacqueline. "Recovery Stores: A Sense of Mission." *Publishers Weekly*, November 23, 1990, 26–31.

Roeck, Alan L. *Twenty-Four Hours a Day*. Center City, MN: Hazelden, 1978.

Rosenthal, Andrew. "After the Riots: Quayle Says Riots Sprang from Lack of Family Values." *New York Times*, May 20, 1992, A1.

Ryan, William. *Blaming the Victim*. New York: Pantheon Books, 1971.

Sack, Kevin. "There Are Two Sides to Every Game in Town." *New York Times*, November 5, 1995, E4.

Sanders, E. P. *Jewish and Christian Self-Definition*. Philadelphia, PA: Fortress Press, 1983.

———. "When Shame Entered the Garden." *New York Times Book Review*, December 25, 1988, 1.

Sandomir, Richard. "The Big Daddy of the 'Inner Child': John Bradshaw." *Newsday*, July 8, 1991, 36.

Sartre, Jean-Paul. *Being and Nothingness: An Essay*. 1943 reprint. New York: Citadel, 1974.

Saul, John Ralston. *Voltaire's Bastards: The Dictatorship of Reason in the West*. New York: Free Press, 1992.

Schaef, Anne Wilson. *Laugh! I Thought I'd Die (If I Didn't)*. New York: Ballantine Books, 1990.

Schaefer, Tom. "A Little Shame Could Do a Lot of Good." *Knight Ridder Newswire*, February 18, 1995.

Schneider, Carl D. *Shame, Exposure and Privacy*. Boston: Beacon, 1977.

Schneiderman, Stuart. *Saving Face: America and the Politics of Shame*. New York: Knopf, 1996.

Shales, Tom. "Merlin of the Media." *Washington Post*, February 17, 1983, C1.

Shapiro, Jerrold Lee. *The Measure of a Man: Becoming the Father You Wish Your Father Had Been*. New York: Perigee Books, 1995.

Shaw, George Bernard. *Man and Superman*. 1905 reprint. Baltimore, MD: Penguin, 1966.

Singer, Milton B. *Shame and Guilt: A Psychoanalytic Study*. New York: Norton, 1971.

Smith, Sid. "Scream TV: Cashing in with Trash." *Chicago Tribune*, March 19, 1995, C1.

Somers, Suzanne. *Keeping Secrets*. New York: Warner Books, 1988.

Sommers, Christina Hoff. *Who Stole Feminism? How Women Have Betrayed Women*. New York: Simon & Schuster, 1994.

Stacks, John. "The Powell Factor." *Time*, July 10, 1995, 22–5.

Staples, Brent. "The Chain Gang Show." *New York Magazine*, September 17, 1995, 62–3.

Steinhauer, Jennifer. "No Marriage, No Apologies." *New York Times*, July 6, 1995, C1.

Stevenson, Robert Louis. *Dr. Jekyll and Mr. Hyde*. 1886 reprint. New York: Bantam, 1967.

Strachey, Lytton. *Eminent Victorians*. New York: G. P. Putnam's Sons, 1918.

Strathern, Andrew. "Why Is Shame on the Skin?" In John Blacking, ed., *The Anthropology of the Body*, 99–110. New York: Academic Press, 1977.

Swift, Jonathan. *Thoughts on Various Subjects*. In William Eddy, ed., *Satires and Personal Writings*, 406–16. New York: Oxford University Press, 1965.

Sykes, Charles J. *Dumbing Down Our Kids: Why America's Kids Feel Good About Themselves But Can't Read, Write, or Add*. New York: St. Martin's Press, 1995.

Szasz, Thomas. *The Myth of Mental Illness: Foundations of a Theory of Personal Conduct*. New York: Harper & Row, 1961.

Taylor, Gabriele. *Pride, Shame, and Guilt: Emotions of Self-Assessment*. New York: Oxford University Press, 1985.

Tolstoy, Leo. *The Death of Ivan Ilych*. 1886 reprint. New York: Viking Penguin, 1960.

Tomkins, Silvan. "Shame." In Donald Nathanson, ed., *The Many Faces of Shame*, 133–61. New York: Guilford Press, 1987.

————. *Affect/Imagery/Consciousness*. New York: Springer, 1963.

Wakefield, Dan. "Robert Redford's 50, Then and Now." *New York Times Magazine*, August 21, 1994, 26 ff.

Webster, Noah, et al. *The New England Primer*. Hudson, NY: Asbel Stoddard, 1801.

Wesleyan University. *Catalog*. 1995.

West, Mark. "Guilt and Shame in Early American Children's Literature." *University of Hartford Studies in Literature* (1986), 18 (1):1–7.

Wetzstein, Cheryl. "Thinkers from Both Right and Left Back Concept of Shame." *Washington Times*, March, 16, 1995, A2.

Whitehead, Barbara Dafoe. "The Failure of Sex Education." *Atlantic*, October 24, 1994, 55-80.

Williams, Bernard. *Shame and Necessity*. Berkeley, CA: University of California Press, 1993.

Wilson, James Q. *Crime and Human Nature*. New York: Simon & Schuster, 1985.

————. *The Moral Sense*. New York: Free Press, 1993.

Witham, Larry. "Japan, U.S. Diverge at Moral Crossroads: Group Shame, Personal Guilt Guide Different Ideals." *Washington Times*, January 11, 1994, A9.

Woititz, Janet. *Adult Children of Alcoholics*. Pompano Beach, FL: Health Communications, 1983.

Wood, Christopher. *The Dictionary of Victorian Painters*. Woodbridge, Eng.: Antique Collectors' Club, 1978.

Wurmser, Leon. *The Mask of Shame*. Baltimore, MD: Johns Hopkins University Press, 1981.

Yardly, Jonathan. "What the Victorians Can Teach Us." *Tampa Tribune*, April, 2, 1995, 4.

Zhang, Sheldon X. "Measuring Shame in an Ethnic Context." *British Journal of Criminology* (1995), 35(2):248-62.

INDEX

INDEX

INDEX

Pulitzer, Joseph, 96
Punishments. *See under* Criminal behavior
Puritans, 48, 184
Puttnam, Robert D., 79
Pyne, Joe, 104

Quayle, Dan, 2, 99–100, 172, 177–79
"Queen for a Day" (TV program), 18
Quin, Bradley J., 163–64
Quiz Show (film), 94

Radio, 76–77, 80, 83
Rage and Fire (Gray), 106
Random House, 66, 124
Raphael, Sally Jessy, 11, 18
Rawls, John, 60
Reagan, Nancy, 106
Reagan, Ronald, 180
Reckless Youth, 106
Recording industry, 5, 21, 108–12, 192
Recovered Memory movement, 140
Recovery movement, 11–12, 21, 117–41
Recovery Store Network, 122
Redbook magazine, 116
Redford, Robert, 94
Reeves, Rosser, 76
Religion
    decline in proscriptive role of, 10, 12, 142–55, 169
    Recovery movement and, 123, 130, 139–40
    as shame mediator, 41–44
Renaissance shame, 41–45
Responsibility, individual vs. group, 15, 51–53
Revlon, 87
Rice, Donna, 5, 100
Richardson, Elliott, 174
Riley, Debbie, 19
Rivera, Geraldo, 18
RJR-Nabisco, 191
Robinson, Chris, 99
Rogers, Fred, 131
Rolling Stone magazine, 133
Roman Empire, 195–96
Romanticism, 57, 60, 130, 184
"Rough music" ceremony, 42–43
Rousseau, Jean-Jacques, 57, 140, 184

Rowell, George, 66, 80
Rubin, Jerry, 61
Ruckelshaus, William, 174
Ruskin, John, 156
Ryan, William, 60

Safe Place Publishing, 126
Safire, William, 177
Sallman, Warner, 149
Sampson, Robert, 205
Sanders, E. P., 148
Sartre, Jean-Paul, 26
Satir, Virginia, 132
SATs, 13, 163–65
Saudi Arabia, 37
Scarlett Letter, The (film), 10
Schaef, Anne Wilson, 124, 126
Scheler, Max, 32
Schlessinger, Laura, 216
Schmitz, Jonathan, 17–18, 19–20, 21, 22, 25, 36
Schneiderman, Stuart, 21
Scholastic Assessment (Aptitude) Tests (SATs), 13, 163–65
Schools. *See* Education
Schwarzenegger, Arnold, 5
Scott Fitzgerald: Biography (Meyer), 106
Sears Roebuck, 2, 191
"See It Now" (TV program), 173
Segal, Erich, 60
Segmented sponsorship, 78
Self-esteem, 12, 14, 121–24, 139, 140
Self-help books, 121–29
Selfhood, 20, 22–23, 29–30, 51–52, 119–21, 139
Self-improvement, 56
Sex education, 5, 145
Sexuality, 32, 33, 111–12, 144–49
Shame
    contemporary vs. 1950s' view of, 1, 94–95
    cross-cultural commonalities, 30–34, 39
    cultural-specific gestures, 37
    definitions of, 23–24
    guilt vs., 37–39
    historical overview of, 41–45, 50–62, 195–97
    institutional proscriptions and, 142–69
    physiological manifestations of, 24–29

242